Praise for The Debt-Free Graduate

"All students and their parents will be able to read this book with profit and amusement in mind."

The Globe and Mail

"Absolutely loaded with practical tips on financing your education and living simply and cheaply."

The Toronto Star

"...contains a wealth of information for students facing the double jeopardy of increasing post-secondary school costs and shrinking job prospects."

The Halifax Chronicle-Herald

"A superb resource! Humorously presented with useful tips and strategies on how to make your dollar go further."

Dr. Jack Russel, Counsellor and faculty member,
University of Western Ontario

"Every student or parent of prospective post-secondary students should read this book."

The Canadian MoneySaver

"...creative ideas about everything from decorating and detergent substitutes to travelling and investing are useful well beyond the garden walls of student life."

The Queen's Journal Reader

"This book will be helping today's bright young things long after they have forgotten their Latin verbs."

The Vancouver Sun

"This is a marvellous book for both students and professionals, which blends useful techniques for fiscal management with an emphasis on self-discovery."

Dr. Michael Doyle, Assistant Professor in Counselling,
Memorial University of Newfoundland

"...practical, occasionally ingenious cost-cutting tips."

Report on Business Magazine

"*The Debt-Free Graduate* is chock-full of great money-saving strategies—thankfully, in a style that is humorous and highly readable.

Richard Zajchowski, co-author of the bestselling
Learning for Success

"With ongoing government cutbacks, the cost of a university education will continue rising. *The Debt-Free Graduate* offers students and parents realistic strategies to make education more affordable. Buy the book and apply the strategies and you're guaranteed to make back your investment 100-fold."

Jim Harris, co-author of
The 100 Best Companies to Work for in Canada

"A must-have for any student."

The Toronto Sun

To my Mom and Dad,
who taught me the value of a dollar, and, far more impor-
tantly, through their love, faith, and support also showed me
the value of things that money can never buy.

Every effort has been made to make this book as current as
possible at the time the book went to press. This book is sold
with the understanding that neither the author nor the pub-
lisher is engaged in rendering professional advice.

http://www.debtfreegrad.com

First published in trade paperback by HarperCollins
Publishers: 1996
Revised edition published by HarperCollins Publishers: 1998
Current edition published by Money$marts Publishing: 2014

Canadian Cataloguing in Publication Data

Baker, Murray, 1961-
   The debt-free graduate: how to survive college or university
without going broke

Rev. ed

ISBN 0-9733806-0-8
   1.   College students – Canada – Finance, Personal. I. Title.

LB2337.6.C35B35 2003   332.024'375   C2003-904864-0

08 12   WEB   10 9 8 7 6 5 4 3 2 1 14
08 14
Printed and bound in Canada

THE DEBT-FREE GRADUATE

HOW TO SURVIVE COLLEGE OR UNIVERSITY WITHOUT GOING BROKE

MURRAY BAKER

VISIT US AT:
WWW.DEBTFREEGRAD.COM

FOLLOW US ON TWITTER:
DEBTFREEGRAD

VIEW OUR BLOG:
WWW.DEBTFREEGRAD.ORG

Money$marts Publishing

Contents

Acknowledgements

Perhaps one of the most unexpected parts of writing this book was the chance to relive my university experience of looming deadlines and hair-pulling editing, fuelled by potent coffee and excessive perfectionism. However, the hard work and long hours were shared by the many people who assisted in their special and individual ways. To these people I owe a great deal of gratitude.

I am grateful for the many people who provided initial encouragement. Richard Zajchowski, who encouraged me in the process of taking this to print; Michael Young, who was my first contact at HarperCollins and who lent his expertise in the publishing field; Gordon Pape, who gave his encouragement and suggestions; Al Magrath, for his helpful advice; and Sandra Weese and Kendrew Pape, for their feedback early on in the process.

An enormous amount of information is contained in this book, which I could not have collected without the professional expertise of: Gary Mason, Frank Arroyas, Tom Burnett, Doreen Whitehead, Glenn Matthews, Joan Van Housen, Andrew Holt, Fran Wdowczyk, Rob Tiffin, Rod Skinkle, Dave Caves, Maura Helsdon, Steven Daniel, Karen Mackenzie, and numerous others. I am extremely grateful for the wealth of information they provided and their willingness to take time out of their already busy schedules to share it with me.

A great deal of thanks goes to Andrea Hajdu, who squinted and waded her way through my often undecipherable chicken scratching to convert it to more humanly legible computer form and who did much in the way of legwork to verify facts, figures, and details. Also thanks to Carl Baker,

Wendy Magrath, and Nancy Amos, who assisted in the various proofing and editing stages, and Paul Milligan for his input from the fringe.

I particularly want to thank my editor, Marie Campbell, for the encouragement, support, and expertise she provided throughout the process. Her patience with deadlines, her very thorough and helpful editing, and her constructive advice were invaluable in attaining a more polished product. I also want to thank Scott Mitchell for his editing expertise. Thanks also to Iris Tupholme, Carol Bonnett, Nicole Langlois, Susan Broadhurst, Andrea Orlick, Michaela Cornell, and the rest of the HarperCollins team for their support of this project and commitment to it.

Much thanks goes to the rest of my family, friends, and co-workers for their personal support: Loreen Baker, Roger Baker, the Magraths, Jack Russel, Sandra Dunlavy, and the Hunters. Their understanding of my absence from many social commitments was greatly appreciated.

Thank you to Laurie Hunter, whose contributions to the project were many. Her diligent word processing and editing were invaluable. Much more important, however, was the personal love, support, and encouragement she gave through the long and often stressful process.

Much thanks to Tecla Jenniskens for her love, humour and great soup during the writing of the second edition. Thanks also to Glenda Chin and Helen Yagi for their support and feedback through updates of *The Debt-Free Graduate*.

A very special thank you to Maria Isabel Bunning for all her love, continual encouragement and great sense of humour during the writing of the 2014 edition of the book. Her passion and dedication were a great source of motivation.

Finally, I wish to thank the numerous students I have the privilege of working with. Their energy, enthusiasm, and dedication in assisting others are a constant source of inspiration and a reminder of the student within us all. Who says you have to leave school when you graduate?

Introduction

This is a book that will tell you how to earn, save, and spend smart. It will give you tips on finding the best summer and part-time jobs and making them really pay, strategies for making your hard-earned money go a long way, and advice on how to avoid being gouged by those who prey upon students' financial inexperience (including those who write get-rich-quick books for students). It will tell you how to find optimal housing for the best price and how to furnish your palace for a pittance. It will tell you the things you need to know to eat like a king on a shoestring budget, save on school supplies, and travel cheaply. It will also suggest ways to turn your student status into a financial advantage, how to make sure you have the cash you need when you need it, and how to make your money grow without using a roll-of-the-dice approach. No fancy formulas, just good sound methods.

When I was still a student, it would never have occurred to me to write this book. However, as graduation approached, I began to see more and more of my classmates afflicted by one of the great plagues of modern society: debt. The university students I knew were no longer swallowing goldfish for fun; rather, they were viewing them as a potential food group in their student diet. The milestone of graduation, which once represented a time of great joy, now signalled a time of having to pay back the long string of debts that had accumulated during student days. I no longer envisioned a graduation ceremony in a hall full of parents brimming with pride, but rather students convocating in front of the person they had grown to know best these past few years—their local bank loan officer.

Graduating students are now commonly facing principal debts of $25,000–$30,000, and sometimes as much as $50,000, or $60,000 with thousands of dollars on top of this to be paid in accumulated interest. These figures represent more than merely a debt that will force recent graduates to live frugally for a couple of years. Rather, they reveal a situation that will have a profound impact on the lifestyles of graduating students for many years into their working lives. The ability to afford vacations, to get married, to own a house, to have children, to buy cars, boats, and other consumer goods will all be severely hampered. Even the ability to create projects by which to generate capital (to pay off these loans), such as starting a business, will be impaired. Perhaps worst of all, graduating with a huge debt will affect an individual's ability to take advantage of such tax shelters as RRSPs and Tax Free Savings Accounts (TFSAs) to plan for their own future and RESPs to plan for the future education of their children. Sounds like a pretty grim situation. But it need not be.

This book is not about the burden of debt that can hang over a person's head for much of his or her adult life. Nor is it a financial book filled with graphs and charts and technical formulas, as you're sure to get enough of that in your economics and business textbooks. Rather, it is a book about some simple measures students can take to stay out of debt while still having the time of their lives at college or university.

It is also unlikely that you will use every single tip or idea that is included within these pages, and indeed it is probably unnecessary that you do. However, many of these ideas will go a long way towards improving your financial wellbeing and making you a debt-free graduate.

CHAPTER 1

Smart Financing, or, Where the Heck Am I Supposed to Get $60,000?

That first talk between parents and their kid is not an easy one. There is uneasiness as parents fumble for the right words, while children are perhaps equally uncomfortable as they anticipate what will trickle from mom or dad's mouth. It's a topic that pervades our society through advertising, movies, television, and other media. It's on everyone's mind as they mature, yet it's not an easy thing to talk about. Yes, I'm speaking of money. Along with sex, it's probably one of the most alluded to, but avoided, topics in the house.

However, as the start of university approaches, it's one issue that is key to pursuing an education. Too often, the issue of financing an education is left to miscommunication and assumptions. "Yeah, I'm headed off to university—got my trunk, computer, and slightly broken-in Doc Martens ready to go, but I'm not quite sure where the money's coming from."

But you can do a lot to avoid this stress and uncertainty. Your next two to four years will be less stressful if you do something now. Assess your situation carefully. Talk to anyone who may be helping finance your education: parents, other relatives, significant others, etc. For many students the biggest source of financial support will be parents. Talk with your parents about financing your education! It's something you may have to bring up yourself, and the discussion may not go perfectly, but it will start things off in the right direction. Here are some tips on what to talk about:

- How much money do you think you can reasonably contribute to the whole process? Don't be unrealistic by assuming you'll pick up a senior management job for the summer, or that you are bound to pick the right lottery numbers sometime in the next year. Be conservative in your estimate of how much you can contribute from savings, summer and part-time jobs, and other earnings.

- Talk about how much your parents can contribute each year. Get a firm commitment (oh, the dreaded "C" word). I'm not suggesting you show up accompanied by a lawyer and a 20-page contract, but it's important to get some clear figures or a commitment to cover specific costs. For example: "We'll pay your residence and transportation costs" or "We'll pay for books and tuition," not "We'll do what we can" or "We'll see how the year goes"—only the government can get away with such vague promises.

- Find out what your parents' expectations are. Do they expect you to work part-time? Do they expect straight "A"s? Or do they expect both, along with you being VP of the student council and captain of the basketball team? Their expectations can greatly affect how much you need to have them assist with the funding.

- Look at what your major expenses are going to be. If you are leaving Montreal to go to the University of British Columbia, then you'll be looking at moving, as well as trips home at Christmas and perhaps at Spring Break. If you're living at home but having to drive to campus, then you'll have some auto expenses. If living in residence, consider expenses such as food, accommodation, and activity fees (and a good supply of water balloons).

- Come up with an estimate of what it will cost you. Include everything, right down to entertainment, personal care products, clothing, and so on. Obviously, your costs will be higher in places like Vancouver or Toronto than they will be in London or Winnipeg. Be realistic. Don't claim you'll get by on $10 a month for entertainment when you are used to spending $50 a week. It's better to overestimate. If you are unsure, ask for a sample budget from your college or university financial aid office. The sample budget below shows you a very general cost breakdown.

Sample Budget (based on an eight-month term)		
	AWAY FROM HOME*	AT HOME
Tuition Fees	$ 6,253	$6,253
Compulsary Fees	750	750
Books and Multimedia	1,160	1,160
Entertainment (32 wks. × $28)	896	896
Clothing (8 mo. × $33)	264	264
Transportation ($277 per term)	554	554
Rent (8 mo. × $451)	3,608	—
Telephone (8 mo. × $53)	424	—
Utilities (8 mo. × $81)	648	—
Food (8 mo. × $262)	2,096	—
Miscellaneous	208	208
TOTAL	**$16,861**	**$10,085**

*These costs are estimated for students living off-campus and preparing their own meals

The reality is that a sizeable number of students don't have the proverbial Bank of Mom and Dad to tap into. Many students are from single-parent families, families where one or both parents are unemployed, or families that are simply not in a financial position to contribute. However, if the financial support of your parents is out of the question, there's still plenty you can do to pump up the money flowing in and dam up the cash draining out.

The Four-Step Game Plan

By having a rough idea of what you have and what you need, you'll save costly unexpected financial mistakes and stress. Prior to each year, go through the following exercise:

1. List all resources that you have: scholarships, bursaries, money from parents (or guardian or spouse), job earnings. Then list all expenses: tuition, books, food, housing, transportation, entertainment, etc. (Be realistic. If you inhale food like a vacuum then account for this; if you guzzle beer like one big Oktoberfest then figure this in. You may of course want to do this exercise when your parents aren't looking over your shoulder.)
2. Compare the two to see differences and examine where you can cut your expenses and/or where you can increase your resources. For example, cut out one night a week of eating out, have three roommates instead of two, work five hours a week researching for a prof.
3. Plan for the money you will need and when you will need it. Think, for example, of tuition at the start of the year, extra money at Christmas, money to move home at the end of the year, etc.
4. Map out where you'll keep your money, and where it will be when you need it. For example, Canada Savings Bonds for half of the money, a money market account for a quarter, and the rest in a bank account.

The sample budget is equally important for the student not receiving parental support. Where the real difference lies is the increased necessity of tapping into scholarships, bursaries, loans, and various summer and part-time jobs. By maximizing these sources of cash and using cost-saving strategies, you can go a long way towards narrowing or even eliminating any shortfall from lack of parental funding. Summer and part-time jobs are discussed in chapters 3 and 4. Below are some guidelines for finding and making the most of other sources of funding.

Scholarships

One of the most lucrative ways to haul in the cash is to excel in the classroom. In fact, as colleges and universities fight for top students, the size of scholarships has increased plenty. That means it may be more worthwhile for you to aim for the grades than toil away flipping burgers.

Why are scholarships such a great thing? 'Cuz they're free money. No EI deductions, pension deductions, union dues, payback—it all goes to you. It's like having your cake and eating it too. And the news is now even better. Scholarships, fellowships and bursary income received by post-secondary students is now exempt from income tax by eliminating the former $3,000 exemption limit. (See Addendum 1)

Scholarships are, for the most part, based on the marks you pulled off in your last year of high school or your grades in college or university. Brains also beat out brawn. So unless you pack up and head south, your GPA is going to beat your ERA and your point-per-game average nearly every time. Occasionally, colleges and universities also consider such factors as community involvement, extracurricular activities, athletics, and leadership skills. When factors other than marks are considered, the handouts are generally called "awards." Some may be specific to a particular faculty or program. They may range in value anywhere from $100 to $22,000 per year. Now, you don't have to be an accounting major to realize that's not a bad haul! Not only that, some are renewable for up to four years.

Scholarship awards are paid out in different ways. Some deliver the cash, others cover tuition, some pay for residence room and board, and still others give you a certificate to redeem at a campus bookstore or computer store. Some company-sponsored awards even include an offer of summer employment. All in all, they spell out a significant financial bonus.

So where are the big bucks when it comes to scholarships?

The number of scholarships is large and it can be difficult to track them all down. In addition to asking for information at college and university financial aid offices, there is a book published that lists the scholarships available at Canadian universities. Although a bit dated, as most scholarship listings have moved online (see page 12), it will still give you an idea of some companies and organizations that are handing out the cash. The best place to find this book is a high school guidance office, although some universities and public libraries may also have copies.

Ask for:
> EDge Interactive. ScholarshipsCanada.com.
> Entrance Awards Directory 2007, Toronto, Ont.:
> EDge Interactive, 2006.

The key in the scholarship game is to get your eye on the prize early. In your second-last year of high school, start to investigate what the schools you're thinking of attending are willing to fork over to have your presence grace their campus. You may need to apply for certain scholarships a full year before you actually attend.

Main Entrance Scholarships—Often called national or presidents' scholarships, these are like the Oscars of the scholarship Academy Awards. Prizes, including cash and non-monetary gifts, can run as high as $20,000 a year in total value. Some are a one-shot deal, although many are renewed each year, as long as you continue to pull off the high grades. The funds for these scholarships often come from the college or university itself, or from a particular faculty, or out of the deep pockets of some very well-endowed individuals.

Simply by applying for admission to a particular school, you may automatically be considered for many scholarships and awards. However, you will need to apply separately for others. Some scholarships even require you to write a short essay or go for an interview.

If you are a top high school student, your guidance counsellor should alert you to these scholarships—but don't count on it. Sometimes these people are asleep behind their copy of *High School Counsellor Quarterly*, and miss their cue. So don't let thousands of dollars slip away due to a missed application deadline. Enquire at the college or university awards office directly. Keep in mind that deadlines for these scholarships are early at many schools, so enquire well ahead of time—even up to a year or more before you plan to attend.

Other Admission Scholarships—If you don't walk away with the big trophies, not to worry. Unlike the Academy Awards, you can lose the Oscar and still bring home some valuable prizes. There are many other admission scholarships, often funded by distinguished donors (and undistinguished donors with lots of money), as well as by corporations, agencies, and institutions. Many of these are sizeable and therefore worth pursuing, and some also continue each year, provided you maintain a high average.

In-course or Faculty Scholarships—Unlike admission scholarships, in-course or faculty scholarships are based on how you do once you make it to college or university. In the awards scenario, these are like walking away with a Genie Award—valuable, sought after, but only known regionally. Again, these can be substantial and sometimes continuing prizes.

Location—You may be eligible for an award based solely on where you live: province, county, city, or town. If you are from a town where you're the only person furthering your studies, you may be a shoo-in.

Citizenship—Many entry scholarships are available only to Canadian citizens or permanent residents. If you don't fall into these categories, it may be worth it to apply to your country of origin for funding since obtaining citizenship or landed status in Canada can be a lengthy process. In-course scholarships open to all students are a good route after first year.

Extracurricular Activities—Some scholarships, on top of considering your marks, also look seriously at such things as community involvement, leadership skills, and extracurricular activities—sometimes as far back as three or four years, and possibly further. They basically look for a well-rounded person (totally unlike the well-roundedness one develops after living on residence food for a year), so involving yourself in areas outside of academics may improve your chances of receiving an award.

Academic Improvement—Some awards are occasionally given to students showing the greatest improvement. I don't recommend bombing your first year and then working your butt off the following year, just to qualify for these awards. Nevertheless, such awards can contribute to your dwindling cash supply, so it's worth checking with your school to see what's available.

Area of Study—Your chosen field is particularly important in terms of qualifying for financial support. Most faculties have many awards made available by alumni or corporations in that area, so check with both the school and the specific faculty to which you are applying.

Special Skills, Interests, Knowledge—While playing the national anthem by cupping your hand under your armpit isn't likely to net you much in the way of cash, other skills, such as a foreign language, musical ability, or dance, might. Consider any skills you excel at and check to see whether related organizations offer anything in the way of prizes.

Club Affiliations—A poker club won't deal you much, but if you, your parents, or your guardian belong to a club like Kiwanis, Girl Guides, Boy Scouts, Optimist, or 4H, then you may be eligible for some decent scholarships. Dad's club with the funny little hats and the secret handshakes may pay off for you yet!

Place of Employment—The company you or your parents work for may provide scholarships for family members. Check with the human resources office to see what is offered.

Union—Whether you lean to the left or the right, it may benefit you if your parents belong to a union. Check to see if your parents' union offers any scholarships to family members.

Ethnic Lineage—Some cultural clubs and organizations offer various scholarships, which you may be eligible to apply for simply because you are you. Check with cultural or ethnic clubs with which you or your family are affiliated.

Churches and Religious Institutions—Your prayers may be answered when it comes to funding. Some religious institutions offer scholarships to their members.

Cash Competitions—If you love the challenge of competition, you may want to look into contests in areas in which you excel. If you are a good speaker, there are speaking scholarships. If you love arguing, there's debating. Look into these for some extra cash.

Athletic Organizations—There are some awards given by various athletic organizations. If you excel in a certain sport (or sports), check with the clubs or organizations with which you play and train. Although few in number (but growing), schools themselves may also provide some athletic scholarships, usually with a minimum academic average attached.

Permanent Disabilities—If you have a disability, such as a physical or learning disability, you may be eligible for certain scholarships. Check with the campus disabilities office.

Special Situations—A number of other situations may qualify you for funding through awards of various kinds. Being a single parent, female, minority, or international student (the plight of the follically challenged male hasn't been recognized yet) may all lead you to a cash windfall.

Veterans Groups—If your parents were involved in wartime service, you may qualify for scholarships given by various veterans groups. Head down to the Legion to see what they're shelling out of the war chest.

Couch potato—Finally, some scholarships you may qualify for just sitting there and watching TV. Yes, some scholarships are awarded to cable subscribers in Atlantic Canada. Of course, there's a catch. You have to put down the Fritos, let go of the remote and roll off the couch to get to their office for an application. Point is, keep your eyes peeled for unlikely sources that may help pay your way.

To help find some of the charitable foundations and who they give their money to—hopefully you—an invaluable resource is **Grantconnect.ca** (Formerly known as the *Canadian Directory to Foundations and Corporations*). Published by Imagine Canada, this Canadian database contains over 3100 foundations, 150 corporations and 90,000 indexed grants.

Award Search Service

If you want to avoid the search entirely, you can plug into an award search service that will track down all that's potentially available for you. The only catch is the cost: this service will usually set you back $150–$200, with no guarantee it will come up with anything. I liken these services to the kind of modelling agents who'll take your money, let you know what's out there, and then leave you to get it yourself. These services are not worth it. So save yourself the cash. With a little digging, you'll be able to unearth this precious metal yourself.

The Better Option

Rather than shell out money for a fund search service, tap into the following free Canadian sources to help you find the treasures.

On-line check out **scholarshipscanada.com** and **studentawards.com**. Both sites offer good databases, searchable based on your situation. They will come up with a list of scholarships that you may be eligible for. You can find these and other scholarship links for Canada and abroad at: debtfreegrad.com/pages/freeres&tools/sourceofcash.html

Bursaries

If you haven't, er, shall we say, excelled in the academic area, there's always another route to the loot: need. Not to be confused with other pressing needs such as deadline extensions, a date, or a purpose in life, this is good, old-fashioned financial need. A gift of money given to a student who demonstrates a genuine need is called a bursary.

Scholarships for the *Really* Desperate

The Mike Tyson Athletic Support/High Achievers Club—For all students whose total marks are greater than Mike's brushes with the law. Students receive a substantial grant to take the bite out of expenses. Unlimited funding is available, although you are advised to cash your grant cheque ASAP, since the program is administered by Don King.

The Canadian Tobacco Association Endowment Fund ("Reaching Out" to the Youth of Today)— Successful candidates receive no cash but are given unlimited quantities of home-grown Canadian tobacco (along with other, unidentified substances which may appear in their products) for those high-stress periods in the term. Included is a bonus guide called "Suppressing Research You Just Don't Like," a must-have for students wanting to fudge their research findings.

The Larry King Law Scholarship—Awarded to the student who shows particular excellence in the area of divorce law. Drawn from his alimony payouts, this large scholarship also includes placement representing Larry in his next divorce. Awarded annually. Eligibility is very limited since former wives of Larry are ineligible to apply.

Canada Post Scholarship—Open to all high school graduates. A simple scholarship to apply for: simply mail in your form, and if it actually gets there on time and in one piece you automatically receive an award. Last year, two Canada Post Scholarships were granted nationally. Please allow up to three years for delivery.

The Jo Jo Psychic Prize—Awarded to the most tele-pathically perceptive student who has levitated to the top of his or her graduating class. This scholarship covers all educational expenses, both in this life and in future existences, provided an A average is maintained. Students need not apply since Jo Jo, of course, already knows your marks.

Fast-Food Foundation Burger Bursary—A whopper scholarship awarded annually to students whose marks are matched only by their cholesterol level. Scholarships range from basic to the deluxe monster scholarship with everything on it. Awards can be picked up at any drive-through location in Canada.

Greenpeace Scholarship—Given annually to students who have served a sentence of at least 90 days for civil disobedience while maintaining a B average. Not much in the way of cash, but all recycled books are paid for, along with spray paint, shackles, and some "lip-smacking vegetarian recipes." Students who continue their planetary protests may also be eligible for an additional Bail Bursary. Geared towards the up-and-coming activist, this bursary is particularly valuable for the incarcerated protester who really *can't* make it to class.

But before you head out the door to spend this money in advance, remember a couple of things. You may not have to be the brightest bulb in your class, but you do have to demonstrate some sort of academic competency—like passing, and even maintaining, say, a B or C average. Primarily, though, bursaries are based on a demonstrated financial need.

Unlike some scholarships, you need to apply for bursaries. Colleges and universities tend to chase down high-grade students more aggressively than they do students who are broke. What do you need to qualify for these gifts? The following factors are considered:

- How good you look . . . on paper, that is. Some schools will take into account your resources, such as income and savings, along with those of your parents (if you are classified as a dependent student). They will also look to see that you've worked out a reasonable budget of modest spending to arrive at that need.

- Bursaries, like scholarships, are sometimes based on qualifying factors such as ethnic background, single-parent status, or disability.

- Bursaries sometimes look at outside activities that you've been involved in (legal, of course). Community work, athletics, leadership roles, and volunteer work are often considered. Since marks aren't the prime consideration in awarding bursaries, these other factors may be given closer attention.

- Check into bursaries that are offered to part-time students. Some students are part-time for the very reason that they are financially strapped. There are bursaries offered specifically for such students. Check with the department or faculty of part-time studies or mature student organization at your school to see what is offered.

- Many bursaries are specific to certain faculties or areas of study. It could be that some alumnus was cash-strapped as a student, then graduated and actually paid off his loan, and left some money to help other financially struggling students. There are many such bursaries. I have even come across an award for Pest Management—nothing to do with annoying roommates, I suppose?

- If your parents have affiliations with service clubs, organizations, or a generous employer, especially a college or university, you may be eligible for certain bursaries or awards.

- Another potential bursary source is athletic teams or clubs. They may offer bursaries to members in need.

Other points to remember in the bursary bonanza game:

- Bursaries, like scholarships, were taxable on amounts over $3,000, however as of January 1st, 2006 these are tax exempt.

- Like scholarships, some bursaries are open only to Canadian citizens. However, special private-donor bursaries for international students may be available at your school. Check with your campus international student or financial aid office.

- Dates for applying for bursaries will vary. It is best to apply at the beginning of the school year so as not to miss out. However, you should ask for this information from your school well in advance (when you apply for admission).

- Because some bursaries are given out continuously each year as qualified students apply (until the money runs out), you may find it pays big to apply at the earliest date possible (first come, first served!). There are more and more students dipping into a limited pool of funds.

Summary of Scholarships and Bursaries

- Ask at your high school guidance office for information on scholarships for which you may be eligible.

- Read the large course calendars of various universities and colleges for information on scholarships and bursaries (some give quite detailed descriptions).

- Check directly with the financial aid, or scholarships and awards office at the universities or colleges you are applying to (some smaller schools have this office as part of a larger department). Plan your budget early and, if you will be in need of financial assistance such as bursaries, make an appointment two to three months before the start of school to discuss your options.

- Find out what is available to you through your affiliations with clubs or athletic teams.

- Check for opportunities through your parents' work, social, service, and professional affiliations.

- Do a search using the print and on-line resources that are available at your library and on the web.

- Consider whether you may qualify for assistance for being a member of an ethnic minority, female, disabled, or a single parent (or just desperate and dateless).

- If you're already in college or university, check within your faculty or department to see whether any in-course scholarships exist. If you don't think you have a chance at one, drop in to your faculty anyway just to say hi.

- Apply early—12 months ahead for scholarships, and at the beginning of the school year, or preferably earlier, for both government bursaries and those offered by your institution. Avoid missing an early deadline, and therefore a rapidly disappearing pile of cash that you could be enjoying.

Work/Study Plans: The Gift with a Catch

If you still haven't walked away with any of the prizes I've described so far, there's another option to consider: work/study programs. These financial creatures are a cross between a gift and a job: a little cash for a little work. As with bursaries, approval is based on need. The program is often funded by the government but run by your college or university through its financial aid office. Rather than purely a gift, they're a gift that you work off, usually in particular faculties or departments around campus. You may be asked to do anything from typing or photocopying to researching or making artwork to earn your approved amount, although the intent is to give you work related to your studies. Upon qualifying, you apply for the job you're most interested in. The pay for these positions is often decent (though not exorbitant) and may vary depending on the job.

Things to remember about work/study:

- Competition for this funding can be tough, so apply early at your school's financial aid office. Many work/study programs operate only until the money runs out, which happens pretty quickly these days.

- Some schools may approve additional work/study positions in mid-year, if not all approved students take advantage of their funding. Be sure to check back later (usually in December).

- If there's a particular job you want (say, researching for a favourite prof) but there's no money currently set aside to pay you, see if the person you want to work for can create a work/study position. If approved, and you qualify, you may have a job, and they may have a position which they normally couldn't have afforded to create. Definitely win-win all the way.

Government Loan and Grant Programs

Grants and loans are two of the biggest sources of funding for many students. Grants are of course preferable since you don't have to pay them back. This breed of funding has been fast disappearing as governments have decided to cut back on the gifts in favour of loans. There are, nonetheless, some special grants still around, and some increased study and research grants that were added since the 1998 federal budget.

Grants

Grants are awarded on the basis of need, although often there may be additional considerations.

Gender, for example, can mean money if you are female and a grad student in certain areas of study not traditionally pursued by women. Designed to encourage women to pursue an education in subject areas such as engineering and physical sciences, these grants can total up to $3,000 per year.

Permanent disability may also qualify you for federal grants of up to $8,000 and Canada Student Study Grant for students with Permanent Disabilities of up to $2,000. Check with your disabilities coordinator on campus for details.

Part-time and full-time students may qualify for grants federally (Canada Study Grants) or provincially. Eligibility is based strictly on need, along with whether you have family responsibilities. First time, first year post secondary students from low income families may now be eligible for as much as a $3,000 Access Grant.

In addition to checking in your home province to determine whether you are eligible for the above awards, you should enquire as to whether your home province still makes general grants available to students. The provincial guys can occasionally be generous and start giving out money too!

Canada Student Grants Program (CSGP): out with the old, in with the new.

The new grant program replaces the 10 year old Canada Millennium Scholarship Foundation. Gone are the merit based scholarships and the bursaries, all of which have been replaced by grants. In addition to grants for students from low and middle income families, grants for students with dependants, part-time students and students with permanent disabilities are also available under this program.. You will automatically be considered for these grants when applying for a student loan – all except for the Grant for Services and Equipment for Students with Permanent Disabilities. If you're in Quebec, Northwest Territories or Nunavut you'll need to go through their own provincially run financial assistance programs.

Loans

If you think loans are confusing, you are not alone. When it comes to figuring these out, the people that administer them also seem puzzled. Governments are continually changing the rules, just as you finally figure out the game. One thing that's not puzzling is the fact that sooner or later you are normally going to have to pay the loan back, most likely with some form of interest tacked on. Loans can thus be a dangerous trap as they silently grow while you are buried beneath your mound of textbooks. However, by learning what's available and how to use them wisely, you can take advantage of some very deep cash pools.

Canada and Provincial Student Loan Programs: The Products

Government loans come from two sources: the federal government and provincial or territorial governments. You apply each year you are studying by filling out a single application in your home province. It's then sent to your province's central processing office, where a formula is used to decide how much the federal government will contribute and how much your provincial government will kick in.

Canada Student Loans, the grandmother of the loans program, is sponsored by the federal government. Loans are approved by the government. In addition, as of March 1, 2001 rather than negotiating your loan with a participating bank, you have your loan directly with the government through the National Student Loans Service Centre (NSLSC) (loans prior to that time are still held by the participating bank, credit union, or caisses populaires). Presently, roughly $2.4 billion is loaned out to more than 425,000 students under the federal program (which doesn't include Quebec, Nunavut or the Northwest Territories).

Provincial Student Loans vary from province to province and are usually set up as a cost-sharing deal to supplement the funding from the federal government. Together, these two sources make up the majority of student loans.

So what's the big break with the Canada and Provincial Student Loans?

There are five big advantages:

1. These loans are interest-free while you are in school—a potentially huge benefit. Federal and provincial governments have agreed to pay the interest for you until you graduate. But before you go shedding tears of graditute, remember you're young so they'll tax you back later.

2. You don't have to start paying back the loan until six months after you graduate.

3. The interest rate you pay on these loans is limited by the government. The two possible rates are:

   • A maximum floating rate of prime plus 2½ percent
   • A maximum fixed rate of prime plus 5 percent

4. Upon graduating you may be eligible for the student loan Repayment Assistant Plan (RAP) if you are having difficulty making loan payments. Based on your income (and family size) the program will limit (or in certain cases eliminate) the amount of your loan payments while you are in a precarious employment situation until the big bucks start rolling in. It will also limit the length of time for your student loan burden.

5. The interest that you pay on the loan is tax deductable.

To give you every last detail of how these loans work would require a thick, boring book which would be out of date by the time it hit the shelf. I'll leave that to the government, since they excel in producing such publications. What is important to know is what federal and provincial loans mean for you, how you can take advantage of them, and how to use them effectively.

The main thing to remember with student loan programs is that they exist to supplement your funding from other sources: primarily jobs, savings, RESPs, income from other investments, scholarships, and of course the Bank of Mom and Dad. Once your money from other sources is calculated, the loans kick in to lend you whatever your shortfall is (with limits of course). The ultimate criterion here is what they consider your need to be.

Qualification Criteria

In addition to demonstrating need, qualifying for a full-time student loan also requires that you:

- Be a Canadian citizen or permanent resident of Canada or be a designated protected person.

- Be a resident of a province or territory participating in the Canada Student Loans program.

- Be enrolled in and sustain at least a 60 percent course load; the minimum course load is 40 percent for students with permanent disabilities.

- Maintain a satisfactory scholastic standing.

- Be enrolled in an approved program at a designated post-secondary institution, as determined by your provincial government (12 or more weeks in length within a 15-consecutive-week period).

- Not have a previously defaulted student loan (first time applicants 22 and over must pass a credit check).

- Not have exhausted your maximum lifetime limit of financial aid including interest free status.

Applying: In Step with the Government Shuffle

Complete the following steps:

- Pick up a Canada/Provincial Student Loans form from a high school guidance office or college or university financial aid office in the spring (or at the same time as you send in your first applications), or for on-line provincial applications go to **www.debtfreegrad.com/pages/govtloans/index.htm**

- Work through the NSLSC forms, accompanied by the detailed records you kept of your resources and earnings. You may also have to estimate your summer earnings and then report your actual wad when you pick up your loan in the fall. If your actual earnings were different from your estimated earnings, this could change the amount of your loan.

- If you're a dependant, get the necessary information from your parents, such as their income and current financial situation. (Reassure them you won't reveal any of the Swiss bank accounts they have tucked away.)

- Attach supplementary documentation to explain any special situation not reflected in your application. This may apply in cases such as parental bankruptcy, recent divorce or illness in the family, or summer-school attendance.

- Apply early (or even earlier). Within the first one to two months that applications become available is optimal.

- Submit your application to the Provincial or Territorial Student Assistance Office in the province you are applying from.

- Pray hard that the public service union doesn't go on strike and severely delay your application.

Processing: The Loan Ranger Decides Again!

Once you have filled out the loan application form (a multi-page document which the government undoubtedly considers good practice for the income-tax-filing ritual, which you'll also experience soon enough) and submitted it to the appropriate authorities, the following steps are taken to process your request.

You Are Categorized—Government people like to categorize things since it makes it easier for them to understand. You'll be put into a category such as "dependent student living at home" or "single independent student living away from home."

Your Costs Are Assessed—Based on your category, the government decides how much your education is going to cost you. This figure is based on the money required to support a very basic student existence, not the amount required for the existence of the government worker figuring out your application.

Your Contributions From Other Resources are Calculated— The government looks at what you can pitch in to help pay for school. (Better not be hiding that 40-foot yacht, or the condo in Maui—those government people tend to frown upon any toys they don't have.) They look at your savings, and they add up your summer and part-time earnings to figure out how much you should have saved. Any other sources of income—EI benefits, your Family Allowance, along with RRSPs, inheritance, and other liquid assets will also be looked at. In 2014 the government scraped the $5000 vehicle exemption, which means owning a vehicle valued, for example, at $9,000 will no longer affect your expected contribution from assets. If you are a dependent student, they'll want to know how much your mom and dad are hauling in from that chinchilla ranch they own. Your parents are expected to contribute something—how much may depend on factors such as how many of your siblings they are helping through school as well. Some provinces may also assess your parents' assets over a certain amount. If your parents are divorced, the government may look only at the financial resources of your sole-support parent, or they may require documentation outlining child-support agreements. Other resources may also be looked at.

Then They'll Figure Out Your Needs—After subtracting all your resources from your costs, the government comes up with the supplementary amount they believe you will need to live the life of a full-fledged student. (If, for example, all your resources totaled $10,000 and your expenses came to $15,000, then you would probably qualify for a loan of around $5,000.) After that, you'll receive notification of how much you qualify for (Certificate of Eligibility – also called schedule 1) in Canada and provincial student loans. And the government workers? Well, they'll probably take a break, maybe catch some zzz's, or if the weather's cooperating, maybe just take the afternoon off for some golf. Ah, the life of a civil servant!

Bringing Home the Bucks

Expect a reply within four to six weeks (depending on when you apply). Not to doubt the efficiency of government or anything, but never count on your loan showing up at the beginning of the school year when you need to pay your tuition, rent, etc. Always ask for a deferral on your tuition until your loan arrives and have your own earnings available for initial expenses such as rent, food, and other necessities.

Once you receive your loan documents, have your Confirmation of Enrollment section signed at the school you'll be attending (this is sometimes done electronically). Then, run with newfound optimism (along with some photo ID and proof of Social Insurance Number) to any designated Canada Post Outlet (or in some provinces the agent of disbursement) to submit your completed loan forms and obtain your Canada Student Loan Agreement. Expect the money to be tucked into your bank account within one week—if you arrange direct deposit by attaching a voided personal cheque, or two weeks if it is sent by mail.

Appeal Process

No doesn't always mean no—at least when it comes to loans. If you think you should have been approved for one and you were not, you can appeal the decision. Don't hesitate just because it's a hassle. You should appeal in the following situations:

- If the information you provided was incorrect or has changed. Maybe that summer job selling vacuum cleaners just didn't pan out.

- If you think that a calculation or mental error has been made on your assessment. Perhaps that government employee mistakenly got your loan amount and his golf score mixed up.

- If you have extraordinary circumstances that weren't reflected in your application. Your parents may have split up, one of them may have been laid off, or your own summer job may have fallen through. Yes, there is a human side to the government, and they may take a compassionate second look.

Tips on Government-Sponsored Student Loans

- If you have any doubt that you'll have enough cash for the school year and you honestly qualify for a loan, take it out, as it may be more difficult to get the loan later during the year if you suddenly find you are short of cash.. Then sock part or all of it away in a safe investment where you'll earn money and won't be tempted to spend it. The money will be there if you do suddenly find yourself in desperate straits, but if the emergency never arises, then you can pay back the loan in full before the interest kicks in. You'll also help to establish a credit rating for yourself by taking it out and paying it back on time.

- If you have questions, ask at the financial aid office of the school through which you are applying. Even if you're getting frustrated by delays or errors, be patient. School staff are usually very helpful and rarely the ones responsible for delays in your funding. They'll often be able to help you apply for other available sources of funding as well.

- With the recent changes to the program, you may have questions— so a couple of numbers for the National Student Loan Service Centre are worth remembering: Whether you are applying to a public or private institution the numbers are now the same: 1 888 815-4514 (1 800 2 225 2501 outside North America) or 905 306-2950.

More Student Loans

If you don't come home with much in the way of federal or provincial loans, take another look at government programs. There are more treasure chests to be opened.

Part-time Canada Student Loans—If you're not enrolled full time (that is, if you're carrying less than a 60-percent course load), you may be eligible for part-time student loans. Part-time loans just got an upgrade, with the maximum total amounts being raised to $10,000 (from $4,000) and perhaps more importantly, you do not have to start paying these back while in school (See Addendum 2). The best part, however, is that the interest on part-time loans has recently been eliminated while you are in school. If your income is low enough you may be eligible for repayment assistance under the Repayment Assistance Plan (RAP).

Compu-cash—In some provinces, you can obtain a purchase-specific loan. For example, Quebec offers loans for students to purchase computers while the Canada Student Loan Program now allows for this expense in your loan calculations.

Canadian Forces Personnel Assistance Fund—If you are a dependant of military personnel and staring in the face of General Broke, you may be eligible for these loans. Age (under 26), family income, length of service, and compassionate circumstances are all factors. The Department of Veterans Affairs (no, they don't deal with old flings) has information on other programs for veterans' families.

Emergency Loans—These are often available on a short-term basis (usually 90 days) for students in dire straits (e.g., when your provincial loan has been delayed). They're meant to give you money for immediate needs such as food and rent, while long-term financing is sought from other sources. Emergency loans are usually arranged through the financial aid office.

Longer-Term Loans—These are sometimes made available by corporations, organizations, student unions, alumni, and just plain nice people with lots of money. Primarily based on need, they are often given to students in specific situations, including those enrolled in certain programs, possessing a particular ethnic background, entering a specific year of study, or involved in various extracurricular activities. Often the only criterion is being a student who is broke. Usually these loans are administered through the college or university financial aid office.

Special or Emergency Loan Tips

- Ask about what's available. These loans aren't widely publicized, so you must ask about them, usually at your campus financial aid office.

- Some smaller loans even have some flexibility whereby in dire circumstances they turn into grants (i.e., they're non-repayable). Find out whether similar loans are available and what the conditions are.

- If your funds are really low and food is scarce, check whether your school or community has a food bank. Student use of food banks is increasing everywhere, so don't hesitate if the temporary need arises. Think of it as an interest-free food loan you can someday repay to help someone else.

- Don't be afraid to admit to your cash-strapped situation. Take advantage of what's available. School is usually stressful enough without having to worry about how you'll pay for your next meal.

- If you have a permanent disability, you may be eligible for loan forgiveness as part of the Repayment Assistance Plan for Borrowers with a Permanent Disability (RAP-PD).

Bank Loans

Some banks and lending institutions are not involved with federal or provincial loan programs. Not wanting to miss a piece of the action, however, they offer their own student loan setups. Be aware that these are not federal or provincial government-approved loans but rather regular loans with the word "student" attached. Some institutions offer straight loans. Others offer a line of credit where you are given access to, say, $5,000 and allowed to withdraw money as you need it. You pay interest only on the money you withdraw. Interest rates are fairly competitive with government-approved loans.

Sounds OK? Not so fast. The big drawback is that you have to start paying the interest off right away. This can add up quickly and start taxing your cash reserves. What happens if you end up one summer without a job? The interest still needs to be paid. Your best bet is to stay away from these loans unless absolutely necessary. It is difficult enough to pay the interest off if you take one out in third or fourth year; if you start in first year, you're really putting yourself behind the eight ball, as your interest payment on three or four years of loans can be frightening!

For example, if you take out a $6,000 bank loan in first year at a 9 percent interest rate, you may be paying off $45 a month in interest alone, which totals $540 a year. However, if you continue to take out a $6,000 loan every year, by the time you get to fourth year, you may be paying $180 a month, which means $2,160 a year, just to pay off the interest. This is on top of the $24,000 that you'll have to start paying off when you graduate. The danger of this is that by the time you're in fourth year, you need an extra $2,160 on top of the $11,000–$13,000 or so you would normally need to pay for school. It's like trying to dam a river while it's still raining.

Another big drawback of non-government loans is that

you usually need a guarantor (someone who will be responsible for paying your debt if you, for some reason, can't). This may make it more difficult to obtain a loan, particularly if you don't have someone willing to take on this responsibility.

If you do choose to go with a regular bank loan, you should investigate ways of negotiating a lower interest rate. For example, if your favourite aunt has $5,000 sitting around in Canada Savings Bonds, Guaranteed Investment Certificates, or some other long-term plan, you may be able to a strike a deal with the bank. If you convince your aunt to put her money up as collateral (a sort of guarantee that the loan will be paid), the bank may let you borrow against it (this is called a secured loan) and charge you a much lower interest rate (usually around the prime rate). At the same time, your aunt will continue to collect the interest earned by her bonds or certificates. The risk obviously goes to the person supplying collateral, but if it's your parents, or a favourite aunt, they probably have faith you'll pay it back. Over time, your interest-rate savings can be substantial. Even so, you still pay interest on these loans while you are a student.

Being Your Own Bank

In recent years the government has changed the rules to allow a person to borrow from their RRSP (up to $20,000 total) to pay for education. If you have an RRSP set up, it's one more option to choose from. The advantage to you is that it becomes in effect an interest free loan to yourself. You do have to repay at least part of it back to your RRSP plan. A great deal? ... well perhaps—but nothing comes without cost! In this case your cost is really the tax free earnings that you are giving up by withdrawing money from a place where it can grow tax free for retirement. The sooner you are able to pay it back, the quicker it can resume earning money within the tax shelter. Your decision on whether to use this option may be based on whether by withdrawing the money for an education you believe you can increase your earnings potential and thus overcome any temporarily sacrificed earnings within the RRSP.

One other loan route is to borrow against life insurance policies. While whole life or cash value–bearing policies are generally very poor moneymakers, except for the insurance companies, you can sometimes borrow against them at an interest rate lower than you'd otherwise get from a bank (the policy itself is a form of collateral). Imagine, a life insurance policy that benefits you while you're still alive. What a novel concept!

If you choose any loan, there's one major thing you need to remember: you have to pay it back, and usually with some form of interest attached. The obligation is easy enough to forget about when you are eyeing that soft leather coat, or that big-screen TV with the sale sticker attached. In fact, in Ontario the OSAP loan program was, at one time, affectionately known as the Ontario Stereo Assistance Program. However, there are some graduates around who are still struggling to pay off the loans they racked up, while the stereos they bought have long since broken down. If you take a loan, remember to spend it on your education.

Loans: Navigating Shark-Infested Waters

Borrowing money seems to be a fact of life. But paying back more than you need to isn't. If it's your first loan, it may seem like you are at the mercy of the big institutions, a powerless student meekly asking to borrow a few thousand out of the billions in their grasp. All of a sudden, those smiling people from the commercials seem a little less friendly. But there is lots you can do to ensure a loan at a good interest rate without feeling like a groveling desperado.

- Shop around. Try banks, credit unions, and trust companies. If you prefer one place, then ask them to match your best offer from a competitor.

- If you or your family have often dealt with a particular bank or credit union in the past, ask for a preferred lending rate.

- Don't be intimidated by banks when you seek a loan. Remember that you are young and educated (and getting more so), and it is in a bank's best interests to establish a long-term business relationship with you. If you don't like their attitude, go elsewhere!

- Ask for an explanation of any unclear terms on your loan

agreement.

- If you are turned down for a loan, find out why. It could be that your credit rating has an inaccuracy in it (a more common occurrence than you might think). Phone 1-800-465-7166 for an application for a copy of your credit record. It is everyone's right to receive this and it is free.

- Always negotiate the terms of your loan and try to get an interest rate lower than what the institution originally offers. The worst they can say is no, and a yes could save you a substantial amount of cash. Try asking for $\frac{1}{4}$ to $\frac{1}{2}$ percent lower than what they quote.

- Find out if you can pay down your loan ahead of time without penalty. This is particularly important if interest rates are starting to rise.

If you are given a loan, follow these repayment guidelines:

- Make payments on time! This will enhance your credit rating and chances of getting future loans at a reasonable interest rate.

- If you find yourself with surplus money at any time during school, pay down your interest-charging debts as soon as possible, starting with whichever loan charges the highest interest rate.

- Keep records of all payments made—rumour has it that banks have made the occasional mistake.

The Bottom Line

If you receive a government loan, accept it and use only what you need. Put any money you don't need into safe, high-interest-earning investments until you have to start paying interest on the loan. When you do start paying it off, the interest you earned by investing the surplus will help with your payments.

Take a regular bank loan only as a last resort. It could lead you deeper and deeper into debt throughout your years on campus.

Long-Forgotten Treasures

When you're moving, you often stumble upon things you didn't even remember you had. Your public school graduation photo (did you really dress that goofy?), your first baseball glove, your childhood toys, your early comic books (they look a little like the public school photo), and old trading cards. Lots of useless stuff . . . but wait a minute, there could be some big cash in those relics! You'd be surprised at what grown men will pay for rare dolls and comic books.

Take a look at the things you have. I'm not promising that you're sitting on a gold mine, but you may pick up some extra cash from things you've long since forgotten. Here's a sample of current prices in the memorabilia market:

- *Autographs* — Madonna, signed programme: $300; David Letterman: $50.

- *Comic Books* — Incredible Hulk 181: $400–$500; giant size X-Men #1: $500.

- *Trading Cards* — Wayne Gretzky rookie card: $900; O. J. Simpson rookie card: $225 (without the glove—with it, the sky's the limit!).

- *Toys, Games, and Dolls* — Charlie's Angels or Six Million Dollar Man games: $60–$80 (who could part with those?); Beanie Babies: $9-$6,000 (yes, I said grown men are paying big cash for these . . . some guy's version of child support perhaps); Transformers: $2–$200; GI Joe's: $2–$2,000! Which way to the toy chest?

- *Stamps, Coins, Record Albums, Watches, Posters, Celebrity Memorabilia (or any other items you think may be worth something)* — check price guides at the library. If you find you'd like to sell something:

- Look in the phone book for dealers who buy this stuff or the newspaper for collectors' fairs where people buy and trade these items. Get a few price estimates before you sell.

- Remember the price listed in books is probably not the price you'll get. Dealers will want to make a profit. But don't be afraid to negotiate. You have the right to turn down the price they offer.

CHAPTER 2

Investing: Past, Present, and Future

If your parents proclaimed, "She's going to be the next Einstein!" the moment they heard your first garbled words, then they probably started planning for your education early on. There are plenty of ways they may have made financial arrangements while getting a tax break on what they stashed away. Be sure to ask whether your parents, or other relatives, took advantage of these opportunities.

Listed below are some of the ways that parents can get an early start on saving for their children's education.

Registered Educational Savings Plans (RESPs)

RESPs are one way parents can put money away to save for their children's education. RESPs are an investment tax shelter, meaning you can invest money within this plan without the tax man grabbing a piece of the earnings every year. This type of investment is classified as a "trust" because the money is held "in trust" until the child heads off to college or university. There is no tax deduction for the money that is put into an RESP; however, the money is allowed to grow there tax-free. If parents start early, there might be quite a pile by the time the kid heads off to campus. You may now invest up to $50,000 lifetime in an RESP (formerly the limit was $42,000) and the annual investment limit has been eliminated. If for example, your parents had invested $210 month for 15 years, you would now have $72,240, assuming that the RESP earned 8 percent annually. Without the tax break on the earnings, you would have only $55,540 – a difference of $16,700 (assuming a 37.5% tax rate on investments). These figures are approximate. Additionally, the newly created Registered Disability Savings Plan (RDSP) allows parents of children with a disability to contribute even more for their child's education; up to $200,000 lifetime.

But the good news is that in 1998 RESP's got better – 20% better. Under the Canada Education Savings Grant (CESG) program, the government matches contributions by 20% of whatever amounts parents and other contributors put into the plan (now up to $2,500 from the previous $2,000 limit). For low and middle income families the government will kick in up to 40% on the first $500. This means potentially the government could be rolling $500 your way each year on a $2,500 RESP annual contribution ($600 for low and middle income families). Under the RDSP program, parents may receive grants from 100%-300% depending on family income. There is also a $1000 Canadian Disability Savings Bond for low income families unable to contribute. With RESPs it's like earning a 20 percent return right from the start. Alberta, Quebec, Saskatchewan and now British Columbia offer additional grants or refundable tax credits (see Addendum 3) Once the plan is set up, grandparents, relatives, and friends can all contribute. Instead of Aunt Mildred sending you that pair of psychedelic PJ's every birthday, she could contribute to the RESP. So in effect a $100 gift really becomes a $120 gift when the government's "gift" is factored in. Just don't expect a sappy card from the government!

When you begin college or university, you start to withdraw money from the plan. You, as the student, are taxed on the money earned when it's withdrawn. (Did you think the government wasn't going to try to nab something?) Part-time students may now also be able to access RESP payments. The good news is that students are usually in a lower tax bracket than their parents, so you will be taxed at a lower rate or maybe not at all.

These savings plans are often marketed as Educational Scholarship Plans or Educational Trusts. Many of the RESP companies, some of which are non-profit, offer plans that invest primarily in safer investments. These can include government bonds and Treasury bills, which provide a high degree of safety and predictability of returns. You can also buy plans from other financial institutions, some of which offer RESPs that invest in somewhat more volatile investments through mutual funds. The returns over the long run tend to be a bit higher but then at the cost of more risk and volatility. Of course, there's still a charge for these products. There are up-front fees of $100–$200 and usually a small administration fee (approximately 0.5 percent) and/or deposit fees ($5.00–$12.00 per year).

Registered plans come with an important restriction: the money must be used for education. The money in an RESP is sometimes pooled with that of other parents who contribute. If other parents' kids don't end up going on to post-secondary studies, those parents get their initial investment back but none of the accumulated interest. You, along with others who do go, receive a share of their earned interest (along with your own, of course). Others are set up as an individual plan but the money must still go to education. But restrictions have been loosened, making it less of gamble if a parents' "future Einstein" decides that studying "wave motion" would be better done on a surfboard than in a Physics lab! Most funds will now allow the parents to transfer the plan to another kid for education (to your future Edison), put the earnings in their own RRSP (up to $50,000 provided there is contribution room), take the earnings as income (subject to taxation) or even use it for their own education. However, under the new rules, the principal is still returned tax-free and the government education savings grant would go back to the government (easy come, easy go!).

Other Options

There are other ways parents can stow away cash for their sons or daughters through trusts set up in the child's name. A trust plan is simply an account set up for a young person to help him save for things such as an education. One method of setting up a trust is for a parent or relative to open an account in the child's name and deposit money directly. The biggest drawback here is that interest and dividends on the original amount are taxed in the parent's name, while the interest on the interest is taxed in the child's name. In this scenario, the parent with the lowest income should be the one to contribute to the account. For example, if a husband and wife were making $40,000 and $8,000 respectively (she works part-time), it would be best to have the wife set up the trust so that the income would be attributed back to her and thus taxed at a lower rate. It is important in this case for the wife to write the cheques for contributions on her personal account (not on a joint account) so that she could prove to the Canada Revenue Agency, if necessary, that the money came from her and not her higher-income-earning husband.

An even better way is to have the child herself set up the trust, even though the money may still come from her parents. In this case, full control of the money must be given completely to the child. Interest and dividends on money from the parents are still taxed in the hands of the parent, but capital gains (money earned from the actual increase in the value of stocks or bonds) are taxed in the hands of the child. If left untouched, there could be a treasure chest of money when the student turns 18. Of course, the one disadvantage (or perhaps an advantage if you're the child) is that because the money is completely in the child's hands, it is the child who decides what she wants to do with it. If a trip around the country on a new motorcycle has more appeal than a trip to college, then so be it.

Because capital gains made within these trust accounts are taxed in the student's name and dividends and interest are taxed in the parent's or guardian's name, it makes sense to have at least some of that money invested in a vehicle that can make capital gains. These include stocks and bonds, preferably within a good quality mutual fund. I'll talk more about these options later on in the chapter.

The advantage of a trust account over an RESP is that parents don't have to gamble the investments' earnings on whether their kids continue their education after high school. The money invested and the earnings stay with the child regardless of his educational plans. The drawback, of course, is that you don't get the 20 percent grant from the government. Regardless of the plans, the fees, administration charges, safety of the investment, predictability of earnings, and plan flexibility all need to be considered.

Baby Bonus Bonanza

Check to see if there is an account tucked away with a baby bonus bonanza in it.

Many parents invested the monthly "baby bonus," "child tax benefit" cheque, or "family allowance" cheque (a gift that the government sent just because you were born—sort of makes you warm and fuzzy all over, eh?). By setting up an account in the child's name, parents can invest baby bonuses without the earnings being taxed at the parents' higher tax rate. It is thus a good option if this money is invested in an account, fund, etc., separate from other education savings. In 1993 the government changed the rules of the Child Tax Benefit Program so that now only lower-income families can receive the benefits. As part of this program, families of children born after 2003 who are entitled to the National Child Benefit supplement will now receive a $500 Canada Learning Bond at birth (if eligible at that time) in addition to up to 15 instalments of $100 for a maximum $2,000 learning bond which must be put into an RESP.

Minding Your Family's Business

Investing money under a child's name is a good way for parents to reduce taxes on the earned money. As long as a child's income is not more than the basic personal exemption of $11,138 (2014 figure), then she, as a dependant, pays no tax on it. Technically, however, parents cannot just give you money to save without the interest and dividends earned on it taxed back to them. But there is a way around this. If your parents have a business, then it may be time for them to hire you. By doing this they can pay you a salary. They can't just stick you on the payroll and have you take out the trash or wash the car a couple of times. You must perform legitimate business services, such as making deliveries, bookkeeping, office cleaning, or handling reception. This way a salary can be paid to you and taxed at your lower rate. The younger you are hired, the better! Parents get the advantage of your labour and writing it off as a business expense, while you gain investment money for your education and possibly some valuable work experience.

Best Investments Before College or University

Where do you invest the stash of cash earmarked for your education? If you are planning to start your postsecondary education within the next three years, you should keep two things clearly in mind: (1) preservation of capital (you don't want to lose what you start with) and (2) steady, predictable earnings growth. Basically, you want to know that the money you have will still be there when you want it and that it is going to be worth more at the end of that period than when you put it there.

Daily interest accounts are just one step up from keeping your money under the mattress (except you may get some free support from your mattress). The one thing the account offers is security. Basically, this is the place to park a small portion of money for everyday expenses and emergencies. Don't count on making any money here. With service charges and "maintenance fees" (I guess that must mean taping up ripped bills and polishing the coins—must keep the royals untarnished!), you'll be lucky to break even.

Breeding Your Money the Safe Way

There are many ways to make your money multiply. The big obstacle is that there are probably 10 times as many ways to lose it! When it comes to financial advice, everybody has an opinion, and a reason for giving you that opinion. Usually it's to make money. From the self-proclaimed financial expert who promises to make you a lot of money overnight to financial planners who falsely call themselves "Dr." (usually an indication that they want to extract some serious money from your wallet), many people will say they'll show you the way to get rich. Check out the advertising in the financial pages of your newspaper. You'll see plenty of ads that promise you huge returns on your money: mutual funds, real estate, oil and gas funds, options, limited partnerships. All those promises might give you the impression that you'll be able to put the whole family through school!

However, what is crucial to remember is that the impressive statistics cited are often historical and selective—they are not a guarantee of future earnings. Remember the musings of Mark Twain, who pointed out that "there are three kinds of lies: lies, damned lies, and statistics." I am not saying that there are not many fine investments that offer some very good returns; however, they usually carry with them a substantial amount of risk. So play it safe and be leery of anyone who promises a high return with no risks. Stick with guaranteed or very-low-risk investments offered through reputable banks, credit unions, trust companies, mutual fund companies, and security and investment firms.

Canada Savings Bonds

Canada Savings Bonds (CSBs), which include Canada Premium Bonds (CPB) are probably one of the safest investments. They are government-backed and insured, so they are not likely to become worthless (oh, what was Canada's debt again?). The additional advantages are:

- They pay a guaranteed interest rate for three years (with some newer issues offering a guaranteed rising rate each year).

- You pay no additional fees (on top of the amount you invest).

- You can invest relatively small amounts (as low as $100).

- You gain a feeling of empowerment (because you are actually loaning the government money).

- You can have the interest compounded or paid out annually.

- You can purchase Canada Premium Bonds (CPB) at banks, credit unions, caisses populaires, trust companies, investment dealers and brokerages, by phone or through some employers (Canada Savings Bonds (CSBs) only).

- You can now cash them in any time.

The drawbacks are:

- They are only available at certain times during the year (usually mid- to late- October).

- The interest rates are sometimes slightly lower than a bank or trust company's Guaranteed Investment Certificate.

- If you cash them in prior to the anniversary date you only receive interest to the last anniversary date.

Guaranteed Investment Certificates (GICs)

They may not be glamorous. You won't be able to boast how you cashed in on that big gold find. But you'll have the money there when you need it. As the name suggests, these certificates offer a guaranteed rate of return for the agreed-upon time period. The beauty of these investments is that they offer you flexible maturity dates—you can buy GICs for periods ranging from 30 days to 10 years—as well as the option of either receiving the interest as a payment (usually on an annual or biannual basis) or leaving it in the GIC to compound (interest on top of the interest). Perhaps the biggest plus is that the money you put into a GIC is insured (up to $100,000 per bank). These advantages are particularly important for students, since you know exactly how much you are going to get and when you are going to get it—making for a much less stressful existence.

GICs do have the drawback that your money is locked in for the agreed-upon time period. In addition, unlike Canada Savings Bonds, higher minimum investments may be required, from $1,000 to $5,000 depending on the type of GIC you invest in and the financial institution you invest with.

The great thing about GICs is that you can invest and get a good rate of return while the flexible maturity dates ensure that you'll have money available when you need it. By staggering your maturity dates (the dates when your GICs come due), the money becomes free at different times. Say you have $8,000 to invest but know you will probably need it over the course of the school year. If you invest for periods that run in increments of 30 days, you can have a fresh supply of money available each month. You might invest $1,000 for 30 days, another $1,000 for 60 days, another $1,000 for 90 days, and so on. The great thing here is that all the money is not accessible at once, so you won't be tempted to spend it. At the same time, the amount that comes due at the end of the term (when you're probably really hurting for money) will be larger because it will have accumulated the most interest.

Money Market and Treasury Bill Accounts or Funds

If you want to earn a rate of return higher than a general interest account, but also have more flexibility than a GIC, then you might want to opt for a money market or T-bill account or fund. They generally pay a higher rate of return than the savings account, and you can usually take the cash and run when you want, but there are drawbacks as well as advantages.

Advantages:

- They offer a better rate of return than a regular bank account.
- The minimum investment for funds (usually $500 or $1,000) is very reasonable.
- There is no fixed term (great if you are not sure when you'll need the money).
- They are fairly-low-risk investments.

Drawbacks:

- The rate of return is not guaranteed (it fluctuates).
- The money is easily accessible, which could be a pitfall if you are prone to impulse spending.
- Although the money is usually invested by the account manager in relatively safe, highly insured bonds, GICs, T-bills, etc., the account is not insured.
- They usually pay slightly lower interest rates than fixed investments (such as CSBs or GICs).
- High management fees (of some funds) can eat into your earnings.

Caveats and advice:

- Be aware of penalties for early withdrawal from funds. Always,

always, always find out what redemption charges, fees, etc., they charge.

- Shop around. You can often do better than the major banks (some smaller trust companies and credit unions give you a higher rate of return on accounts). Investment planners can shop around for you, and find you the best deal. You can access a rate comparer at the **www.debtfreegrad.com** website.

Mutual Funds

The mutual fund industry has exploded in Canada in the past few years, with an estimated $129 billion being poured into these investment vehicles annually. A mutual fund is basically a pool where you and a throng of other investors put your money to be managed by a professional fund manager. Depending on the type of fund, the manager will then invest all the money in a mix of investments, including anything from stocks, bonds, Treasury bills, and GICs, to international investments. Depending on how much you put in, you will then share whatever money the fund has made (or lost) during the time period you invested. Because of fluctuating markets, traditional wisdom suggests that stock mutual funds pay best as long-term investments (five years or more).

If you have some money you can afford to leave untouched then you might consider putting a small portion into stock mutual funds. You can often start out with as little as $500, and many funds will let you make a monthly contribution from your bank account of as little as $25 per month. The automatic monthly contribution withdrawn from your bank account is the easiest and least painful way to contribute.

Some mutual funds charge a fee, called a "load" (as in "that's a load of money they take from you"), sometimes one to four percent. Your best bet is to stick with high-quality no-load funds, which don't charge you anything. Many of these have returns equal to those of load funds. Some companies are no-load but will charge you a one-time setup fee. Banks and trust companies also offer no-load funds.

The area of mutual funds that has shown the best rate of return over the past 5- and 10-year periods has tended to be resource and equity mutual funds. Some of these funds have delivered average 5 and 10 year returns of 10–25 percent. (The fund advertisements you've no doubt seen, are more than eager to point this out.) Investment firms love to sell these to you because they get a higher commission than if they sell you a GIC. However, the simple fact is that, because these funds are invested in the resource sector, which can be volatile, you cannot predict how much your money will be worth at any particular time (unless you can predict the stock market yourself—in which case you'd probably be on Wall Street managing one of these funds rather than figuring out how to pay for an education). Specialty funds, such as energy, precious metals, and other single-sector funds, along with emerging market funds, tend to be the riskiest of the mutual funds.

Somewhat less risky mutual funds are T-bill, money market, or bond funds, but again no guarantees. These funds tend to place a greater portion of your hard-earned money in more secure types of investments. Historically they haven't made as much money as equity funds, but they are usually more suitable for shorter time periods. What it comes down to is weighing the risk versus the reward. Aren't life's decisions complicated?

Are these investments a good bet for students? Well, it depends. A well-managed mutual fund can bring you some very hefty returns if you are willing to invest for at least a four- or five-year time horizon. As a general rule, if you as a student are going to need the money within the next year or two, then you are probably best off staying away from the more volatile equity mutual funds and sticking with the less volatile money market or T-bill mutual funds.

Also, contrary to what some people believe, the money you put into these mutual funds is not insured. For instance, you could invest $2,000 in a volatile mutual fund (i.e., 400 shares at $5 per share). Eight months later, when you need the money for school, the shares may only be worth $4 apiece. If you withdrew your money, you would only receive $1,600—a loss of $400, not to mention any sales or redemption fees you may be charged. There's no insurance to help you out here.

If you do go the mutual fund route, you need to keep in

mind that not all funds are created equal (and they are certainly not managed equally). It will pay to pick one that is likely to perform well in the long term. Also be aware of the sales charges, management fees, and switching fees that come with each fund. To help you compare Canadian funds and their past performance, check the business sections of papers such as *The Globe and Mail*, *Financial Post*, or *Toronto Star* in addition to databases at **www.fundlibrary.com** or **www.morningstar.ca**. There are also annual guides to mutual funds available. One particularly good reference is Gordon Pape's *Buyer's Guide to Mutual Funds*. Reading this guide will give you a good understanding of the various kinds of mutual funds and which ones have done well and which are likely to do well. No guarantees, but a step in the right direction.

Tax Free Savings Account (TFSAs)

Take advantage of the recently created Tax Free Savings Account (TFSA), which now allows Canadians 18 and over to save up to $5,500 per year, with the earnings tax free. While as a student you may not have $5,500 each year to save, it could be beneficial in avoiding a tax hit on any money you do invest for your post secondary education, as well as when you start saving your post-graduation earnings. As with other tax shelters, the return and risk depends on what investments you hold *within* this tax shelter, along with any fees associated with these investments.

Retirement? You Gotta Be Kidding!

Even if retirement is the last thing you are thinking of, it may pay to take advantage of the tax shelter offered by Registered Retirement Savings Plans (RRSPs). It could mean the government gets nothing, nil, zilch, el zippo while your money is earning compound interest year after year, all tax-free. Basically, an RRSP is a tax shelter that allows you to invest money without being taxed on what you earn until you withdraw it from the plan. You can put almost any Canadian assets into an RRSP—cash, stocks, GICs, CSBs, etc. (On the other hand, Aunt Mildred's pearl necklace may be a sentimental favourite but it can't go into your RRSP.) The result: a huge stack should await you as you get older.

The advantage is that you can deduct what you put into an RRSP against your earned income. If your taxable income for one year is $16,000, for example, and you put $2,800 into an RRSP, then your taxable income would be reduced to $13,200. Assuming a 15 percent tax bracket, you would actually save $420 (15 percent of $2,800).

If, on the other hand, you find that your earnings are slim during one of your postsecondary years, you can redeem some of your RRSP savings and probably not pay taxes on it, since you'll be able to use your educational deductions, thus leaving you in a lower tax bracket (more on reducing the tax you pay in chapter 15).

Putting money into an RRSP is a particularly effective strategy for a student to use if you take a year off to earn cash for school, or if your summer job was especially lucrative (e.g., business at your hot dog stand was just *sizzling*!). In high-income-earning years, put the maximum amount allowed into an RRSP. The most effective time to redeem an RRSP early, if you absolutely must, is during your college or university years, when you don't earn a lot of money (e.g., you studied, travelled, or were on involuntary beach patrol) and have your educational deductions (as shown in chapter 15). Remember that recent changes now allow you to borrow interest free from your RRSP for education purposes (the Lifelong Learning Plan). Under this plan you later repay it to your RRSP rather than just permanently withdrawing it.

Keep the following points in mind:

- If you have money in an RRSP, keep some of it flexible so you can withdraw it if you need to (a Canada Savings Bond or money market fund would work well).

- Watch for service fees and administrative fees, as well as penalties for withdrawing funds early.

- If you withdraw RRSP funds early, the government withholds some money. You will get it back with your tax refund, if you qualify for one; otherwise, the withheld money is deducted against what you owe on your income tax return.

- If you borrow money for your RRSP to pay for school, make sure that you pay it back on time. Otherwise, you may well find yourself penalized along with paying taxes and interest on unpaid amounts.

If you don't have money for an RRSP, you can borrow (usually at a low rate). Doing this usually provides a financial bonus only if you repay the loan in one year. If you make lots of money in the year before you start school, you could borrow to buy an RRSP, thus reducing your tax bill. In the following year (as a student), you could withdraw from your RRSP, repay the loan, and still reap the benefit from lowering your previous year's tax bill.

Your best investments will be determined by your time horizon and by how early you or your parents start saving. If you start saving for your education at least eight or ten years ahead of time, you may want to split your investment, putting some money into a more volatile (but potentially more rewarding) equity mutual fund and some into a more stable investment such as money market, bond funds, or GICs. As you move closer to starting college or university, you will probably want to gradually shift the majority of your money to the more stable, predictable investments. Within most mutual fund companies you can shift 10 percent per year between funds (i.e., from an equity to a money market fund) without being charged a load fee.

Regardless of what investments you choose, check the options carefully. Be aware that some planners may try to sell you the investments that land them the highest commission. (They may try to push a mutual fund over a GIC, for example, since the commission they make can be four to five times higher.) So talk to a planner or broker you trust, and shop around for the investment that fits your objectives.

CHAPTER 3

Your Summer Job: Making It Pay

Targeting a Summer Job

All jobs are not created equal. As students well know, jobs differ greatly in terms of both the experience they offer and the pay they provide. Often a student is faced with the dilemma of having to choose between good experience or good pay. Ideally, it would be best to find a summer job that provided you with both. Pedalling a popsicle cart may pay you well in the heat of summer, but it may not be what you had in mind when you said you wanted to get some travel and sales experience.

How can you make the most of your summer work during those two to four, always-too-short months? The answer lies in aiming for a job that will give you as much of both as possible. If your objective is strictly to earn as much as you can during that time period, then perhaps you will have to opt for the job that pays the most. In such a case, it is probably worthwhile for you to try to obtain the "experience" in a volunteer capacity, even if it is only once or twice a week. If you have the luxury of taking a job that offers poor pay but great experience, it may be worth your while in the long run. Experience may increase your marketability once you graduate, in which case any temporary financial sacrifice will be made up quickly.

A summer job taken for experience may also reveal whether you want to pursue this kind of work as a career.

For instance, working with children at a summer camp or playground may convince you that you want to pursue teaching as a full-time vocation. Conversely, finding out that teaching is definitely not your forte might save you from wasting the time and expense of a year in teacher's college.

Regardless of your financial situation, you should still try to make as much of your money in your summer job as possible. Targeting your job search will not only allow you to return to school with an enviable amount of summer earnings, it will also make your summer job hunt that much easier to begin with, by focusing first on worthwhile employment opportunities.

Ten Targeting Tips
1. Think long term.
Find a summer job that will allow you to return year after year (ideally one you want to return to in future summers). A company or agency that requires you to undergo specialized training, for instance, will probably want you to return, since it is considerably more expensive to train new staff each year. A prime example of this is the job of tour guide. In addition to learning regular duties, someone hired as a tour guide may undergo several weeks of intensive training to learn a variety of tours in different areas. Similarly, a student who has been taught a certain trade or skill within an industry (for example, a specialized machinist or computer operator) is likely to be sought after as a returning summer employee. Although initially you might spend a great deal of time in training, you will ultimately become a more valuable asset to the company. This may put you in the position of being able to negotiate for higher pay in subsequent years, or the company may already have some built-in incentive or bonus to entice you to return in future summers.

2. Search for jobs that are recession-proof.
While no job is immune to economic fluctuations, some areas are more apt to be affected by a downturn in the economy. Sectors that sell or manufacture durable consumer goods such as cars or refrigerators, for instance, are

usually hit fairly hard by poor economic conditions. Thus, if you were working in an automobile plant or a department store, your future would be somewhat more uncertain than if you were working in a grocery store. Simply stated, a consumer may decide to put off buying that new sports car or microwave when times are tough, while it is almost certain that they will still continue to purchase essentials such as food. Other potential employers that usually do well in a recession include service industries such as cheap restaurants, home and lawn maintenance, pharmacies, and discount retailers.

3. Assess the company's financial picture.

Consider the company's financial state, asking yourself the following questions: Is this an established company? Have they been doing well of late? Do they have a good reputation or are people reluctant to do business with them? You can find answers by checking with people in related industries, asking customers, or even by monitoring how busy they actually are. If you really want to research a public company, check out their annual report at your school library, employment resource centre, or company Web site. Factors such as a company's reputation and financial picture may affect not only the stability of your summer job now, but also the way future employers look upon your past work experience. If a potential employer sees that you worked for a disreputable or floundering company, they may question your integrity or even your ability. A summer job as Bernie Madoff's accounting intern, for example, will do little to boost your reputation.

4. Assess the stability of the agency to which you are applying.

A summer position within a government department, for example, may be vulnerable to funding cuts in future years. Such programs are often temporary or test projects. Another factor to consider, particularly prior to an election year, is whether your summer job is likely to be discontinued in future years should there be a change in the governing party.

5. Assess how the company treats employees.
Do they have a history of laying people off when business is slow? Consider the fact that a summer employee would most likely be the first to go should there be layoffs. This is especially true in unionized companies, where layoffs are often determined on a seniority basis. (Keep in mind that even if you are paying union dues as a summer employee, you may not be entitled to full union membership.) Does the company treat its employees well? More specifically, are people paid regularly and on time? Talking to employees can be an easy way to find this out. Alternatively, a newspaper search at your library may give you some past history of the company and its practices.

6. Find out whether you will be paid a guaranteed wage or on commission.
Some companies will pay a combination of wage and commission, or will pay you a minimum amount by way of a "draw." A draw is a fund out of which you are paid when your commissions do not reach a certain total. If you draw from this fund, you are expected to replace this money once your commissions are above a certain amount. If you are paid strictly on a commission basis, find out precisely what that commission rate will be. I'll discuss the caveats of commission sales later in this chapter, as this is one area of employment where students are frequently exploited.

7. Find out ahead of time if you will be guaranteed a certain number of hours.
A summer job may promise a tremendous pay rate, but if you end up getting only a few hours per week then you may not end up with the great stash of cash you had anticipated. If possible, try to get something in writing which clearly states the wage and the minimum number of hours you will work each week.

8. Find out if there will be any opportunity to work overtime.
A summer job can turn into an absolute gold mine if you

can work extra hours at an overtime rate. Some companies pay time-and-a-half for working extra hours or during holidays, while others will pay as high as double or triple time. Some places, however, will simply let you take extra time off during less busy periods (which may not be such a good deal if your goal is to accumulate as much capital over the summer as possible). The pay rate will be determined by factors such as union agreements within the company and labour laws in the industry or area you are working in.

9. **Is the stability of the job you are considering particularly vulnerable to unpredictable forces?**

A prime example is outdoor work that is affected by the weather! While we all start the summer hoping that every day will be sunny, this is rarely the case. And, in fact, some summer jobs are extremely dependent on the weather. Working as a lifeguard at an outdoor pool is a good example: on rainy days you may only have a chance to work a couple of hours, if at all. Some employers will pay you regardless of the weather, while others won't. Clearly, this is something you should know ahead of time, since it may affect your decision regarding which summer job to accept.

Another common summer job that may leave you high and dry in wet weather is house painting. If you are considering a job in this business, find out whether the company you hope to work for has interior painting contracts lined up in case of inclement weather. If the company is dependent solely on exterior painting, wet days will leave you without any work at all—and it may also mean that the days you have off will be too wet to enjoy outdoor leisure-time activities—a double negative whammy!

10. **Find out if there are bonuses or incentives to be earned on top of your wages.**

Know specifically what these bonuses are and precisely how to attain them. Be sure to get the incentive scale in writing. Some companies offer bonuses for reaching a sales goal or for special achievements. Other employers may give you a bonus simply for staying until the end of the summer.

Holiday resorts, for instance, may give you a sizeable bonus for staying with them right through their seasonal rush. They don't want to be left in the lurch by employees quitting at peak season. Bonuses can take a variety of forms. Some employers will give you cash, and others will give you a gift of some kind. You may find that some companies offer free trips. For those of you straining to figure out how you can save enough to go away at Christmas or Spring Break, this might just be the ticket.

How Much Cash Will I Really Haul In? Assessing the Costs and Benefits of a Job

Students will often hastily accept a summer job without considering some of the hidden costs of employment. This is akin to buying a car "as is" without at least giving some thought to the actual cost of getting those wheels on the road. When weighing the costs and benefits of a particular job, keep the following questions in mind.

1. What will you need to wear when you are working?
Will you have to buy any special clothing for the position you are considering? Needless to say, there are probably some of you who have just been dying for an excuse to purchase a new wardrobe. However, you must remember that the purchase of new clothes will cut into your savings. Good outfits for an upscale retailer, or formal office wear, could cost you plenty. It may be that the clothes you end up buying can also be worn to school (which would be ideal), whereas if you take a job as host/hostess or mâitre d' in a restaurant and are required to purchase tuxedos or formal gowns, you may not get much use out of them in the near future, unless of course your parents are planning a debutante ball, coming-out party, or delayed bar mitzvah sometime soon.

In some cases you may be required to purchase a uniform. This may be cheap or expensive, and, unlike other clothes, you may not have any use for it once you leave that job.

Think twice about laying out cash for your uniform at the "Chunky Chicken" takeout restaurant—you may not find many occasions to wear a feathered rooster suit. On the other hand, if it is a job at which you plan to remain for several summers, it may not be such a bad investment over the long run. If you are hired by a company that experiences a frequent turnover of employees, you may be able to buy your uniform at a cheaper price from someone who is leaving. Conversely, you may be able to sell your uniform to someone who is starting at about the same time you are quitting.

2.   Will you need to invest in necessary equipment or tools? Some companies require you to purchase specific equipment needed for your job. Students working in a factory may have to shell out some cash for safety boots, hard hats, or protective eyewear. In some cases, a company may partially subsidize these acquisitions by either reimbursing part of your payment or buying large quantities of the item from a wholesaler and then selling them to employees at cost. Purchasing used equipment is another option. After all, does it really matter if your hard hat is a bit marked? One word of caution, however: if you buy used equipment, be sure that what you buy is safe (i.e., that it meets the standards set by government and/or the company for which you will be working). Uncle Joe's World War I army helmet may have done the job in the trenches at Vimy Ridge, but it won't be considered proper headgear at the auto plant.

   Tree planting is another popular summer job. Although potentially lucrative, it is a prime example of a job that requires considerable capital investment to get started. Equipment for this endeavour, including such items as a sleeping bag, rain gear, and a shovel, may cost you as much as $300–$800 or more. Again, because this is a fairly common job, you may be able to pick up used equipment at a fraction of the cost, or perhaps even borrow it from someone you know who has planted trees in the past (borrowing is a particularly good option if this is your first crack at wilderness work—you may find that after a week of slogging it out in the bush, the world of takeout pizza, air-conditioned theatres, and poolside parties is just too good to give up). Again, check what you buy to see that the rain gear is waterproof, the face mesh is bug-proof, and the shovel handle stays on!

3. Will you be required to shell out some of your own capital for inventory?

Some jobs, particularly in the area of commissioned sales, require you to contribute some of your own cash to purchase inventory when you first begin and/or every time you need to replenish your selling stock. Because you will eventually get the money back, this may not seem like a big factor at first, until you realize that during the time your funds are tied up, you will be losing potential interest. Say, for example, you put $4,000–$5,000 dollars into inventory. At a rate of 7 1/2 percent, you may in fact be sacrificing $100–$125 in lost interest alone during that four- or five-month summer period!

You should also take into account the liquidity of your inventory. In other words, will you be able to convert your excess inventory easily into cash at the end of the summer? If September rolls around and your tuition fees are due, but instead of cash you have $2,000–$3,000 worth of prize-winning purebred chinchillas on your hands and do not have a ready buyer, you are, needless to say, in a bit of a bind. Unfortunately, the barter system has long since passed, and universities are reluctant to accept mammals as payment. The point is, don't be stuck at the end of the summer with unsellable stock or inventory. Some other pitfalls of commissioned sales and jobs requiring a high cash outlay will be discussed later in this chapter.

4. What other job-related expenses will you incur, and will you be reimbursed?

Students who take a job requiring them to use their own automobile, for example, should be aware of the costs they will incur for gas and oil, parking, and, perhaps most important of all, wear and tear on their car. Some may get reimbursed for gas and parking, but few receive anything for the wear and tear. Yet, if driving for your job means putting thousands of miles on your car, then your tires, muffler, brakes, battery, clutch, or transmission may soon need replacing. Even wearing out the interior upholstery can greatly affect your automobile's resale value. Find out ahead of time whether your company will pay you an additional fixed amount (e.g., 48¢ per kilometre) for distance you travel on the job.

If you are required to attend luncheons or receptions, will they be paid for? Or if you have to organize any parties, receptions, or other forms of entertainment, will you be reimbursed for the costs? (The intrinsic value of merely being able to party shouldn't prevent you from wanting reimbursement.)

If your job is in a different part of the country, how much will it cost you to get there and back? Even if it's somewhere you always wanted to go, it could take a big chunk out of your earnings if you have to fork out for your own transportation.

5. Will you be losing potential income by working for free or for a meagre wage during a training period?

Earlier in the chapter, I mentioned that some jobs may require extensive training. You should therefore find out if you will be paid for this training. Some employers will pay you full wages even during this period, while others will only give you a subsistence allowance—perhaps $20 a day. Some may pay you nothing until you have successfully completed the training. The situation will vary with the company, the type of job, and the laws that apply to training and employment. Find out about the training pay before you accept or decline a position, and remember to weigh the potential gains of specialized training against the initial financial sacrifice.

6. What is the earning potential from tips?

Some of the people who earn the most money are actually paid the lowest hourly wages. A large portion of the take-home earnings of waiters, bartenders, bellhops, and cab drivers, among others, comes from cash tips. In some jobs, however, people receive only occasional tips. Find out ahead of time what the average tips are and keep in mind the tax regulations regarding your responsibility to report this income. In the government's eyes, you are expected to pay income tax on everything you earn, including bonuses and tips, even though no earnings receipt (T4 slip) is issued for such income. While I am not advocating not claiming your tips, remember that for some jobs the expectation is that you will have tips to declare, while for other jobs that expectation does not exist.

7. **Are there employee discounts or freebies that will save you money on basic living expenses such as food, accommodation, and transportation?**

When assessing the pros and cons of a potential summer job, you should consider the perks or advantages. In many cases, the extras that go with the job will greatly affect the amount of cash you bring home at the end of the summer. An employer who requires you to travel a great deal may provide you with a company car for the summer. If it is a promotional vehicle, many companies won't mind you driving it around since the more exposure their company logo receives, the better (unless, of course, you are seen racing around with half your friends hanging out the window and your fraternity mascot perched on the roof).

Tour guides often receive free meals and/or accommodation when travelling with their tour group. Working for an expensive charter company could thus translate into a free stay at some of the world's finest hotels. Aside from the experience of true luxury, the most important advantage is reducing the two biggest drains on your summer funds: food and shelter. Even subsidized accommodation at a summer resort or restaurant meals at a fraction of what they cost the customer will benefit your bank balance. Many large companies or hotels have their own cafeteria, where they charge employees only what it costs to prepare the meal. Just what you wanted after a year in residence—more cafeteria food!

8. **Are there any discounts, perks, or job benefits that will save you money on luxuries?**

If you work at a golf course over the summer, you may receive free golf privileges and perhaps even a generous discount on golf equipment that you purchase at the pro shop. This may not seem like a big deal at first, but if you are an avid golfer who would have played on a regular basis anyway (say three or four times a week), you could save several hundred dollars on green fees alone (not to mention all the free golf balls you might find).

Plenty of other summer jobs offer various benefits and perks. If you work in a video store you may get free movie rentals, an airline job may allow you free or cheap transportation, and a hardware store might give you free pocket protectors. Well, maybe that's not such a good example, but the point is to consider the perks. Some benefits will obviously be better than others, but as a general rule, a job that gives you a break on things you would purchase anyway (food, clothing, or even something like a bicycle if you're a cyclist) will be of the greatest value.

Summer Job Caveats

Although summer jobs are usually a great source of money for your education, they can also turn into absolute financial disasters. Just as there are many employers who pay well and provide good experience, there are also some dishonest employers who seek to take advantage of enthusiastic and capable students. To avoid falling prey to these vermin, keep the following caveats in mind.

Commissioned Sales

Selling on commission can be very financially rewarding. However, it can also lead to great disappointment for students. The money that you actually make is often far less than the money you were led to believe you could make. You should therefore be very careful before devoting your time, and possibly your money, to this type of summer work.

Ask people within the company, as well as within the industry, what type of commission you can reasonably expect to make. Find out if you will be servicing existing accounts, or making cold calls, or strictly doing telephone sales. The type of selling you do will affect the amount you make, as well as your willingness to ever pick up a phone again.

Pyramid-Type Organizations

Pyramid schemes are one type of commissioned sales that often target students for employees. While many types of pyramid sales schemes are now illegal, there are others that have a pyramid-type structure and yet still operate within the confines of the law. A pyramid structure is a multilayered system in which a cut of each person's sales goes to the person immediately above them in the hierarchy. Therefore, the higher up the pyramid you move, the more money you make. Companies of this type should be approached with great caution, as they can leave a student penniless, or worse still, in debt. This is not to say that money cannot be made, but rather that there are many companies in which even the best salesperson would be hard pressed to come out ahead.

Some of these companies make great claims: "Earn $1,000+ in one week" or "Fred Flatbrush made $20,000 last summer." However, if you read the fine print, you may discover that $1,000/week in sales means only $150 of that is profit, or that Fred Flatbrush may indeed have made $20,000 last summer, while his fellow employees made very little. It is important to talk to those at the bottom of the pyramid to see if they too are making money. Keep in mind, though, that sales people in a pyramid-type industry are likely to say they make money—after all, they want to get you involved so that they can also make a commission on your sales. In the past, students have been burned selling products such as water purifiers and cleaning supplies. Check with the Better Business Bureau to see if any customers or employees have lodged complaints against the company that wants to hire you. It's better to learn from other people's bad experiences than your own.

High-Pressure Hiring Tactics

Beware of a company that tries to pressure you into signing a contract or agreeing to something before you've had time to consider the offer (be particularly leery of these people if they are wearing undersized polyester suits with wool ties). If the company is truly confident in their product, they will not hesitate in letting you think it over for a day or two before you commit yourself. If you are not sure (or even if you are), ask for a day or two to consider the pluses and minuses of the job. This will also give you a chance to come up with any questions you need answered prior to accepting an offer.

Student-Run Organizations

In recent years, there has been a proliferation of student-run businesses, as young people parlay innovative ideas into profitable ventures. College Pro Painters, a Canadian outfit started many years ago by a group of young entrepreneurs, went from a summer business to a company doing $40 million in sales per year. They were so successful that they began to compete on a seasonal basis with companies that operated year-round. Once the success of companies like College Pro became apparent, other student entrepreneurs rushed to get in on the action. Originally confined to painting, these ventures now encompass products and services ranging from window cleaning and car washing to installing decks and lawn sprinkler systems.

Among the new companies, there have been some tremendous success stories. However, at the same time, there have been far too many businesses that flopped and left students short of both cash and work. This is not to say that you shouldn't work for one of these new ventures, but if you are counting on making money to finance your university or college career, you should be very selective about the enterprise you get involved in. If you are willing to take a chance on an idea, you may want to start your own business on the side rather than risk your whole summer's wages on another student's venture.

If you are thinking of taking a job with a student-run company, there are a number of things you should check out first. Some of these things have already been covered in this chapter, under targeting and assessing employers. I recommend that you also give careful consideration to the following suggestions.

1. Find out about the structure of the company.

You don't need to do a complete financial analysis of the company by tracking down its auditors, but you should verify that there is some sort of structure and order to the business. As in most companies, there should be a clear division of roles and responsibilities. If there is no one in charge, or if no one is quite sure who is in charge of what, then important decisions may not be getting made when they need to be. Be wary of businesses where the people you are trying to get in touch with are not accessible, or don't get back to you when they say they will. If you as a potential employee are not able to reach them, there is a good chance that their customers would have the same problem.

2. Check to see how the business is run.

Some companies have a great product and an excellent reputation, but certain branches or franchises may be terribly managed. You could end up working for a franchise with a horrible manager, over whom the central office has little control. Look for signs indicating such things as whether they are organized and professional in their operations.

3. Ask about opportunities for advancement within the company and the option of returning in future summers.

If you plan to work for a student company for a few summers, you should check to see what opportunities there are for promotion. Student-run companies often have a high turnover of managers, as former managers usually move on once they graduate. In one of Canada's largest painting businesses, for instance, 60 percent of its franchise managers each summer are new to the job. Those starting out as regular workers may later have the opportunity to run their own franchises.

Moving up in the ranks means not only the potential for much more money, but also the opportunity to gain experience in organizing, accounting, and supervising, all within the same company. This expertise could greatly increase your earnings potential and employment marketability once you graduate.

4. **Ensure there is enough actual work lined up to keep you employed for the summer.**

In the past, some summer companies have hired staff to work without having the contracts to support them. The result: some very broke and bored students working few or no hours for much of the summer.

"Student-Run" Knock-Offs

Some businesses, capitalizing on people's soft spot for hard-working students, use terms like "student," "youth," "university," or "college" in their company name. The obvious implication is that the business is run by students and that students benefit from it. However, some of these are scams run by slimy characters who basically use poorly paid students as fronts, and thus reap the benefits and profits themselves. Coupon-book marketers and landscaping outfits are possible examples. Check them out thoroughly through the Better Business Bureau and campus employment centres.

Fire the Boss and Hire Yourself!

Finally, many students are motivated—by an entrepreneurial spirit, displeasure with a tyrannical boss, or lack of success finding anything else—to start their own business. Some enjoy the freedom of running the show, others the personal challenge and thrill of taking a risk, and still others the opportunity to reap significant personal as well as financial rewards. Student innovation has led to some tremendous success stories. From retail concepts to painting businesses, from landscaping companies to rollerblade rentals, student ventures have sometimes rivalled full-time businesses! For instance, summer businesses started on venture capital (loans or grants given to start a new business) in Ontario had sales averaging $15,000, with some hitting upwards of $80,000—not bad for a summer's work! However, before throwing all your money into a business, be aware that with any venture there is the possibility of a shortfall in the finance department. Most small businesses won't make you rich right away. However, the money you do make, along with the experience you gain, can be invaluable for your future career ventures.

While information on running a summer business could take up a whole book by itself, here are a few suggestions that will improve your earnings and minimize your risk of loss:

- Start planning well in advance. A good business plan and a good marketing plan are the most important predictors of success for a student business. There are many excellent books available to guide you through preparing a complete business plan (see the list of suggested readings below).

- Compile a list of all of your business needs, such as equipment, supplies, transportation, time, and, most critical of all, the initial or up-front financial outlay. Before you begin, make sure you have access to what you need, and that it will be available when you need it.

- Start small at first to keep things manageable and to avoid a huge outlay of time and money. You may want to try a very small venture on the side one summer while you have another job, just to see if there is potential to make a go of it full-time the following summer.

- Consider balancing a summer business with a part-time job so that you will have at least some cash coming in to live on.

- If you or your family have friends who operate a small business (a successful one I might add), talk to them to get some advice. They will be able to tell you the things that they did right, as well as the things they did wrong (which may save you from making the same mistakes).

- Take advantage of local community or provincial Small

Business Centres, which are set up to assist potential entrepreneurs. They may provide information, counselling services, and a resource library free of charge, as well as clinics, consulting, and other services at nominal costs. Some campuses may also have similar business centres.

- Explore possible avenues of financial assistance. There are various venture capital loans and grants available to encourage student entrepreneurs. Although the federal government pulled the plug on the student small business loan program, some provinces and territories have summer business funding programs of their own. Ontario's Summer Company program, for example, offers up to $3,000 in the form of a grant, while Nova Scotia weighs in with up to a $5,000 interest free loan. Some programs will even give you non-monetary support in the form of mentoring. Check with your local small business centre to see what is provided in your province, or check out your province's program(s) online at www.canadabusiness.ca to see what they offer to help you start and run your business. Keep in mind that although the deadlines for these programs differ, all will require an application and business plan outlining how you intend to rake in the cash for the summer.

- When estimating how much money you will haul in, be conservative. Allow for unforeseen expenses such as advertising costs, equipment repairs, taxes, and leftover inventory or supplies, as well as setbacks such as inclement weather and slow sales. Being prepared will help prevent you from coming up far short of your expectations when September rolls around.

Suggested Reading

Many excellent books on starting your own business are available. Before splurging on all of the titles recommended below, check out the selection at your public or school library. Then decide on the one(s) that best fit your situation. A good start is to get one that includes (as each of the books below does) a step-by-step plan you can work through.

Douglas Gray. *The Complete Canadian Small Business Guide*. Toronto: McGraw-Hill Education, 2012.

Walter Good. *Building a Dream: A Canadian Guide to Starting Your Own Business*. Toronto: McGraw-Hill Education, 2011.

David Schincariol. *Start and Run a Profitable Student Run Business*. Vancouver: International Self-Counsel Press Ltd., 1995.

David Bangs. *The Start-Up Guide: A One Year Plan for Entrepreneurs*. Chicago, IL: Dearborn Publishing, 1998.

Job-Search Musts

1. Start early.
"The early bird gets the worm" is more than a cliché when it comes to finding a job. Many companies start thinking of their summer employment needs in early winter—a time when summer may be far from your thoughts. The time to start thinking about your next summer job is while you're finishing this summer's job. If you plan to return next summer, let your employer know, in writing, before you leave. (Even if you don't want to return, keep this option open.) If you want a different job, start thinking of what you need to get it now.

2. Tell one, tell all.
Let everyone know that you are looking for a summer job. Most summer jobs are found through word of mouth, and you never know who may have a lead, so let your chiropractor, manicurist, bank teller, and psychic know you are looking. I heard of one person who actually had a parking attendant assist him in his job search. Many of the parking lot's regular customers worked in the industry in which this man was hoping to get hired, and the attendant offered to hand out the job hunter's résumé to the appropriate people.

3. Use your connections.

Whether you like it or not, who you know often counts for more than what you know. Make use of friends, relatives, their connections, their connections' connections, and so on.

4. Be persistent.

As long as you aren't abrasively pushy, an employer will admire your eagerness. Never take no as a final answer. I once received a rejection letter for a summer job in Banff, Alberta. I ignored it, left Ontario anyway, and visited the personnel manager in person. He interviewed me and, despite an enormous stack of applications on his desk, hired me on the spot. While I'm not saying you should go to this extreme, the point is that a no today may not be a no the next time you ask.

5. Have a super résumé.

Pay the extra expense to have your résumé professionally designed and printed on quality paper (or posted on-line). (A photocopy on the back of that anthropology essay just won't cut it—even if it was an "A" paper.) The extra cost is nothing compared to the better job it may help you land. Student employment or career resource centres sometimes offer free workshops and assistance with résumé preparation—a much cheaper option than paying a commercial service. A couple of excellent books to consult are:

Yana Parker, Beth Brown. *The Damn Good Resume Guide: A Crash Course in Resume Writing*. Berkeley, CA: 10 Speed Press, 2012.

Quentin J. Schultze. *Resume 101: A Student and Recent-Grad Guide to Crafting Resumes and Cover Letters that Land Jobs*, Berkeley, CA: Ten Speed Press, 2012.

Check your campus career centre for these and other titles, as well as sites such as ResumeEdge which offer some useful free articles and resources (**www.resumeedge.ca/articles**).

6. Proof, proof, and proof again.

Any applications and résumés you submit must be thoroughly proofread. Nothing is more likely to get your application filed in the wastepaper basket than submitting one full of spelling, grammatical, or punctuation errors. Referring to a Ms. as Mr., or calling someone the vice president when they are really the president, isn't going to win you any bonus points either.

7. If you get an interview . . . prepare
Appropriate dress, manner, and attitude are all essential to getting the job. Studying up on the job and the company and preparing for all possible interview questions are also crucial. Your guidance, campus placement, or career counselling office should have videos, books, and workshops on interviewing techniques—usually available at little or no cost.

8. Follow up.
Follow up with a thank-you letter after any interaction with the employer—particularly after an interview. Employers will appreciate the courtesy. If it doesn't land you the job you originally applied for, it may very well lead to a different or future job with the same employer or a referral to another employer. (Remember: connections, connections, connections!)

9. Explore all areas.
Service Canada Centres for Youth (SCCY) have been handed their pink slip with the focus now on-line through the Services for Youth (**www.youth.gc.ca**) website. But there are many other places to take your search: Campus employment centres, want ads, job fairs, bulletin boards and student job banks (www.jobbank.gc.ca/job_search.do?source=jb) are only a few of the many routes to employment. If you apply many places and receive many job offers, then all the better. Nothing is greater than having to choose. "Hmmm, do I take the $14-an-hour job with the company car and weekends off, or do I take the $18-an-hour job with night shifts but possible overtime pay?" Oh, those decisions!

10. Do an excellent job once you get it.
The best way to land next summer's job is to leave this summer's job with a return offer or a glowing reference. If

it's a reference letter you are after, ask *before* you leave. In this age of corporate downsizing and job elimination, your supervisor may no longer be around when you actually need the reference!

The summer is such a critical time for a student in terms of funding an education. The amount you make during that period can greatly determine your lifestyle, level of stress, and academic success during the school year. Ultimately, it can determine how much debt you ring up during your school years, and your financial health long after you graduate. So be strategic and make pay while the sun shines.

CHAPTER 4

Part-Time Employment: Finding a Job You Can Afford

If the mountain of cash you brought back from the summer looks more like a Saskatchewan wheat field, you may end up looking for a part-time job during the school year to top up your funds. In fact, roughly 40 percent of university students end up working some type of part-time job. Whether it's greeting customers and laying on compliments at your local Gap store, or bouncing unruly patrons out of the neighbourhood pub, you'll find that some jobs leave you with very little money at the end of the week.

So how do you choose what to eat at the employment smorgasbord that lies before you? By following some simple strategies, you can be certain of coming away full—full of cash, that is.

Sizing Up How Much You'll Really Make

When is a wage not a wage? When it's gobbled up by a lot of costs that dig into your paycheque. If you size up your costs, you'll have a better idea of how much you are really making.

- Your transportation costs—gas and parking, bus fare, or taxi (for the chronically late)—can take a big chunk if you have to pay to get to work. I knew one friend who used to drive to a retail job and spend $8 on parking for a seven-hour shift. She was automatically losing more than $1 an hour right off the top.

- Clothes you buy for work can also drain your wallet. If you have a job in a retail store, you're often required to dress well. Depending on how chic you need to look, this could set you back anywhere from $300 to $1,000. If you work 10 hours a week, or about 300 hours for the school year, you could end up spending between $1 and $3+ an hour just on clothes. A job where you can dress down is optimal.

- If you work in a store, you may be given a discount, commonly about 10–25 percent off the original price. Sound like a good deal? Well, if you are like most people, the lure of a discount will entice you to buy more than you normally would, perhaps leading you to become the store's number one customer. Your employer will love it because, even with the discount, he's probably still making a profit. You may be better off to work in a place where you hate the products! The point is, discounts can be great, particularly if you get things at cost, but they can also sucker you into spending a lot of what you make.

The bottom line: go for a job that pays well and that will cost you little in extra expenses.

How Much Do You Really Work? Assessing Your Time Costs

Time *is* money. A common maxim but a very true one. Students may not be trained to think in these terms, but there are many ways that a job can rob you of money by taking up your time.

- If you spend a lot of time travelling to and from a part-time job, not to mention the time it takes to go home and change after class, you are almost giving a gift to the time robber. You may spend so much time commuting and getting ready for work that you have less time to actually do the part where you get paid. Say you have a 12-hour-a-week job but you spend five hours getting there and dressing up and down. You may be better off taking a job that's closer to home and requires less prep time, even if it pays a bit less.

- Consider positions that will allow you to study on the job. If you work as an attendant or answering phones, for example, you may have a lot of idle time. If you have a job where you can get two hours of studying done in a four-hour shift, that's almost like getting paid 50 percent more. While it's not likely you are going to be able to whip through a copy of *War and Peace* while waiting tables on a Friday night, you may be able to read a Tolstoy anthology while working in some sleepy boutique.

- If you have a teaching or instructing job, make sure the pay is good enough to warrant the extra time you put in preparing lessons and marking assignments.

I'm not saying you should never devote extra, unpaid hours to a job, particularly if you like it or the experience is excellent; rather, consider the time you lose for studying, as well as for extracurricular and social activities.

The "What Am I *Really* Getting" Equation

$$\frac{(\text{Hourly Rate} \times \text{Paid Hours}) - \text{Expenses}}{\text{Paid Hours} + \text{Travel Time} + \text{Unpaid Prep Time}} = \text{Real } Hourly \text{ Wage}$$

Where to Search

Where do you find the jobs that will actually *make* you money? Here is a list of the most important resources.

Connections, Connections, Connections—Many jobs don't even get advertised. As with summer employment, many of the plum jobs are found through word of mouth. So let *everybody* know you are looking—family, friends, relatives, even strangers—and keep your eyes and ears open.

Targeted Search—If there's a particular type of job you want, because either it's going to pay the big bucks or provide the experience you need, ask around at companies, agencies, and services that are likely to offer these positions. Even if they aren't hiring, they may know who is.

Campus Employment Centres—One of the best places to find out about advertised part-time jobs is right on campus. University and college employment centres specialize in jobs aimed at students, which saves you having to sift through a lot of unsuitable jobs advertised in newspapers and government employment centres. Most campus centres now post their jobs on-line, which means you should be able to access them from a home computer.

If you visit the employment centre, go early in the morning. Many job postings are faxed or emailed to the centre overnight, which means they're usually posted at the centre just before opening. If you're first in the door, you'll get to check out many of these jobs before hordes of other students come sniffing around.

Campus Newspapers—You may find some decent help-wanted ads here, although they're also highly visible to everyone else. When it comes to jobs, there's no such thing as friendly competition. Find out when and where on campus the papers are first delivered, or appear online, and grab one while it's still hot off the press.

Bulletin Boards—Tucked between the posters advertising the next Campus Pacifist Club "sleep-in" and the Pistol & Rifle Club's next "shoot-out," you may find some job postings on campus bulletin boards. Sift through these ads carefully, as they're often for jobs with fly-by-night operators who prey upon students.

Off-campus Government Employment Centres—These centres can offer some opportunities. However, many jobs are not geared to students, so you'll have to wade through the unsuitable ones. August may be your best time here to track down some part-time jobs of interest, although cutbacks may have reduced the service, so don't expect a lot here for part-time fall jobs.

City and Community Newspapers—These are a reasonable source as well. The only problem is that they're seen by many people, so you'll have more competition. You'll also have to spend time sifting through for suitable student jobs.

Temporary Agencies—These are another possibility, particularly for clerical-type office positions. If you have regular days off, this may be a good option.

The Web—Numerous job postings are now available on-line. Your best bets are your campus employment centre web site and the Canadian Government's Job Bank listings: **www.jobbank.gc.ca/home-eng.do**. The Youth Resource Network also provides a good list of job sites at: **www.youth.gc.ca/eng/topics/jobs/looking.shtml**. You may also be able to launch your résumé into cyberspace on your own or through a campus service. Sites such as **Monster.ca** and **LinkedIn.com** also allow you to launch your résumé for free.

Still a better option is to make use of job search engines, which scour many job boards and deliver matches to your email. A couple worth using are: **www.indeed.ca** and **www.wowjobs.ca**.

On sites such as Craigslist and Kijiji you may find some decent job opportunities, however caution is in order, as there is no real screening of potential employers. Thus some jobs may not be as legit as they appear. As a caution, never send money related to so called "opportunities" and only meet someone in a legitimate commercial office or in a public place.

On-Campus Employment—Still Your Best Bet

Your best bet for part-time jobs is to stay on campus. There are some very good reasons to earn your cash here:

- The most obvious advantage is that jobs are close to where you study, so you'll save money and time getting to and from work. Finish your class, grab a coffee, and be at your job within minutes. Larger and more spread-out campuses may be a little less convenient this way, but they're still the preferred location.

- Employers on campus are usually more flexible than off-campus employers in terms of working around your class schedule. This will be a big bonus when it comes to time off for exams and other scholarly commitments. You may even have a job where you can work, duck off to class, and then come back to work.

- It depends on the job, but often campus employment is more flexible than others when it comes to attire. Sure, you may have to slap on an old lab coat, or sew up the holes in your jeans, but this is tons cheaper than having to splurge on a new wardrobe to work at Fashion Heaven.

- You'll usually have a secure paycheque. A university is much less likely to go bankrupt than a business. It may go into debt a lot, but you are less likely to get a bounced cheque.

Traditional Jobs on Campus

Retail Outlets
Bookstores, variety stores, clothing outlets, disc shops, drugstores, postal outlets, etc.

The Good:	Usually steady, flexible hours.
The Bad:	Usually low to moderate pay.
The Ugly:	You may grow delusionary after hours spent folding crested paraphernalia, or stocking shelves of the latest sparkling juice craze.

Campus Restaurants

The Good:	Usually flexible hours, with frequent shifts at non-class times; it may pay well if tips are involved ("Hi, my name's Tip—Tip your waiter."); sometimes free food; can also pay well if unionized.
The Bad:	Sometimes tedious work; can be low-paying, depending on setup (e.g., whether you get a cut of the tips).
The Ugly:	After numerous shifts, you may need to have the perky smile you wear at work surgically removed.

Bars, Pubs

The Good:	Often a social atmosphere; biggest hours are mealtimes and evenings; you can make some very good coin, depending on tipping arrangement (e.g., do the waiters keep all

tips or are they shared by bartenders, coat check, bouncers, etc.?).

The Bad: Can be late nights; may be low pay, depending on whether you're waiting tables or washing dishes; can be tiring work.

The Ugly: May have to deal with unruly, loud, obnoxious people—usually your friends . . . and other undesirables.

Campus Services

Includes registrar's office, employment centres, financial aid office, info booths, grounds maintenance, etc.

The Good: Reasonable pay; usually casual attire; the boss is likely to be understanding of a student's schedule.

The Bad: Sometimes only temporary (e.g., beginning of school).

The Ugly: You may be the target of irate students sick of lineups, computer errors, cutbacks, and rising tuition fees, along with full-time employees that have been axed to save on pensions and benefits.

Security Staff, Special Events

The Good: Often pays decently; great training for police wannabes (sorry, no free doughnuts until you make the big leagues).

The Bad: Sometimes odd hours and lousy weather; occasionally you are garbed in outfits that make you look like a cross between a bus driver and an usher at an alternative cinema.

The Ugly: You may be the occasional target of misdirected chilli dogs, hurling students, and wayward body surfers at football games and concerts.

Lesser-Known Jobs on Campus

There are many jobs floating around that may not be the

first occupation that comes to mind, but they pay in the same cold hard cash as the others.

Sports and Fitness Facilities—On-campus athletic facilities offer great part-time jobs, usually in something you enjoy anyway. The hours may be few, but they usually fit in well with your classes. Jobs range from refereeing basketball or teaching aerobics to tending the locker room or lifeguarding in the pool. Usually they'll train you for referee and sports official jobs, although the greater your experience and qualifications, the more cash they're likely to toss your way. So if you are going to be dribbling around the basketball court anyway, why not shove a whistle in your mouth and get paid for it?

Student Councils—Serving the body that serves the student body offers great opportunities to earn some coin, and they sometimes pay fairly well. Since some councils have a long-standing tradition of occasionally mismanaging money, you may find they'll pay you for the wildest of things. From poll clerking elections, proofreading directories, or selling tickets, to simply running around in some ill-conceived costume promoting an unlikely cause, you'll be able to pick up jobs here and there. Also, contrary to your experience in high school, elected student council positions at many Canadian universities actually pay, often at a decent salary.

Campus Media/Expose Yourself to Money—OK, so you want a job that gives you more exposure—consider campus media! Newspapers, radio, and TV stations are common on campus. While you may not walk into your own prime-time network show, you can often write, talk or play your way up to an editor or managerial role—at only a fraction of the pay, of course. The great part about these jobs is that although you might have to start out volunteering, you still end up getting some great career experience. And you'll be first in line when a paid position becomes available.

Professors—If it's relevant experience you're looking for, why not tap into the cash that's floating around the academic circles. Universities drink from the Bay of Funding, so why not you too? Professors hire students throughout the year to do research, marking, editing, and basically compensate for their absent-mindedness. The work is usually very flexible since professors are likely to understand that your classes come first. The key to these jobs is hunting them down in the first place, since they're usually not advertised. So hit up the profs you like (the best picks are the ones whose classes you've actually attended) and tell them you're interested. If they're not hiring a student, chances are they'll know other profs who are.

Teaching Assistantships—Also floating around those musty faculty corridors are jobs as teaching assistants. Although they're usually reserved for upper-year or graduate students, you can sometimes grab a teaching assistantship in your area of study. The cash can be fair, although graduate students generally get the higher-paying jobs. (Don't be surprised, however, if you're hired as a teaching assistant and suddenly experience a sudden dramatic loss of all fashion sense, developing the occasional urge to mismatch your socks and shorten your pant hems. No job's perfect, I guess.)

Exams—Another employment opportunity is proctoring mid-term and final exams. This mindless job requires an intimidating look and a keen eye for crib sheets. Coffee is a must for this yawner way to make some cash. Inquire at department or faculty offices.

The Tweet Sound of Money—Who better to turn to for social networking than those who are among the biggest users of it? Many college and university departments are turning to students to help maintain and provide content for their social media platforms. Many of these are paid positions and provide some great experience.

Residence—If you've survived a year in residence (i.e., you can still utter coherent sentences of four or more words and have left your roommate basically intact), you may want to consider a job in residence as a member of the staff. Frequently known as residence advisors and dons (although terminology varies), these positions can offset your food and accommodation costs by offering you a free or subsidized rate on both. They may even pay you a small salary as well, although the benefits are sometimes better than cash, since you aren't taxed on them.

Responsibilities vary from campus to campus, but commonly you are in charge of a residence floor or wing. By acting as an advisor, an occasional referee, a confidant, a sympathetic shoulder during traumatic viewings of *The Young and the Restless*, and generally being available, you'll acquire some good experience in addition to the financial perks. While being a supervisor is time-consuming, it may not even seem like work if you enjoy the residence experience.

If you live off-campus, some universities and colleges offer paid positions for upper-year students to work as advisors for off-campus, first-year students. Check at the first-year programs office or student services department.

Residences also sometimes hire students for such part-time projects as clerks, reception, and programming, for those who enjoy residence but at a safer distance.

On-Campus Jobs You Never Knew About
There are plenty of other jobs on campus that will send a few pesos your way. The trouble is, you often don't hear about them or even realize they exist.

Be an Animal!—A guinea pig, that is. Universities, and to some extent colleges, do plenty of experimental research. This could mean money in your pocket. You'll find that experiments are particularly common in the psychology and behavioural science departments. This doesn't mean they'll be fixing an electrode to your head and giving you sudden shocks; instead, it usually means pen-and-paper tests given at your convenience. Chances are, the people in lab coats are looking for a correlation between snoring and the male animal's inability to remember to put the toilet seat down—something that's really going to lead to a better tomorrow! The important advantage of these studies is that they often pay cash on the spot. In addition, the time commitment is usually very short, and you can withdraw if you object to something about the study.

The best places to find out about these opportunities are campus bulletin boards, departmental offices and websites such as psychology or medicine, and notices or classified ads in campus newspapers. If you're a real animal, check out the zoology department, where they may even give you a turn on the hamster wheel!

Specialty and Standardized Exams—If you are sick of writing exams yourself, make others write them . . . and get your paid revenge! There are plenty of standardized exams written to get into professional programs: meds, law, business, ophthalmology, graduate school, etc. Many schools hire students to administer these exams. A bit of a bonus over our dollar's value. Check with professional schools on campus to see what department administers these exams and tell them you are interested.

The government also likes to test more than our tolerance. They administer exams for the foreign and public service and pay the test proctors quite well.

One last way to help alleviate exam anxiety is administering exams to students with disabilities. Most campuses now have special arrangements whereby students with disabilities can take their exams under special supervision. Students are often hired to proctor these exams, and are paid reasonably well. You can usually do your own studying while supervising—a real bonus. Enquire at the office responsible for services to students with disabilities.

Tutoring—If you excel at a particular subject, tutoring may be one of the best jobs you can find, because you set the hours and rate of pay. You should be able to set up this service with little expense: some business cards, a few posters, and you'll be all set. After you get started, much of your business will come through word of mouth. Some campuses have referral agencies that will refer students to you. The only possible drawback is that, in exchange for their referral, the office may put a maximum on the rate you can charge. Leave your name and posters at department offices and help centres around campus, not to mention some large posters plastered outside the football team's locker room. The big bonus is that tutoring in your area of study can actually reinforce your knowledge of the subject you're teaching.

Show and Sell—On campus you'll find many companies aiming the big money grab at students. These companies are peddling anything from cellular phones and magazines to perfume and video games. Keep one hand on your purse or wallet to protect it, but your other hand free to apply for positions with these companies. These jobs commonly involve marketing or sales, so they're usually looking for outgoing, motivated self-starters.

Who are these companies? Service or marketing firms, credit card companies, and long-distance carriers are prime examples. They often pay all or some of your wage based on commissions. For example, a credit card company may pay you $5 for every person you sign up. If you're considering such a position, pay attention to the service you will be selling (e.g., how good is the product, what's the cost to the student?). Signing someone up for a free credit card with a recognized company is probably much easier than trying to peddle a card with a service fee for an obscure company.

Travel Companies—Tour operators love to scoop up student dollars, and they'll usually use the three Ss to do it: Sun, Suds, and Sex. However, they'll also rely on the fourth S to sell the first three: Students. Many travel companies market their Spring Break Bash through student representatives. They'll pay you to market their product, offering some financial rewards and/or free trips in the process.

But is this a good way to pick up spare cash? It depends on the company. Some are reputable travel firms, while others are fly-by-night operations: Gus rents a bus and a flea-bitten motel in Florida, California, or Mexico and all of a sudden he's in the travel business. Such companies may offer the "road trip of the year," but you may find these guys take their own vacation when they can't make a go of it—leaving you, the unfortunate travel rep, on your own. All of a sudden you're stuck with no pay, and an angry mob of boom-box-toting students dressed in surfer shorts demanding their money or your head. Not a pretty sight. Your best bet is to check out the company with your provincial Travel Registry and the Better Business Bureau. You'll find out which travel operators offer serious cash opportunities and which ones are likely to offer only serious headaches.

Merchandiser—It seems like everybody is trying to sell something. From clothing to personal safety devices, to "revolutionary new health care products," the options are limitless. While many of these products appear to have stepped straight out of a bad infomercial, some can be a good deal. Usually these products need someone to sell them. I've already talked about sales in chapter 3, but here are some of the highlights:

1. Avoid pyramid schemes. Unlike the great pyramids of Egypt, these usually don't stand up for long.
2. Approach any cash-up-front or straight commission sales jobs with an apprehension bordering on paranoia.
3. Stick with reputable companies that have a proven track record, pay at least a partly guaranteed rate, and offer solid support for your efforts. It's amazing how many "rapidly growing new companies" crash and burn overnight.

Off-Campus Jobs

If you decide to venture into the wonderful world of work off campus, you'll find numerous job possibilities. Some jobs are easier to work into your schedule than others, and the rates of pay will vary greatly. The most obvious places to look include retail outlets, restaurants, entertainment venues, manufacturers, and service providers. But there are also some nontraditional jobs in the community:

- Special events can offer some extra cash now and then. If your city attracts fairs, exhibitions, trade shows, and so on, there may be openings for work. A good place to find out is at the local employment centre, or check out tourist and convention centres for a list of upcoming events and the names of organizers.

- Elections offer you a chance to win and, unlike the politicians, still keep your promises. Two choices appear on the ballot: (1) a job registering (enumerating) voters, which pays fairly well and is somewhat flexible, but is rapidly being replaced by computerized registration, and (2) running a polling station. Always phone the political party in power. They hire the deputy returning officer, while the official Opposition party hires the poll clerks. Deputy returning officers get paid better than poll clerks for virtually the same work. The great thing about both jobs, however, is that on election day you can usually capitalize on Canadian voter apathy by cracking open the textbook you've been avoiding and still get paid for your time.

- There's a way to put the skills you learned as class clown to work. Some urban centres in Canada are doing a booming film business, which means that film companies may be hiring extras. (Gone are the days when two students with a videocam were the Canadian film industry!) Vancouver (not all U.S. actors share David Duchovny's hydrophobia) and Toronto are prime locations, but even smaller centres are attracting Hollywood money. There may even be a film made on your campus . . . an *Animal House* sequel perhaps? The pay isn't great, unless you catch the attention of the director, but you'll sometimes get a feeding or two out of the deal, and maybe even a free haircut.

- Many places such as malls and restaurants have special promos. Check to see if they hire for these occasions. I once strolled around a mall asking trivia questions for $17 an hour.

Making the Most from Off-Campus Jobs

- Keep in mind that the hours you work may vary according to the season. If you work in retail, you can usually count on fairly good hours during the fall when people toss around cash in the run-up to Christmas, as well as during other holiday periods. However, hours can be pretty sparse from January to April, as shoppers stay home and recover from their excesses. If you go the retail route, knowing the seasonal trends can help you plan out your course load.

- Don't be a dumb waiter. Wait staff make their big bucks on Friday and Saturday nights, when customers are relaxed, relieved the week's over, and have recently been paid. This can mean happy diners and drinkers, who tend to throw the bucks around more freely. But there's more. People tend to get caught up in the holiday season, so that even a true grinch will be doling out cash. Therefore, be strategic and try for Friday and Saturday night shifts, and extra hours in late November and December.

- Target jobs that benefit from increased holiday sales. Liquor and beer stores, for example, can give you great cash and lots of hours!

- If you plan to be employed over the Christmas holidays, try to arrange your class and exam schedule to free up large blocks of time for paid work. Some employers may be more apt to hire you if you have three or four solid weeks of free time to give them. Some schools may be more flexible on this than others.

- If you work for a company that pays overtime, you may be able to turn holidays such as New Year's Day and Boxing Day into paydays! Check first to ensure that as a part-time worker you qualify for the holiday pay rate (usually time-and-a-half, and sometimes even double time).

- Always check your pay cheque for vacation pay. Employers are required to pay you this bonus but occasionally they're on vacation when it comes to remembering. So a little jogging of their memory could be healthy for your bank account.

Summary of Tips to Remember

- To figure out what your real wages will be for a part-time job, subtract your total expenses (travel costs, wardrobe, etc.) from your total projected earnings, and then divide by the number of hours (including paid, unpaid, and prep time) you'll work.

- Apply for a part-time job early, before the start-of-school rush, when everybody else gets the same idea.

- Before taking a part-time job, ask how flexible an employer is willing to be with your class and exam schedule.

- Remember that your time is valuable.

- Look for jobs that allow you to study while you work. If you can get two hours of studying done while working four hours, that's similar to increasing your wage by 50 percent.

- If you have a summer or part-time job with a large company in your home town, see if there's an opening with the same company in the city where you'll be going to school.

- If you work part-time in a job that pays part of your wage in tips, bank the cash as soon as you get it. It will spare you the temptation of spending the wad of bills that's weighing you down.

- Avoid the temptation of succumbing to discounts that stores offer to part-time employees. A 10–25 percent discount may sound good, but it could mean you end up spending much more than you normally would.

- Ask if your employer will automatically deposit your pay to your bank account, which allows your money to start accumulating interest right from payday, and will help you to avoid bouncing cheques.

- If you are working part-time, always keep an eye out for a better job. Becoming settled in a part-time job can sometimes be hazardous to your wealth.

- Watch for changes in your employer's financial situation. If the company falls on rough times, you want to avoid being stuck with uncashable paycheques.

- Governments don't pay interest. If you are a student working part-time, take a moment to fill out yet another government form (a TD1, available from your employer) that allows you to have only the minimum deductions taken from your pay-cheque. Bank the money that the government would other-wise have taken. This way, if you have to pay income tax at year's end, you'll at least have earned some interest on the money you set aside (something the number crunchers in Ottawa wouldn't have given you). If you don't have to pay tax, you'll have a nice bonus saved up.

- Some employers will allow you to purchase various invest-ments, such as Canada Savings Bonds, through automatic payroll deductions. These plans are a great way to save money from your part-time paycheque.

CHAPTER 5

Everyday Banking: Avoiding the Big Bank Heist

If you've ever left the bank feeling bewildered about who the money in your account actually belongs to—you or them—then you're not alone. With service charges, maintenance fees, transfer fees, and other hidden goodies, it's little wonder your money seems to be shrinking. In fact, it probably is! It's gotten to the point where I'm afraid to sneeze in the bank for fear of being charged a service fee.

Have you ever wondered why:

- *You* actually have to pay banks a fee to get *your* money from *your* account?

- Banks try harder to give you a credit card when they know you can't afford to pay it off?

- Statements telling you that you owe money arrive on time, but notices of increased service charges tend to get hidden or lost in the mail?

- The interest earned on your savings account is a fraction of the interest you pay on your loan, and an even smaller fraction of the interest charged on your credit card?

- Bank clerks are now called personal financial representatives, but give you the same service at a higher fee than a teller?

- Despite the increased service fees, the pens in the bank still rarely work?

The important thing to remember is that when you deposit money in your account, you are loaning the bank money. (They in turn re-invest it and make a tidy profit.) This having been said, there are numerous ways that you can avoid being a victim of the big, yet subtle, bank heist.

- Try to find an account that levies little or no service charges (it'll probably pay an equally paltry interest rate). Use this account for your daily transactions only, and keep just enough money in it to cover these expenses, along with a bit of a cushion to avoid bouncing cheques (the charges are steep).

- If you have numerous accounts sitting around with small bits of cash, condense them into one or two, thus avoiding the extra service fees that may be charged on accounts with small balances. I'm not quite sure what servicing the bank does on accounts holding only $5 or $10, but you can deprive them of the pleasure of digging their hands any deeper into your pockets.

- Do a search to see if you have any unclaimed bank accounts sitting around with cash in them. You can do a free search by contacting the Unclaimed Balances Service at info@bankofcanada.ca or at 1-800-303-1282, or visit http://ucbswww.bank-banque-canada.ca/scripts/search_english.cfm

- Always ask for the schedule of fees on your account and find out how long they will be in effect.

- If you're not sure of a charge or policy, get it in writing. I've asked a question in one major bank and received three different answers from three separate staff members, all in about five minutes. Obviously the interest rate isn't the only thing that frequently fluctuates.

- Many accounts provide you with a debit card. The positive side of debit cards is that you can't spend more than you have, but their convenience makes spending what you do have all too easy. Transaction fees can also add up quickly. Keep debit cards for emergencies or preplanned purchases.

- Determine how much money you'll need for a given period, then withdraw that amount at one time, rather than making frequent withdrawals. You'll save on transaction fees.

Fat Fee Service . . . er, *Flat* Fee Service

Flat Fee Service is a one-time monthly fee that banks offer in exchange for waiving the individual service charges on your account. The monthly fee covers everything from chequing, withdrawals, and pre-authorized bill payments to free traveller's cheques, laundry . . . nope, I guess I was wrong, they just sent my dirty laundry back.

Flat Fee Service might be a good deal if you make frequent transactions in your account, although in some cases you'll find that it is still cheaper to pay the separate service charges. Before signing up for this service, check your passbook for the past two months. See what items you were charged for and add up the service charges. If the monthly total is consistently higher than the flat fee service, then perhaps you should enter into this type of flat fee arrangement. If you're only ringing up charges of about $2 per month, why pay an $8 monthly service fee?

Banks will try to wow you with a list of benefits that you'll receive if you subscribe to this service. They may sound impressive, but chances are you probably won't use a lot of them. Remember, quality counts, not quantity.

Be wary of some charges that are not covered under the flat fee service, such as overdraft transfers and NSF cheques. There are still ways the bank can tack additional charges onto your statement.

One recent development is that some financial institutions, in order to entice students and other new customers into opening accounts, are offering a student pseudo–flat fee service, which may be less than half the regular rate or even *free!* It will often cover the main transactions, such as chequing, bill paying, and record keeping; however, it does not usually cover traveller's cheques or money orders. Nevertheless, it will probably give you all you need. Ask your bank, credit union or trust company if they offer this no-charge account or student rate—it may just be a good deal.

Choosing a Bank, Credit Union, or Trust Company

Deciding where to park your wad of cash can be puzzling. If you watch the commercials, billboards, and ads, you'll see bank people doing a lot of handshaking and smiling. Makes you wonder if they've spent a little too much time sealed in the vault. But let's assume they're just very happy about being around you and all that money. You still need to decide which institution is going to give you the best deal before you plunk your piggybank down on their counter. Here are a few suggestions to help you choose:

- Consider how each bank treats you. If they're smart, they'll give you good treatment now, regardless of the fact you are a starving student, in order to encourage long-term customer loyalty.

- Look for a bank that is not going to clobber you with service charges and transaction fees. Some banks allow a certain number of transactions per month without charges. Ask if there are any service fees that kick in if your balance falls below a certain amount—say $1,000.

- To help compare service charges, check out the service fee computer tool at **http://www.fcac-acfc.gc.ca/Eng/resources/toolsCalculators/Pages/BankingT-OutilsIn.aspx.** This government site will help you compare the various fees and packages, based on your banking needs.

- Shop around for student deals or discounts. Some financial institutions give special rates on service charges, flat-fee service, etc. Some even offer these free!

- Look for an institution that offers convenient locations. If you don't have access to a vehicle, this is particularly important.

- Check to see which bank has ATM machines on campus and near where you live. If you are constantly using another bank's machines, you'll pay big-time Interac service charges over the year.

- Make sure the institution you choose is insured.

- Keep an eye out for bank promotions that offer cash incentives or fee reductions to get you to switch to that bank.

- The on-line bank may save you money as financial institutions switch to offering this type of operation. Some banks have even offered financial incentives if you make on-line transactions. Much has been hyped about this service as some middle-aged bank executives recruit their 60s musical icons to extol their virtues. Can a bank change? Can a musical idealist be bought?

• Virtual banks now offer accounts that charge no transaction fees, require no minimum balance and pay around 2–4 percent interest on your balance. You may still need a regular account to use some of these, but using the two accounts together may save you money and earn you a reasonable return at the same time.

Remember that if you'll be dealing with a bank for the next three or four years, you should pick one you're comfortable with. If at any time you feel you are being treated poorly or overcharged, ask to speak to a manager. If you're still unsatisfied, switch to another bank. Chances are they'll be happy to have your business.

Tip-off Signs That Your Bank May Be Shaky

1. Pencils stolen from local pro shop.
2. Safety deposit box is actually manager's briefcase.
3. Credit check replaced with frisking.
4. Bank deposit form asks for next of kin.
5. Tellers named "Squeaky" and "Eddie the Worm."
6. Manager is constantly humming "I Go to Rio."
7. Loans office located in side alley.
8. Weapon check at the door.
9. Family members accepted as collateral.
10. Same-day money-laundering service.
11. Bank staff closely resemble the cast of *Crime Stoppers*.
12. Loan rate determined by spin of the roulette wheel.

Credit Cards

Credit cards can be the downfall of many students (not to mention their parents). They offer excellent convenience and can sometimes save you money, but on the other hand, they can lead you into a maze of continuous debt, in which you may wander for years. Use them poorly and you'll pay. Use them wisely and you'll sometimes benefit. If you have any doubts at all about being able to use them without problems, avoid them altogether!

Credit card companies are sure of one thing: the easier it is for you to use credit cards to buy products and services, the more likely you are to make those purchases. Is it any surprise that credit cards have become easier to obtain, and that the number of businesses accepting them is rapidly expanding? They are now accepted in many grocery and liquor stores. (Will that bottle of Scotch soon carry a warning: Drinking and charging may impair your shopping judgement?)

It seems like everyone and his dog has a credit card these days. In fact, a 70-year-old retired navy man in the U.S. was able to obtain a card for his Brittany Spaniel, Ginger. The credit card company didn't discover this until they followed up on a rather large takeout dinner order . . . of the canine variety of course.

How can you use credit cards to your advantage?

- Obtain a card that charges little or no yearly fee.

- Shop around for your card. Some offer an interest rate competitive with a cash loan. You usually pay a yearly fee, but if you think you will be carrying a balance on your card, it may be better to opt for the fee in order to get the lower interest rate. These cards can sometimes offer an interest rate six or seven points lower than standard cards. To compare which option is the least costly for you use the free comparison calculator at: **www.fcac-acfc.gc.ca/ Eng/resources/toolsCalculators/Pages/CreditCa-OutilsIn.aspx**

- Never choose a card based solely on incentives or reward programs. These include such gimmicks as auto reward points and air travel miles. These "rewards" lead you to do what the card companies want: spend more money. You may end up rationalizing your purchases: "Sure, I bought an XBOX, plasma TV, jacket, skis, and four pairs of shoes that I didn't really need . . . but I got half a ticket to Florida."

- Stick to one or two major credit cards. Avoid specialty-store cards which often charge an interest rate six or seven points higher than the major bank cards. (That Bloomingdale's card may be prestigious, but it's an extra worry you don't need.)

- Avoid cash advances—they often carry a service charge as well as an interest rate that starts accumulating the minute you receive the cash.

- Avoid carrying around too many cards. Aside from wearing your pockets out, it makes it easier to lose one without even knowing it. By then the "finder" could have had a great vacation on your tab!

- Always keep a list of your card numbers written down in a place separate from your cards. This way, if they are stolen you can cancel them immediately and shorten the spree someone could have at your expense.

- To protect yourself from impulse buying, lower your spending limit. Despite credit card companies' frequent "generosity" in raising it for you, you're better off to keep it at a manageable amount (an amount that you can easily pay off every month). Remember, their generosity in increasing the limit is not matched by a willingness to help you pay it off.

- When you make planned purchases of things you really need, a credit card can be great if you promptly pay it off in full. If you're a confessed window shopper, leave your credit cards and chequebooks at home when you go "just to check out the new spring line." With strictly cash in hand, you'll be much less likely to succumb to those impulse purchases.

- Some basic credit cards will automatically extend your warranty on purchases by up to an extra year, with no cost to you. For computer and other electronics or appliances this can be valuable. To get the maximum benefit from this feature, charge it and pay your card balance off in full.

- Never use your credit card as ID. Use your driver's licence or student card instead. People can easily use your number online or over the phone to make purchases.

- Most important of all, pay off the complete balance monthly and escape interest charges. Credit card companies won't benefit, but you will.

Other Money Tips

- Never, ever, ever give out your bank card's personal identification number (PIN) over the phone (or in person, for that matter). If anyone tries to get your PIN from you, trace the call and report it to the police.

- Don't leave money slips lying around, even the ATM receipts. Even if your account number or PIN is not on it, thieves can still use the receipt to track down information about your account.

- You've seen the three elated guys walking out of the money retail store, having cashed a $100 cheque—a "privilege" they paid only $3 for. Sure they're excited, they can party, but they just paid 3 percent to cash a cheque—that's $30 on $1,000. I'd want a drink too if I got ripped off like that! Avoid these cheque-cashing places that prey upon people with poor credit (and who can usually least afford the charges). Stick with reputable trust companies, credit unions, and banks.

- Save a Tree - Electronic money transfers through Canadian banks, or third party providers such as Paypal, are usually a cheaper option than money orders or cheques.

- If you do need a hard copy money transfer, opt for money orders rather than certified cheques or bank drafts since they are usually cheaper. A Canadian money order from the post office will often cost approximately 40 percent less than one from a bank or trust company.

- If you have both a U.S. and a Canadian account at your bank, you may be able to get a better rate when exchanging currency. Transfer the money between accounts and then withdraw it rather than trying to convert actual cash. Depending on the amount, the savings may be significant.

The Smart Card-Holder's Creed

(Repeat aloud whenever you feel the buying impulse)

- I will always pay off my credit card on or before the payment due date regardless of floods, sleet, snow-storms, Bay Days, or Midnight Madness Sales.

- I will buy only those items which I would otherwise purchase in the course of daily living, without the prodding of TV, radio, magazines, and other advertising media.

- Despite the strong bond between me and my credit card, I will never invite my card into an establishment where I will be consuming alcohol.

- I will remain faithful to my regular credit card and not discard it for a more prestigious or glittery card unless there is a clear financial advantage in doing so.

- I will not give my card number over the phone unless I am absolutely certain of the credibility of the merchant on the other end, and only when I have initiated the call.

- I will not let TV and my credit card mix, regardless of how glittery those cubic zirconia look or how much Anthony Robbins or Susan Powter promises to change my life.

- I will respect my credit card and not burden it with the pressure to lift me from a rut, the February blahs, or the exam-time blues.

- I accept that everyone and everything has a limit. I therefore pledge to not push my card to its limit or beyond.

CHAPTER 6

Housing: In Search of Paradise Lost

A beautiful condo overlooking the city: Jacuzzi, sauna, exercise room, squash courts, skylights . . . your typical student housing . . . NOT! In fact, the average student residence, in contrast to the comfort of home, is often a place where:

- The four-legged family pet has been replaced by the eight-legged nocturnal variety.

- The skylights have been replaced by an annoying hole in the roof.

- Running water now means the sink leaks.

- The crisp aroma of a roaring fireplace has been replaced by the smouldering odour of the garbage incinerator.

- The climate-controlled exercise room is now the 10 flights of stairs used because the elevator rarely works.

- A view of the park is now a view of the "park 'n' drive."

Well, you get the picture. Leaving the comforts of home for student housing can often be an unappealing and expensive undertaking. Staying at home can cut a big chunk out of your expenses. With the cost of education increasing dramatically, more students are choosing the latter option whenever possible. For instance, some students are postponing breaking out on their own by living at home during their undergraduate degree and thus saving their money for an out-of-town graduate or professional school.

Living away from home will not only require a rent

cheque every month, but also mean added expenses for transportation, groceries, and other items. Equally important, the location you choose will affect the amount of time you spend in transit. Do you want to spend more time riding the bus than you do in class (well, I guess that depends on the class) simply to save $25 per month in rent? If you're fortunate enough, you may be able to continue your education while living at home. For many, that may not be an option (or perhaps one you wouldn't want to consider).

It's a jungle out there (usually because landlords don't weed the lawn), but you needn't be stuck crashing in some lowly cellar deep in the heart of a student ghetto. There are a variety of options to save you from this fate.

On-Campus

Mention residence and people often cringe. The word conjures up the image of flowing kegs of beer, water-balloon fights, 3 AM guitar jam sessions, hallways filled with shaving cream, and other hijinks that would have your mom pacing the floor at night. But relax. Residences have changed a lot in recent years and, more often than not, only periodically give way to a "zoo" mentality (usually at the end of exams). While this will vary from campus to campus, many residences have even gone so far as to have extended quiet hours on their floors.

Many students compare living in residence to bungee-cord jumping—it's great once, but that's enough. Little wonder that most students venture off-campus after first year. However, there are advantages to living on-campus. Residence offers a great social environment with the obvious convenience of being on-campus. The big question is, How much is it going to cost you to live on-campus?

How Much Will You Pay for the Residence Experience?

Usually, you'll pay a residence accommodation fee, along with a fee for meals (or whatever that stuff is that they feed you). Your meal plan fee usually hinges on how much food you're actually going to eat. How much you pay for a place to sleep depends on how many roommates you're stuck with and such things as the size of the room, whether it has kitchen facilities, a bar fridge, or other appliances, and so on. You may also find that you pay a fee that goes to your residence council for social events, orientation, intramurals, and other festivities.

The amount you pay will vary from school to school. On average, a school year's accommodation will run you anywhere from $2,800–$5,100 for a double room to $3,900–$5,800 for a single. In addition, meal plans can cost anywhere from $2,300 to $4,400 or more, depending on whether you are a nibbler or a gobbler. Many residences will now let you choose a specified meal plan and then either add to it or get a refund on unused portions. Some schools will allow you to donate your extra points to a local food bank or charity.

Residence council activity fees may cost $25–$99 or more. Additional costs include coin laundry and possibly parking charges. Laundry is usually cheaper in residence than at commercial laundromats.

In all likelihood, the residence experience will cost you between $5,100 and $10,200 per year, depending on the arrangements. If you don't have to purchase a meal plan, you are probably looking at $2,800–$5,800 plus whatever you spend on food.

Space is often more limited in residence rooms than off-campus apartments, so if you have lots of worldly possessions, you may decide to put some of them in storage. A dry corner in your parents' attic or a friend's basement is the cheapest option. Otherwise, you may have to pay for off-campus storage. Factor this into your budget. Off-campus storage may cost anywhere from $60–$150 per month or more, depending on the size of storage space you need.

As a general rule, it is cheaper for a person to live in residence than it is to live alone off-campus. The off-campus option starts to become cheaper, though, when you have roommates.

Financial Advantages of Living in Residence

- Meals are cooked for you (cheaper than eating out, plus no tips).

- You're not locked into a 12-month lease.

- In most cases, your social life will be cheaper, since many activities are provided right in residence.

- Your transportation costs are reduced.

- The furniture is usually provided, so you don't have to drop a ton of cash to furnish the place or pay the movers.

Financial Disadvantages of Living in Residence

- Meal selection is limited. (Is that mystery meatloaf going to look even remotely appealing by April?) A repetitive diet of cafeteria food could drive you to eat elsewhere at an additional cost.

- On some meal plans, you may have to pay for three meals a day whether you eat them or not—a real negative if you skip meals a lot.

- You may spend more (on the latest clothes, gadgets, etc.) to keep up with your neighbours, in what sometimes becomes a competitive environment.

Off-Campus

Home Sweet Home: Renting or Leasing

If you're leasing off-campus, you'll be meeting one of the most unpredictable of all creatures . . . the landlord. This experience can leave an indelible mark on your life. Depicted in sitcoms as key-juggling, tool-toting, noise-hating, neurotic snoops, real landlords usually fail to live up to their TV portrayals. Many even border on normal. Sometimes, however, you get one that doesn't have all his or her coals in the furnace. A landlord's attitude is often affected by whether he's paid by the owner to manage your place, or owns and lives in the building himself, or is an absentee landlord (living far off in some distant city).

When you live off-campus, you may be asked to sign a lease which basically commits you (sorry, there's that "C" word again) to paying rent for the house, apartment, room, trailer, tent, etc., for a specific time period. The lease specifies how much rent you'll pay, how long you'll pay it, what costs are included (e.g., parking, utilities), what the landlord is responsible for (e.g., property upkeep, painting), and what you are responsible for (e.g., telephone, cable). It also sets out any rules by which you must abide (e.g., no BBQs, no golfing in the hallways, no animal sacrifices on the balcony . . . your basic standard requirements). The length of time you will be expected to commit to will vary from province to province and will depend on the type of place, the situation, etc. A 12-month lease is the most common, but others may be longer or shorter. The bottom line is that a lease is legally binding once you sign it (in some provinces, a verbal agreement may be binding), so read it carefully. If there is anything you don't agree with or anything missing from the agreement, have it changed or added before you sign.

When entering into any kind of lease agreement, use the following guidelines to avoid being stung by unforeseen expenses:

- Know what you are signing. Be sure the lease clearly states, in writing, exactly how much rent you must pay and who is responsible for paying the other expenses (hydro, cable, heating, etc.). Don't assume the landlord will pay for something just because it isn't mentioned in the lease.

- If your landlord promises to fix something or renovate your new place prior to you moving in, have it in writing before you sign the lease. When it comes to doing promised repairs or maintenance, landlords are sometimes prone to memory loss (ironically, the amnesia often only lasts as long as the lease). So, if they promise that your badly stained walls will be painted or that a shower will be installed, *get it in writing*!

- Make sure you inspect the premises and fill out a damage report prior to moving in. Otherwise, your landlord may try to blame that missing chandelier on your end-of-term blowout party and demand that you fork over the money for it.

- Make sure all occupants' names and signatures are on the lease (no matter how well you know your roommates). If not, any damage charges come to the person who signed. If you're the only one, you alone may be legally obliged to cough up the full rent and any additional charges.

- Some places will require you to pay first and last month's rent. If you do this, you are entitled to interest (at government-set rates) on the last month's rent for the length of time the landlord holds it. Make sure that this interest finds its way to you at the end of your lease.

- When disputes arise, seek the free advice offered by many college and university services for resolving such matters. Some campuses have housing mediators who provide advice and outline the options open to you, while sparing you the expense and time of taking legal action. Other campuses have law students or legal aid professionals who can advise you on housing matters and disputes.

- Remember to give proper written notice prior to leaving. The amount of advance notice required by law varies from province to province (often 30 or 60 days). Don't assume that just because your lease is up you don't have to give notice. Many students have been stuck having to pay one or two months' extra rent because they neglected this detail.

Choosing a Place: Location! Location! Location!

Probably one of the biggest considerations is going to be the location of your off-campus housing. You may pay slightly more if you're close to campus, but you'll save money and time on transportation.

Location will also affect how much you pay for things like groceries, health and beauty aids, and pharmaceuticals. It may be worth paying an extra $50 a month in rent to be near a cheaper shopping centre.

If you plan to use public transportation, consider not only whether your new home is on a bus route but also how frequent the local buses are. Do the buses run every 10 minutes or once every hour? If they run infrequently and you miss one or the bus is delayed, you may end up shelling out for a last-minute cab to class.

How Many Can We Cram In? The Price of Privacy

A constant tradeoff when choosing a place to live is deciding whether you prefer privacy or cheap rent. Living alone is expensive, but to some, privacy is everything; to others, privacy equals isolation. How many people do you want sharing your space? Consider your personality and decide which of the following statements is true: "I love to socialize constantly and work the crowd." Or: "I love the quiet of a house to myself without the distractions of the TV and stereo constantly blaring." Are you used to inhabiting space with lots of people? ("I loved living with my 14 brothers and sisters in that little log cabin." Or: "I was an only child in a five-bedroom house.") Assess how tolerant you are of others. ("It drives me bonkers when someone leaves their straggly hair in the sink.")

If you choose to live communally, choose your roommates with care. Decide whether you will be able to tolerate these diverse characters for long periods of time, especially during stressful periods like exams. Sure, they might seem great the first week, but are you going to feel so amicable when the dishes are piled to the ceiling, your roommate's kitty litter hasn't been changed since last term, and your bathroom counter looks like the chemistry lab? And, yes, you may like your five roommates, but will you also like their half-dozen friends loafing around the house for days on end?

The more people you share a place with, the less you'll pay for rent and utilities, provided you split the costs.

A common arrangement is to share a house or apartment with one to three roommates. Any more and you may find that the shower is cold by 9 AM and the fridge is overstuffed with half-rotting food. What cost in privacy are you willing to pay? Bear in mind that while living with five other students may seem like fun in first or second year, by fourth year you may crave a little more peace and quiet. It is important to strike a balance between what you can handle financially and what will safely preserve your sanity.

Adding Up the Costs

You've just seen a great place. Dishwasher, washer and dryer, exercise room, skylights, Jacuzzi, sun deck, two-inch shag carpet . . . OK, forget the carpet—it's still a nice place and the price seems right. It's a bit out of the way, maybe, far from campus and far from downtown, but it's still nice—what a place to impress a date. What a year it's going to be (better downplay that part to mom). But then you remember that utilities are extra. It's a big place—expensive to heat—and all those appliances are expensive to run. Oh yeah, cable is also extra, and the phone. A nice place, yes, but all those extras add up. Maybe it's not such a great option? You get the picture. Basic rent is only one part of the cost to consider. Extra expenses can add another 25–50 percent to your monthly bill.

You'll no doubt end up paying some of these extra costs, but keep them in mind before signing a lease and try to keep them to a minimum.

Kitchen Facilities—Check to see what appliances you have to cook with. If there's no place to cook, you'll end up spending a lot more on pre-made or takeout food. A microwave is better than no stove at all, but even nuked food can lose its appeal over time.

Having a fridge or freezer can save you lots of cash by allowing you to buy food when it's on sale and then store it, or to prepare food in large quantities and freeze it. (A large freezer also makes a good home for those edible parental care packages.)

Appliances—These gadgets can tack dollars onto your monthly bill but can also save you money in the long run. One of the deciding factors, of course, is who pays for "the juice." If you pay for your own hydro and water, these devices can jack up the bills. A busy water heater can use $30–$60 in electricity per month, an air conditioner $15–$60, a dishwasher $2–$10, and a washer and dryer $8–$22. But remember that some appliances are time savers and may prevent huge mounds of clothes and dishes from piling up. Taking your clothes to a laundromat or a dry cleaner can also cost a lot, particularly if you have to pay to get there as well.

Storage—This may seem minor, but if you have lots of stuff and your place is small you may end up having to pay to store some things during the year, or in the summer if you sublet your place. Make sure the storage area is clean and dry. Numerous friends of mine have come back after the summer to find their possessions submerged in ankle-deep water or their couch repossessed by rodents while they were gone.

Bad Location—Living in the middle of nowhere can not only cost you in terms of extra transportation, but, if you're on a 12-month lease, can also affect your ability to sublet your place during the summer while you're away. (I'll talk more about subletting later in this chapter.)

Heating—Global warming can only do so much: heating can add up big. If heating is included in your rent, that could be a huge plus for you. If not, take a good look at what it's going to cost. An old house with high ceilings may be charming, but you might spend half your food money trying to heat it. Consider what type of fuel is used, how well the house or apartment building is insulated, and whether you or the landlord controls the thermostat. Oil and electric heating are generally more expensive than gas. An attic apartment might be cheaper to heat than one in a basement, because heat rises.

I had one friend at university who lived in an amazing place that didn't have any insulation, and was therefore very difficult and expensive to heat. The electricity was included in the rent but the heat wasn't, and he would resort to opening the door of the electric oven and turning it on to heat the place. Pretty desperate and unsafe measures to save a few hundred dollars.

It's also difficult to heat rooms with large windows or gaps in doorways. Check those things out before you move in. And don't rent a bigger place than you need; it's a waste to heat rooms you don't use. A sun room can be great in the summer, but if there is no way to block it off from the rest of the space, you may pay big time to heat it in the winter.

If you have to pay your own heat, insist on seeing the heating bills from previous tenants (make sure you see the one from January, which is likely to be the coldest month).

Air Conditioning—Just as you'll need warmth in the winter, you'll want to keep cool during those scorching summer days. Air conditioning makes it comfortable but it can be expensive. If you don't plan to use your place in the summer, it's not such a big factor. If you do plan to stay for the summer, ask to see that July utility bill too.

Cable—Many students can't seem to survive without those timely television talk shows and gripping daytime soaps. If you're among the TV majority, remember to add the cable fee to your monthly costs and perhaps an installation fee as well. If you want the more elaborate channel packages, you'll have to dig a little deeper. Find out whether cable is included in your rent.

Phone—If you want to be connected to the outside world, you must shell out for phone service. If you're boarding with a family, you may have local landline phone charges included in your rent. Otherwise, expect a monthly fee, initial setup charge and of course, your potentially monstrous long-distance charges on top. If you go the cell route, you may have these plus some additional charges (see cell phones).

Parking—If you don't have a car, parking is a non-issue. Otherwise, keep in mind that some places, particularly in urban centres, charge extra for parking or limit you to one spot per house or apartment. A bit of a problem if you and your three roommates all have cars. (I'll try to dissuade you from owning a car in chapter 12.)

Pool, Tennis Court, Sauna, etc.—These can be nice accessories, but will you actually use them? You'll pay extra for an outdoor pool, but if you're only at school during the fall, winter, and spring, you'll likely never even see poolside.

Juggling the Numbers

With some simple calculations (and I mean really simple), you can figure out how much the various options will cost you for the year. Simply approximate your monthly and yearly costs, then plug in the numbers to compare different types of accommodation.

The "Where Will I Be Crashing" Budget

Rent:	_____
Utilities:	
Gas	_____
Water	_____
Heat	_____
Electrical	_____
Cable:	_____
Phone:	_____
Internet:	_____
Laundry:	_____
Transportation:	
Local transit	_____
Parking	_____
Furniture:	_____
Necessities:	
Cooking utensils	_____
Toiletries	_____
Bedding and linen	_____
Subtotal:	_____
Projected Sublet Income: (subtract)	_____
TOTAL COST:	_____

Finding a Place: Avoiding the Shack Attack

Searching for a place can be an adventure (the first three places you visit), a task (the next three you check out), and a downright pain (every place you visit after that). But keep in mind that since you'll probably spend $3,600–$6,300 or more over the next year in rent alone, time invested now will save you money and hassles later. Shop around at least as thoroughly as you would for a car or a good stereo system.

You can keep the time and cost of your search down to a minimum by making a list of your priorities (e.g., close to campus, a good kitchen, a fireplace) and deciding clearly what you can afford to spend (have a range, including the absolute maximum you will pay per month).

For students, there are some convenient places to look for leads. Here are a few of the best bets:

- Most campuses have their own housing office. This is a natural place to start since the housing that is listed is geared to the needs of students in terms of location, price range, etc. Listings are sometimes categorized by type of place (e.g., two bedroom in high-rise), geographical location, (west section of the city, two kilometres to the university) and price ($400–$600/month). This makes it easier to find the places in your price range and thus stick to your money saving strategy. Most campus housing offices now have all housing listings on-line for easy access. These are usually accessible through your school's home page.

- Many campuses operate their own apartment complexes, usually on or close to campus. They're run like any other apartment, except that they are typically cheaper than what you'd pay for a similar place elsewhere. Some are reserved strictly for upper-year or graduate students. Check with the campus housing office on how to apply.

- Bulletin boards on-campus often have postings by landlords, local families with rooms to let, and other students seeking roommates or wanting to rent out their place. The best selection usually appears on these boards during the last four to six weeks of school.

- Most campuses have student school newspapers, and these are often filled with housing listings. Again, the best time is during the last four to six weeks of term. Newspapers may also be put out for the school's staff and administration, and while most administrative publications are as interesting to the average student as an accountant at a dinner party, they often contain rental listings. These tend to be somewhat better and more expensive accommodations, such as faculty homes (while they are away on sabbatical), and housing geared to upper-year and grad students.

- Some of your best free resources are on-line. Particularly good are free posting sites **www.craigslist.org** and **www.kijiji.ca**, (for accommodation and roommates, as well as items ranging from computers, bikes, events and dates) Both have listings for most major Canadian cities.

- Local papers often have accommodation listings, although it is time-consuming to sort through them all to find housing that suits student needs.

- An often forgotten way to find a good place to stay is through word of mouth. Frequently the prime housing is snapped up before it is ever advertised. The obvious strategy is to let as many people as possible know that you're looking for a place and to keep your ears open.

- If you know you want to live in a particular area, you may want to search for a place by walking through that neighbourhood and looking for signs. With apartments, condos, or town homes, check with the landlord or property manager to see if any vacancies are coming up.

- Avoid any house-finding services that charge a fee. Even ones that don't charge you directly will charge the landlord something, which usually gets passed on to you indirectly. There are enough free listings available elsewhere.

Something to keep in mind when using housing offices and other resource centres is that the listings are rarely screened to ensure that the information in them is accurate. Always write down the information, particularly the price, and bring it with you when you go to look at a place. Students have shown up at appointments in the past only to find out that the landlord is asking more than the notice indicated. If there is a discrepancy, insist on the advertised price. If they refuse, steer clear of the place altogether—chances are it wouldn't be the last disagreement you'd have with that landlord. Another common trick is that the landlord tells you that the unit you want to see has been rented but there just happens to be another place available—at a slightly higher rent of course.

Reading Between the Lines: What the Rental Ads Really Mean

AD SAYS:	COULD MEAN:
Apartment with charm	Twenty years behind in repairs—you'd better take a course in plumbing and carpentry.
Quaint Victorian style	Better dump any friends over five feet—they ain't going to fit! Old Queen Victoria herself couldn't have squeezed in here.
Cool lower-level apartment	Scotchguard the furniture and get your cat to higher ground when it looks like rain! Great if you want to capture that wine-cellar ambience.
Newly renovated	The landlord found a sale on military grey paint and swag lamps. You'd hate to have seen it before.
Great location, close to downtown bars	Next to city jail. Best forgo the "meet the neighbours" party—they don't get out much (or so you hope!)
Located on very quiet street	Quiet? It's deserted! . . . And on the far end of town! Everybody packed up and left this slum years ago!
Suitable for couple	The place is a shoebox! If you and your roommate aren't a couple now, you will be after a few weeks here.
Great backyard	The place is a dump, so bring a tent and a good BBQ and enjoy the backyard! You'd better pray for a mild winter.
Nestled in rustic setting	The landlord hasn't owned a mower or garden shears in his life! Stock up on the snake medicine and set those mousetraps!
Complete with loft bedroom	Attic still needs a fourth wall. Better hope you're over that sleepwalking phase!

More Apartment-Hunting Tips

- Phone ahead to verify details of places you're interested in. Save your time and money by confirming the price, size, lease period, and what's included. Some housing offices have free local phones—so make your calls there and save your cell phone minutes.

- Some landlords and property managers are notoriously unreliable, underhanded, slimy, and sneaky . . . and those are their good points! If you are suspicious of a landlord, ask at the housing office whether other students have had problems with him or her. This may prevent you from being gouged.

- Campus housing offices and provincial housing ministries often have publications on renting that spell out your rights and obligations under the Landlord and Tenant Act. These publications are great resources, so familiarize yourself with them, particularly if your experience with renting has been limited. Especially useful is the *Guide to the Landlord and Tenant Act*, which is usually available free.

- If you're a first-year student, downplay or conceal this fact if you can. Many landlords will not rent to first-year students, and in some cases to students at all (yes, this practice is legal in some provinces).

- If possible, ask previous or current tenants about the landlord. Does the landlord repair things quickly? Is he or she honest?

- Many listings in campus housing offices are dated. If the place sounds good and has been posted for several months, it could already be rented. If it isn't, you may want to ask why it hasn't been. Toxic dumpsite delight? More bugs than an RCMP switchboard? The best place to start is with the most recent listings, which haven't been picked over yet.

- Students may hesitate to negotiate for a lower rent, and they often shy away from asking that the place be repainted and cleaned before moving in. Landlords know this and may try to intimidate you to prevent you from asking. But just remember that you deserve the same respect and treatment as any other renter. If you want a lower rent, ask for one; if you want the carpet steam-cleaned before you move in, ask. The worst they can do is say no, and quite likely you'll earn their respect and send the message that you are not a pushover.

- If there is a high vacancy rate in an apartment building or the rental posting has been up for months, use that to your advantage. Ask for a month's free rent or an eight-month lease. You have more leverage to negotiate a better deal since they're likely to prefer $50 a month less in rent to having a place stand empty.

- If you're negotiating rent for a shared apartment, bring your roommates when you meet to discuss the rent—there's a psychological advantage to outnumbering the landlord.

- Agree ahead of time what you and your roommates are willing to pay. This way you won't slip and accept an offer you don't all agree on.

- Present yourself as someone who is an ideal tenant: studious, quiet, neat, likely to pay your rent on time. The landlord is more prone to accept your offer for lower rent if he thinks you'll make a great tenant, rather than an up-and-coming revolutionary.

- If you don't mind sacrificing selection in order to save some cash, you may want to wait until the month prior to the start of school. Rather than having to sign a 12-month lease (which is allowed in some provinces), you can sometimes pick up an eight-month lease this way.

- Find out the vacancy rate in your area. Some cities and towns have vacancy rates of one percent, others five percent. The higher the vacancy rate, the more leverage you'll have in negotiating a better rent.

- Be creative in your negotiations. For example, if you find a place for $400 a month including utilities and you know that the utility cost to your landlord is $70 a month, offer to keep your energy consumption low. If you manage to conserve $20 a month, ask the landlord to give you a $15 rebate. It's good for you, good for the owner, and good for that nice clean air we like to breathe!

- In condo complexes and apartment buildings, you will often find similar units renting for different amounts, since they are sometimes owned by different landlords or property managers. Don't assume that all rents in a building are the same. I once moved to a nicer place eight floors up and actually ended up paying $90 a month less. Compare carefully and you may end up saving a substantial amount.

- Let's make a deal. If you rent in a house, you may be able to work some sort of arrangement to lower your expenses. You may be able, for instance, to offer to cut the lawn or shovel the sidewalk in exchange for free use of the laundry facilities or a reduction in rent. (It's better than getting paid, since you're not taxed on a reduced rent.)

To Buy or Not to Buy: That Is the Question

Although it's not an option for everyone, if your parents are in a position to invest some cash, you may want to raise an idea with them—having them buy you a place. Well, not really buy you a place, but buy one and rent it to you or let you stay there as a property manager. The advantages are:

- It'll ensure that you have suitable housing while you are at university—and you may even get some input on the place they buy.

- It'll give them a property investment that could appreciate in value.

- It'll give them a property manager who lives in the building (this means you).

- At tax time, your parents can write off mortgage interest, property taxes, insurance, utilities, repairs, and upkeep on rental property.

- Parents can pay you a salary as property manager and they, in turn, can write off the expense.

- It'll generate income from the other renters, which may cover or even surpass your parents' costs. This is a particular advantage when there are numerous rooms to rent. It gives your parents the advantage of you keeping an eye on things and restricting renters to people you know and trust.

Buying a house may be a good choice when:

- There are multiple family members going to the same college or university.

- There is a shortage of good, affordable rental housing.
- The housing market is stable in the area.
- You are the worst possible tenant and nobody but your parents would ever think of renting to you.
- Your parents need to defer taxes.

Sound too good to be true? Owning can be a disadvantage when:

- You don't want the extra burden of acting as property manager.
- You can't cook and would rather eat residence food.
- The vacancy rate is high, and you're not able to rent enough rooms to cover the mortgage.
- Real estate markets are unstable and may head down—perhaps making it difficult to sell when you want (parents should plan to hold it for a minimum of three years).
- Your parents want to buy a decrepit slum with 1970s shag carpeting, while you had your mind set on a downtown house with a sun deck overlooking the park.

Keep in mind that if you and your parents go this route, you will need to make sure you're familiar with the building and fire codes, rent controls (if applicable), and any other relevant provincial or municipal bylaws. These codes and bylaws are usually available at your local municipal office or provincial ministry housing office.

Work with a reputable realtor and, perhaps of equal importance, one who knows the student market. There are plenty of places out there that not even the most desperate of students would live in or, on the other hand, are beyond what most students can afford. Another key is to make sure you get each renter's parents on the lease as guarantors—even lifelong friends can fall short of rent money halfway through the year.

Subletting

If you are stuck in a 12-month lease and your school year is only eight months, you may not want to be paying rent for your break period. Those extra months can drain $1400–$2200 or more from your pocket. Fortunately, there is a way to recoup some of that cash: subletting. After all, why should your place be left idle when others could partake of its charm and ambience?

Subletting has a number of advantages. Not only does it provide some cash but it also means there will be someone around to deter thieves. If you sublet furnished, you won't have to spend the time and money moving your worldly possessions elsewhere, or paying for storage. Sounds pretty simple, right? Well, not exactly. Plenty of other students will be trying to rent out their Chateaux de Shack at the same time. It's a renter's market. But there are things you can do to ensure that your place is rented first. The key here is: *Advertise big! Advertise early!* If you can grab the attention of more people, you will generally be able to charge more for your place. Equally important, you'll be able to be selective about who you rent to. (Do you really want to rent at the last minute to the Mick Jagger lookalike with the exotic snake fetish?)

Some tips on subletting:

- Start advertising well in advance (usually three or four months prior to school's end). Stay ahead of the competition, who usually leave it to the last month to advertise.

- Word of mouth is still the best way to sublet your place. Let people who are trustworthy know that you are subletting. Also, keep your own ears open for people who may be looking for a summer rental.

- Advertise on campus. Bulletin boards and newspapers, online classifieds as well at the campus housing office, for maximum exposure.

- Avoid local city or town papers unless you're absolutely desperate. There are people who prey on student renters, by renting for the summer and then disappearing with their apartment contents.

- Ask for references and check them out.

- Arrange to have you and the summer tenant, along with a witness, sign an agreement. (Ask for a sample sublet agreement at your campus housing office or legal clinic.)

- Ask for first and last month's rent. You may also want to ask for postdated cheques for the other months. This will help save you from having to chase after rent while you're in another city.

- If you have a landline, transfer the phone to your summer tenant's name so that you don't get stuck with a lot of long-distance calls on your bill. This is usually a much cheaper option than having the phone disconnected and then reconnected when you return.

When setting your price, you should consider the following factors:

- Consider the features of your house or apartment. Remember, you're competing with a lot of others who want to sublet. A place with air conditioning and a pool, located close to campus, will likely rent more easily than a cellar apartment, next to the sewage plant, on the other side of town.

- Set your rent below what you pay, but leave enough room to negotiate an even lower amount. It's very rare that you can recoup all your rent. Start by asking for two-thirds of your normal rent and be prepared to drop it to half (even lower if there are no takers). By advertising well ahead of time, you can drop your price later if you have trouble finding a tenant.

- If you pay utilities, you may want to have the renter cover them for the summer. That way, if you rent to Perspiration Pete, you won't end up getting a shock when you find he air-conditioned himself *and* half the neighbourhood during the summer.

- If you share a place with roommates who are all staying for the summer while you want to sublet, you'll probably want to agree on a suitable summer tenant. If you make the decision on your own to rent to Chainsmoking Chucky, the late-night drummer with the hygiene problem, you might not be too popular with the roomies when you return at summer's end.

- You may want to set a price for your place both furnished and unfurnished. If your furniture is taking the wear and tear and the summer renter is getting the use of it, you should receive something extra (usually 10–20 percent more).

Remember, your main goal for subletting is recouping some of your lost rent, while keeping your place and possessions safe and secure until your return. Anything above that is a bonus.

Money in Asphalt: Parking

If you have an apartment that includes parking but you don't have a car, you're still indirectly paying for a parking spot. Why not recoup some of that expense by subletting it? There may be others in your building who have two cars and pay $50 a month extra for another spot. Why not rent your unused spot to them for $40? They save $10 a month and you reduce the rent on your apartment. Stick up a notice in your lobby to let people know you have a space available. This arrangement can be particularly valuable in cities where a parking spot can be as hard to come by as clean air.

Summer Rentals: Your Advantage

If, on the other hand, you are trying to rent a place for the off-school months, then the deck is stacked in your favour. The ratio of students wanting to rent their places versus those who need a place is often 3:1 or more. You can be choosy. Here are some tips:

- If getting a cheap place is your main concern, wait until three weeks or less before school ends. People get desperate and tend to lower the rent.

- Don't be afraid to negotiate. If you're a good tenant, the sub-letter may easily be willing to take $50/month less than the advertised rent, simply to have someone trustworthy there for the summer.

- If you're going to look at a place, dress respectably. A person subletting will be far more willing to rent at a lower price to someone who looks neat and trustworthy than someone they have doubts about.

- Take an agreement with you to have signed so that the terms of your sublet agreement are clearly spelled out on paper.

- You can look for luxuries that you wouldn't normally consider for student housing. For example, you may be able to rent a place for the summer with a pool and tennis court at no extra cost.

- You can sometimes uncover a bargain summer rental with an option to take on the lease at the end of the summer. This can be a great bonus since you get the cheap rent for the summer months, can try it out before having to sign a full lease, and could end up with a good place for the following year. It's the best of all worlds.

CHAPTER 7

Furnishing and Decorating: Fit to Live In

You've found the space you are going to inhabit for the next year—possibly longer. Now the question becomes: How will I furnish the place? The furnishings you choose can make or break how nice your place looks. Unfortunately, they can make or break your finances as well. The great news is that you can furnish your place both well and cheaply with some basic strategies.

Before you start your furnishing quest, check with your roommates to see what they already have. You can save money by not buying a kitchen table when your two roommates each have one. Try to avoid being the one who buys the high-wear-and-tear, but less-durable, stuff: sofa, TV, DVD player, etc. Offer to provide the low-wear, durable things: end tables, pictures, bookcases.

Remember, when you are a student it generally doesn't make sense to pay a lot for furniture. Why? Because:

- You'll probably move often as a student and things will get banged up a lot.

- If you have roommates, your furniture will take more abuse than later when you have your own place (if it's cheap, you won't sweat it when your roommates hold their mixology course on your couch).

- Tastes change rapidly—your choice of decor from the "early academia period" may seem great in first year but may turn

out to be "the most despicable, tasteless piece of home furnishing on the face of the earth" by fourth year. Why pay big
bucks for something new that will last 15 years when you
might be sick of it in three?

Posters, Toasters, Coasters (and Other Freebies)

Freebies and cheap furnishings can get your place looking
so good your parents might even consider staying there.
And there's lots you can do to scoop up these ultimate in
bargains.

Look for the PG Rating—Some of the furniture in your
house is rated PG . . . that's right, "parental giveaway." Just
prior to school, most houses have the Parental Warehouse
Don't-Pay-a-Cent-Event. Excess furniture, appliances, pictures, bedroom furnishings, wedding gifts that were never
used, cottage castoffs, etc. are often available at the
absolute best possible price—free.

Beggars Can Be Choosers—It's great to get a lot of stuff for
free, but you can graciously decline the embroidered
Niagara Falls souvenir pillows or the 1970s macramé wall
hanging. After all, do you really want the extra responsibility of caring for those masterpieces? Be selective and avoid
loading up on too much of the stuff you don't need.

Tell One, Tell All—Let everyone know you are going off to
school and furnishing your own place. Tell all your relatives
and your parents' friends—especially the ones with a sense
of decorating style. You'll be surprised at the furniture,
appliances, pots, pans, wine racks, pictures, TVs, and other
gadgets that will descend upon you. People tend to have a
hard time throwing away their excess possessions. This
gives them a way to get rid of their accumulated stockpile
without the bother of having a garage sale, and they feel
good about knowing it's going to good use. Best of all, it

means that you spend less on furnishing your place. What a deal!

Furnishing Formula #1: New Apartment + Party = Housewarming Gifts—Throw a housewarming party to help with decorating. A good way to ensure practical gifts is to set a theme. For example, if you desperately need plants, consider a "deck the halls with plants" party. Then watch your place be transformed from a barren wasteland into a tropical rainforest.

Curbside Castoffs—You may not make a habit of it, but students often get good furniture at, of all places, the street curb. Good furniture often gets tossed simply because people get sick of it. Take pleasure in their displeasure by relieving them of these things. But remember, a lot of stuff in the garbage is there for a reason. Don't drag anything home that looks like it could be bug- or rodent-infested (a good dating strategy also!).

Creating Your Own Shelves—There's no need to shell out for a bookcase when there are cheaper ways to go.

- Sticks and stones. A great way to make shelves is with simple bricks and boards. Pick these up new or used. They work great and are easy to move around.
- Buy metal brackets and mount boards on the wall. Simple and cheap, and you'll end up with much more floor space.

Table Talk—There are many creative ways to come up with the tables you'll need around the house. You can do this quite cheaply.

- Dining, kitchen, and coffee tables abound in the student exchange pools, and any sturdy table can be transformed with a good covering and/or nice placemats.
- Use a patio table or picnic table to give your place that outdoor look. Chances are you have parents or relatives who would love to store their garden furniture at your place for the

fall and winter. Add a couple of palm trees and you'll think you're on a tropical island.

- Crate Nouveau. Those infamous plastic milk cartons are great for making stacking shelves to hold books, DVDs, CDs, files, etc. They're made to toss around so they'll last for years, and when you move they become instant packing boxes. You can also mix these with wooden boards for that combo natural/artificial look.

- Crate au Naturel. Wooden crates work well as shelving too. Though somewhat harder to find (check food markets and grocery stores), they give a natural, rustic look to a place.

- Budget Brothers Special. Computer, TV, and stereo boxes are usually big and sturdy. If you cover them with a nice big cloth or blanket and set lamps, pictures, or small stereos on top, nobody but the chronically nosey will ever know. You can also fill them with things you want to store. If you plan to put heavier things like the big-screen TV on this "instant table," be sure to have it filled with nonbreakable items, like books, in order to make it sturdier.

Buying Furniture Cheap: When, Where, and How

After you've taken stock of all your freebies and giveaways, figure out what you are still lacking. Then look to the following places for some cash-saving deals.

Broken-in and Tested: Buying Used

Buying used is the best way to go when it comes to furniture and some small appliances. You'll get things for a fraction of what you'd pay new, and in many cases, you'll get much better quality than you could afford to buy new.

Furnishing Formula #2: Year End + Move + Graduation = Bargain—Bulletin boards and student newspapers are absolutely the best places to get good stuff *cheap*. There are bargains available on everything a student needs: furniture, school supplies, appliances, etc. The key here is timing. Scour the boards regularly for new postings during the last eight weeks of the school year (for semestered schools, the last four to eight weeks of each term are good). People are selling their things here for some very good reasons:

1. It's the end of the year—they need money.
2. They are done for the summer and it's cheaper to sell their stuff than to store it or move it home.
3. They're graduating and want to get rid of the stuff. Perhaps they're moving to a new job or doing that Europe thing. The absolute lowest prices are during the last two weeks of school, when the stress of exams and an expiring lease put students into an "I just want to get rid of the stuff" mood.

If you don't purchase at the end of school, there are a few other good times, although you'll usually pay a bit more.

- The start of school is a good time. Other students will sell things when they show up and discover their roommate has a duplicate item: "Wow, we both have the same velvet Elvis portrait! And they told me it was an original!"

- At midyear, some students get their marks and they read like a weather report in January—new record lows. A quick withdrawal from the academic scene can mean a furniture liquidation sale (a real one). Okay, it's vulturous—but good training for law school. The bottom line is that you are apt to pick up bargains here.

Check Your List—A loaf of bread, a carton of milk, and a queen-size bed. That's right, bulletin boards in grocery stores often list cheap furnishings for sale. Stick with stores in student neighbourhoods, while avoiding suburban stores (you tend to find a lot of lawnmowers and baby cribs there).

Word of Mouth—Keep your ears tuned for news of friends who are leaving or graduating. Chances are they may be selling or giving away some things. Let people know what you're looking for.

Don't Lift a Finger Solution—Check with the people moving out of the place you are moving into. They may be glad to part with some things. The big advantage is that they won't have to move it out, you won't have to move it in. Everybody's happy! This strategy works particularly well for that bulky freezer stuck in the basement, or that hard-to-move couch. Other things that are great to pick up this way include blinds, curtains, and area rugs, since these items may not fit into the old tenant's new place.

Moving or Garage Sales—Both can be good, but choose a moving sale over a garage sale. Moving-sale people tend to sell better stuff and have a sense of urgency about getting rid of it because they have to. At a garage sale, it seems like you get more "we're not moving but we just don't want the junk in the house" kind of stuff (probably all the stuff they bought from other people's garage sales over the past 10 years). Moving sales are frequently one-shot deals (whereas some people seem to be having a garage sale constantly), and you generally find more furniture at these sales. The key rule is to go early (earlier than the advertised time), while the good stuff is still plentiful.

If you are moving and have access to a truck or van, check the "free" section of on-line classifieds. At months end people often give good household items away (especially large items such as furniture) as it is not worth it for them to have to rent a vehicle to dispose of it. It is usually first come first serve, so you have to act fast.

Buying Used: Caveats

- Keep portability in mind when you buy. A great way to lose friends is to ask them to help move a pull-out sofa bed, and other monstrous pieces of furniture. Some woods are lighter than others, and some pieces of furniture are collapsible. Check the dimensions: a fold-up futon will fit into almost all houses or apartments, whereas a queen- or king-size bed may not. Try to avoid bulky stuff before shelling out cash on something you won't be able to use. My roommate once waited six weeks for a custom-made sofa and loveseat, and when it arrived—you guessed it—it didn't fit into our apartment.

- Exercise caution when buying used upholstered furniture such as a sofa. If it has been stored in damp areas or left unclean, it may be mildewed, rotted, or even house certain members of the insect or animal kingdom. Even if it was free, your savings would soon be eliminated if you had to pay to bring in the pest control.

- Test electrical furnishings and appliances before you buy them. Plug in the lamp, turn on the microwave, fire up the BBQ to make sure it works. There is some risk in buying electrical appliances, but usually the low cost justifies this risk. Try to buy from people you know or check the item over carefully for signs of abuse.

- Don't, as a rule, buy appliances that "just need minor repairs" unless you can easily fix them yourself. The minor repairs on a blender or toaster, for example, may cost you more than if you bought a new one.

Buying New: The Other Route

If you've taken stock of all your freebies and cheap used furniture, and you still need to buy some things, you can save substantially by paying attention to where and how you buy.

- Consider buying unfinished furniture. This doesn't mean you'll have to make a couple of table legs or anything. You'll usually pay less if you buy furniture unstained or unpainted and slap on a stain or varnish yourself. Tables and futons are great for this.

- Purchase unassembled furniture. By doing some simple assembling, you can cut your costs. Believe me, it's easy. Even I, who thought a Phillips screwdriver was a cocktail served to the royal family, was able to master this task.

- In stores, look for floor models and demos. Whip out the magnifying glass and start combing items for scratches and dents. If you find one, start negotiating for a discount. Remember, any minor scratch can usually be touched up cheaply, and chances are you'll get more scratches moving it in anyway.

- Look for genuine sales at stores. Many stores are constantly advertising 40 to 50 percent or more off. But that seems to be the norm. Are these things ever sold at the so-called regular price? (Some major Canadian store chains have actually been charged recently for such misleading sales practices.) True sales are usually at year-end or on discontinued items.

- Buy directly from the manufacturer. If you know what you like and want, why pay a sales clerk to pester you in a store? You may have to go outside the city to find the factory, but the savings can be worth it.

- Buy from furniture warehouses. Sometimes these high-volume, low-price retailers have great deals. But be cautious, many places are not warehouses—just big stores that advertise as warehouses to make you think you're getting a good price.

- Check out bankruptcy sales. Yes, the bank can be your friend, as long as it's the furniture place they're foreclosing on.

- Auctions are a little more time-consuming and sometimes dangerous if you are prone to impulse buying or sudden twitches of the appendages, but you can often get good buys on new and used furnishings.

- Surplus stores carry a wide though often unusual assortment of items, but prices are right for a student budget.

- Dozens of dollar discount stores have sprung up recently. While they don't tend to sell many large furnishings, you can usually get smaller items such as kitchenware, utensils, glassware, bedding, and bathroom accessories at cheap prices. They may not be top-of-the-line brand names, but do you really need a Gucci shower curtain?

- One little-known place you can get good-quality kitchen utensils and appliances at low prices is at restaurant supply companies. Many sell to the general public, and the quality is usually very good since it is industrial-strength and built to last.

The Living Room: Tips for the Couch Potato

Sofa—You may spend more time on the couch than any other single place, aside from the bed. Whether you are parked for your evening TV fix, or sitting down for an afternoon of Hemingway, or simply engaged in some recreational flossing with that special someone, you'll want something that you're comfortable with, physically as well as financially. If you or one of your roommates haven't benefitted from a giveaway, keep in mind the following when choosing a couch:

- Go for materials that can be easily cleaned. Synthetics tend to be much easier to clean than natural fibres such as cotton. If you room with the varsity drinking team, you may want to go completely waterproof ("Does this couch come in Gore-Tex?").
- Futons are a cheap option. A true friend of the student, these pieces of furniture combine flexibility (a bed and a couch) with portability. They are also much easier to clean, since the cushion and the frame are separate.
- If it's new or expensive, go for the can of Scotchguard. It's worth the extra expense to prolong your couch's life.

Chairs—An essential for handling the overflow on those Thursday sitcom-viewing nights, chairs can usually be picked up cheap. Go for the space savers. If it's not going to be used all the time, why give it space? Your best option, in this case, is probably folding chairs that can be stored away when you want.

Lamps—Everybody seems to have plenty of lamps they want to get rid of. Yes, lots of them are ugly-looking and tucked deep in the corner of the family rec room—perhaps your mother's short-lived attempt at ceramics? But you can take some pretty scary lamps and add a unique lampshade and/or decorate the base to give it a fresh new look.

Kitchen Deco: Chopping Prices

To some, furnishing the kitchen means finding a fridge, a coffee pot, and a couple of beer mugs . . . mission accomplished. However, others may want to actually cook in the kitchen.

The good news is that with minimal effort and little expense, you can have a well-equipped and convenient kitchen at your fingertips.

Kitchens are a breeding ground for gadgets and surplus pots, pans, and appliances. Chances are, your parents, relatives, or family friends would love to give away some of the clutter. So offer to relieve them of it.

Appliances

There are lots of appliances to choose from, but your best bet is to avoid the gadget trap. Buy only what you need. If you have roommates, figure out who has what gizmos and then divide up who buys what is still needed.

Tea Kettle—I don't know of many houses that don't have at least two or three kettles. See if you can borrow one. The whistling ones are great for keeping you awake during late-night cramming sessions.

Coffee Maker—A staple for any student with morning classes. You can usually get them dirt-cheap. Friends or relatives who are true coffee addicts may willingly part with one of the caffeine-delivery devices they've accumulated over the years.

Microwave—Once a luxury, they now give you one of the best values for your money. They're cheap (as low as $100 for a basic one), use little electricity, and you'll probably end up eating both better and cheaper since they're so quick and convenient. Prices have come down, so you can pick one up cheap, either new (at electronics superstores, discount department and hardware stores, and furniture warehouses) or used (since people upgrade to better models). Prices vary depending on options and size, but avoid really old models, which may be of questionable safety.

Toaster—A true basic for the student kitchen. You can usually get a hand-me-down toaster with one element burnt out or a sticky lever. It'll still do the trick.

Toaster Oven—Toaster ovens are particularly good if you live alone and/or pay for electricity. They can also eliminate the need for a separate toaster.

Blender—For the tropical drink freak or the milkshake fanatic, a blender can be great. If you use it regularly, it can be worth the fairly small expense. Otherwise, go with a covered juice pitcher and a few minutes of vigorous shaking.

BBQ—Great if you have a patio. Some students use these all year round. Propane BBQs can be an inexpensive alternative to grabbing some fast-food burgers. And while you will have to pay to fill up the tank occasionally, you really can't put a price on the sweet smell of Spam being cooked over an open grill. Small charcoal hibachis can be picked up cheap. Trouble is, propane is so quick that charcoal seems to take forever, and meanwhile you've polished off most of the snack food in the house. If you have an apartment, fire regulations may prohibit you from having a BBQ. Check first, before you buy.

Here are some ways to save when buying appliances:

- Buy company seconds or refurbished models at factory outlets.

- Buy simple products and basic models rather than the deluxe versions. Do you really need a blender with 16 speeds when one with eight will do? Most people never even learn how to use the extra features. When was the last time you read an appliance manual cover to cover?

- Demonstrator models or discontinued lines offer good value since they are often discounted substantially. The colour may be different from new models, but at 20 to 40 percent off, who cares? Buy them just before the new models come out in February and late August.

- Appliance repair places often fix and sell off unclaimed items that people have left. You can get some real deals here.

- With the advent of discount department stores and warehouse clubs, you can pick up name-brand appliances cheap. Warehouse clubs may not offer you a wide selection (e.g., one colour instead of 10), but their prices are usually better.

- You needn't drive halfway across town to buy an appliance advertised as on sale. Most large chain stores will meet or beat a competitor's prices on identical items. Take the sale flyer to the closest store and save yourself the time and travel expense.

- When buying used appliances, don't pay too much. If it's not under warranty, you take a bit of a risk. Ask to try it first, and check it over closely for signs of abuse. (Does the toaster look like it's been used for the odd game of touch football?)

- Generally, with appliances it's a good idea to stick with recognized brand names. That way, if there's a problem, it will be easier to find a repair place that can fix it. You don't need to go with the most expensive brand name, but at least choose one you've heard of.

- Keep the warranty card, manual, and box if possible. If you resell it you'll get more if it's in the original box. It also saves the wear and tear if you pack it before moving.

Other Kitchen Furnishings

Many of the little things you'll need around your place may be passed on free from the family canteen: pots, pans, plates, mugs, tablecloths, etc. To run out and buy these items adds up. But again, there are ways to save.

Kitchen Cutlery—In our house, it took us guys a few months to figure out how to use this stuff, but once we did, boy did those knives and forks prove helpful. Spaghetti wasn't the problem it used to be! Try dollar stores, where stainless steel cutlery (your best bet) sells at giveaway prices.

Plates—If you have roommates, go for cheap, durable stoneware or plastic. Before you load up on dishes, remember that the more you have, the higher the dirty ones will pile up.

Pots and Pans—Again, an odd assortment is all you need. A frying pan (non-stick), a couple of different-size pots, and a cookie sheet are best to start. You can spend hundreds on pots and pans—but don't. If you buy them, go for a cheaper set to start. If you're a novice cook, you'll probably subject them to every abuse imaginable.

Plastic Containers—They are a must! Tupperware-type containers can be picked up cheap (they are almost constantly on sale). An even cheaper option is to reuse airtight plastic food containers from margarine, peanut butter, etc. Try to get the clear ones if possible so you can remember which one really has the margarine in it and which of the other 10 similar containers has the leftovers.

Cups and Mugs—Go for plastic if you can. Company giveaways, those frequent restaurant promos, and school promotions such as Frosh Week and Homecoming are excellent providers of free drinking containers. You may already have a collection of beer steins that mysteriously followed you home from previous drinking escapades.

Napkins and Tablecloths—Get washable and easy-to-care-for stuff. Plastic wipe-and-wear is the least hassle to clean, but machine-washable fabrics are also good. Avoid white—you'll feel less guilty for drooling over your gourmet creations. Red is a must for spaghetti lovers.

Miscellaneous Gadgets—Bowls, spatulas, drainers, can openers, and other utensils to fill up your drawers can be had free or cheap. Most of these tools can be found for a couple of dollars at moving sales and dollar stores. Avoid the gourmet cooking stores, boutiques, and upscale department stores, where they'll usually charge you more.

Some Overall Tips on Kitchen Utensils

- Avoid electrical gadgetry if you can, such as electric can openers. They cost more to buy and run, and are more likely to break down.

- Use plastic utensils for cooking and non-abrasive cleaners for scrubbing. Your pots and pans will last longer and therefore save you money.

- Never cook on the highest temperatures, as it will shorten or end the life of pots and pans. Even a full warranty does not usually cover such abuse.

The Executive Chambers

Most students will have a room that at least vaguely resembles an office or study space. The good news is that, aside from your techno tools, it's pretty cheap to furnish. As with other furniture, see what the freebie situation is like at home.

Student bulletin boards are again a super way to pick up office furniture. You can usually buy something cheap from a student, use it for four years, and then sell it for what you paid. (If only things worked this way with cars.)

Many companies sell off their surplus used office equipment cheap. This industrial-strength furniture tends to be so durable that it will outlast even the most perpetual of professional students. If you have family or friends who work for a company, have them check into the situation, since sometimes employees get first shot at this stuff. Check with large companies or in the local paper for sales.

An even better bet is a good old, down-home, "it's gotta go" going outta business sale. Sure, you may feel like a vulture hovering over the slightly-used-but-the-price-is-right merchandise—but it'll pass.

Avoid used furniture stores if you can. All they're doing is buying from the places I've mentioned above and then reselling at a much higher price. So cut them out of the action and save!

If you insist on new office furniture, check the wholesale

clubs or office superstores. Prices are good at both, while the selection tends to be better at superstores. If you do buy from an office supply store, see if your family, friends, or relatives can get a corporate discount as a private business owner or through the company they work for. Many office supply companies charge a much lower price to regular corporate customers.

The Desk—The most important piece. The basic features you'll want are a smooth writing surface, drawer space, and something that can support a personal computer. Again, portability is key. That cherrywood conference table may look good in the IBM boardroom, but it probably won't fit into your attic loft. A collapsible desk is ideal.

Try the do-it-yourself special: Take a couple of two-drawer filing cabinets (see below) and place a flat door (available new and used at building supply stores and building wreckers) over them. Fasten with two-sided carpet tape. Voilà: a desk with drawer space.

Filing Cabinets—These are important for keeping your notes and other paperwork organized (or for hiding your desk mess when parents visit). They're also great for holding up the door you call a desk (see above).

Filing alternatives include legal - or letter-size boxes, which can be picked up free at stationery or printing places. If you want to "splurge," cardboard or plastic file boxes can be bought relatively cheaply at office supply stores.

Chairs—Probably the one place you should spend a little extra money for good quality. Long hours spent cranking out the term papers can take their toll. In the long run, you'll save your back (and reduce your chiropractic bills) by spending a little extra. If you're buying one used with the upholstery a little worn, you can always throw a hockey jersey over it to give it a sports motif.

Bulletin Boards—Buy from an office supply store and you'll pay a lot for a simple corkboard. Go to a lumber place, or a do-it-yourself store, and have them cut the corkboard to size. You'll pay less by avoiding the packaging and the retailer's cut.

Other Accessories—File baskets, a wastepaper basket, and so on can usually be picked up used, or from dollar discount stores, while rewired lamps can be found at electrical repair shops.

Bed and Bath

Your deepest thoughts can occur in the bed or the bathtub, so decorate these rooms well for inspiration. It need not cost a lot.

Towels—You probably have a matching set already ... OK, so they all say "Holiday Inn," but still they match! Avoid big bulky towels that take up more room in the washing machine and cost you extra quarters.

Shower Curtain—Buy the cheapest washable one you can find (nylon or plastic). Unless you give detailed bathroom tours, guests won't know it's not a designer model.

Laundry Hamper or Laundry Bags—Save your cash. Laundry bags often float around as freebies in frosh kits, or you can pick up a couple of cheap cloth sacks (one for light clothes, one for dark is ideal).

Mats—Rather than buying a pre-cut mat, pick up a cheap remnant or leftover piece at a carpet place and cut it to size.

Bed—As mentioned above, a futon will give you more versatility than a standard bed. If you do go the bed route, avoid a waterbed as some places won't allow them and you may have to run out and buy another bed. Stick with something basic and simple to move. Remember that the retail markup is quite high on new beds and they're often on sale.

Bedding—Don't tell me you have this from the Holiday Inn too!?! A discount department store is probably your best bet. Splurging on a higher thread-count may be worth it, but don't be lured into buying designer labels.

Personalizing Your Humble Abode

Student apartments are unique and often lack the unimaginative Department Store Decorating Doldrums that our parents' places sometimes fall into. With a few creative touches, you can create your own Student Setup Extraordinaire.

Dealing with Your Hang-Ups

Chances are, you'll want to look at something a little more exciting than four bare walls, but you certainly don't have to spend like you are furnishing the Louvre to have a great-looking wall display. First of all, check out the amazing freebies:

- Travel agencies usually have some great posters of exotic destinations (places you might be able to afford to see on Spring Break because you are not tossing money into overpriced artwork).

- Music retailers and movie rental shops often have promo posters plugging the newest overrated and overpromoted flick (thank goodness for big Hollywood budgets), while sporting goods stores frequently have great ski, tennis, sailing, or snowboarding posters. Campus film and sports clubs may also have some freebies.

- If this all sounds too superficial and you really want your place to make a statement, you are still in luck. Educational and political organizations often spend a lot on awareness campaigns. While you may not want a mug of a beleaguered Mike Duffy, (or any suspended Senator for that matter), on your wall, many organizations put out some really slick posters promoting everything from drinking responsibly to spending quality time with your neutered pet. Contact groups you're interested in.

- Posters advertising festivals and theatre events are often given away. They want the publicity and you want the free artwork.

Some Other Ideas for Pictures

- Have photos from high-quality calendars, magazines, and greeting cards framed.

- Pick out favourite photos and have them colour-photocopied and enlarged at copy centres. You'll have personalized prints or posters at a reasonable price.

- Frames and unique photos can be found at garage sales, flea markets, etc. Spraypaint frames and they can look like new.

- If you find old or historical portrait photos, put them in a frame and hang them up. People are fascinated by these, and it's great to make up some bizarre story about the people in the pictures and watch the enchantment on your friends' faces as you recite the tale to them.

The Frame Game

Framing will often grab more of your cash than whatever it is you are actually framing. This is a notoriously high markup area, but you can save if you shop wisely.

- Never pay full price for custom framing. Instead, check on-campus for an art studio or graphics department. Some places will show you how to do your own framing, and charge only for materials, saving you as much as 50 percent. Another option is retail do-it-yourself framing places, which may save you slightly.

- For cheaper posters, do-it-yourself plastic laminating or dry-mounting can be done at a fraction of the cost of framing. Check out the on-campus art studios or map libraries.

- Custom lamination is a cheaper alternative to framing. The less expensive materials save you money, and if you spill a beverage on your Mona Lisa print, you just wipe her off.

- Buy pre-cut frames for prints and posters. It's much cheaper than custom framing (and quicker too). Best prices: warehouse clubs, art supply shops, and discount department stores.

Get adventurous. Don't limit your wall displays to just prints, posters, and paintings. *Awaken the artist within*! Just as T-shirts make a statement, so can your walls. You can hang a lot of stuff to form a wall display: musical instruments, sports equipment, bikes, pots and pans, dried flowers, rugs, quilts, flags, concert programs, sheets, blankets, roommates (a definite statement), ceramics, and so on.

Plants

Okay, so you've got your place looking like it's right out of the pages of *Shack and Shingle* magazine. But it still doesn't have that homey look—maybe a few magazines for the table, some soiled sweat socks draped over the lamp, or maybe that stuffed school mascot hanging from the ceiling or . . . that's it: plants!

You might cringe at the mere suggestion of having plants—don't want to be tied down or anything. But, before you skip this section, at least read a few words from a guy who couldn't grow mould on bread. A true friend to even the most artistically inept, plants add colour, warmth, and life to your place and even clean the air. Best of all they're cheap! After all, what other living things can you keep that cost virtually nothing to obtain, and can live for years on dirt and water?

Walk into many plant stores and you'll find some great-looking exotic plants that carry equally exotic prices. But there's a much cheaper route to tropical paradise.

Watch-Your-Money-Grow Tips

- Go for easy-care plants that thrive on neglect and abandonment—Marginata and Canes, for example.

- Look for plants that require little watering (e.g., Pathos, Philodendrons). Unfortunately, I have one plant that sops up liquids like Lindsey Lohan on a weekend—a real pain for the frequent traveller or forgetful waterer.

- Try to get plants that thrive on low light (e.g., Chinese Evergreen). If you are a "cellar dweller," this is key. Stores often include tags on their plants that say how much light is required.

- Try for quick-growing plants (you'll need fewer of them). They'll fill out easily and will give your place a lush appearance (a large keg will do the same).

- Choose plants that are particularly good at cleaning and purifying the air—the Molly Maids of the plant world. Spider Plants and Peace Lilies are great for this.

Where to Get Them Cheap

- Clip and Save—Grab your scissors and stake out the home of everyone you know. Clippings from plants can be used to start new plants by simply sticking them in water or soil. Examples of plants that root easily are Philodendrons, Pathos, and Wandering Jew.

- Check with friends and family that are moving. One thing that people are glad to place in a good home is plants.

- Look for end-of-season sales at plant stores, when they clear out cheap plants to make room for the new greenery. Late summer and winter are particularly good.

- Campuses sometimes host plant sales, usually early in the year.

For those of you suffering from aquaphobia, there's an even easier approach: dried flowers. Who says you never got anything out of that past relationship? Dry the dozen roses you got from Lance Romance or that bouquet you tackled everyone for at the last wedding. Just hang them upside down to dry.

I know some of you are still convinced that the chemistry between you and your green friends (or brown by now) just isn't there. Well, there are still two or three last-hope solutions.

Silk flowers and fake plants can offer a good solution to your foliage follies. While they're usually more expensive than the live variety, they don't require any care. A good compromise is to buy a few fakes and place them in the low-light areas and put your real plants where the lighting is good. If you live in a virtual bomb shelter, this might be the ticket.

For the really cheap and desperate: plastic flowers. Better suited for ending relationships, plastic flowers are probably best in extremely low-lit areas: a basement closet comes to mind!

Straight Talk on Pots

Avoid costly pots from home-and-garden stores. Be imaginative—use decorative jars, plastic containers, or plastic-lined tins from food products and dollar stores. Spice them up with paint or a ribbon. An environmental freebie. You can also let your imagination run wild. An old shoe (closed toe only), hat, jockstrap (support your plants), or hockey helmet used as a planter can add a personal touch.

Getting the Gear: Sound Advice on Home Entertainment Products

Sounds like your apartment is going to be pretty complete. But now, time for the really essential stuff, the things that really make a ramshackle, run-down, leaky apartment a home. Yes, you guessed it: the home entertainment system.

No matter where you attend school or where you live—in residence, at home, in a house full of students—you are likely to spend a fair amount of time either watching TV or listening to music. But you needn't let high-voltage electronics short-circuit your wallet. You can enjoy these "essential" pleasures with some simple saving strategies.

Television

Whether it's the stellar acting of *Big Brother* or the fast-paced excitement of a parliamentary debate, or the heart-wrenching testimonial of the woman who wants to marry her minivan on *Oprah*, basic TV entertainment comes fairly cheap. The television is probably the most used piece of entertainment equipment in the house, but when it comes to size and gimmicky features, buy only what you can afford. The better the picture, the higher the price, so consider whether you can endure paler tans on *Survivor* or duller ties on Don Cherry.

If you're thinking of acquiring a TV, consider the cost-sharing option. Most good TVs, VCRs or DVD players last an average of five to seven years. Divide this number by the amount you are thinking of paying and you'll have your cost per year. Then check into whether it would be cheaper to go the rental route based on the cost of a year's rental. If you have five roommates, the cost per person may be very low and you may avoid any roommate resentments when the TV breaks down and you're stuck with the big repair bill.

If you all pitch in together to buy one, the problem will be deciding who keeps the TV at the end of the year. Perhaps a better solution is, say, to have Sally buy the TV and have Al and Tom give Sally what they would have paid towards a rental. It's a great deal for Sally and a good deal for Al and Tom. This strategy can be used for other large purchases, including the stereo and the bar fridge.

The main rule for home entertainment equipment is: Buy only what you need, and govern your spending by how many roommates (if any) will be helping pay the cost.

DVD Players/Recorders and VCRs

DVD players ($40–$70) and Blu-ray machines ($70–$150) have dropped in price, driving the VCR ($40–$100) the way of the 8 track. Combine this with the expense of movie theaters (and the huge cost of munching on concession stand food) and these devices have almost become an entertainment cost saver. Even the VCR's ability to record shows cheaply has been supplanted by the price decline of DVD recorders (in the $100 range) and more recently, the introduction of the PVR ($200–$400 but sometimes free with a cable subscription.) It all means that many inexpensive choices now abound.

Regardless of which device you choose to keep you entertained, go simple on the machine's features. Decide ahead of time which ones you really need and stick with them. Probably the most unused things in the world are these machine's features ... cuz most people can't figure out how to use them. The ironic thing is that most salespeople fumble around trying to demonstrate the features when they have no clue about them either. I've always felt there's a university or college program in there somewhere—"Hi there, I'm an undergrad at DVD U."

Sound Systems

Students spend plenty of time listening to music (or reasonable facsimiles), and now that you're away from home, you have the chance to annoy your neighbours and roommates instead of just your parents with your rhythmic appreciation. While high end multi-component systems still exist, digitized music now means a good set of speakers paired with a computer, MP3 player, cell phone, or numerous other electronic devices, can provide decent sound at a reasonable price.

Used Hardware

If you live by yourself, buying may be the better long-term option. However, if the funds are pretty dry, a new TV, DVD or stereo may be too big of an investment. Although there's some risk, buying used may yield some great deals. Consider the following options:

- Student sell-offs are a great source. The best time to buy is later in the year, since a low bank account often means an electronic liquidation sale. After Christmas is also good, because people who got new TVs, stereos, DVD or MP3 players (or whose roommate got one) often sell off their old system.

- Also, check out TV and DVD rental places, since they often sell off some of their older models at low prices.

- Pawn shops are an option, although prices aren't as good and they only occasionally have a warranty.

- Check classified ads for used equipment. People often sell basic, yet good, equipment when they upgrade

- Old School for Freebees. Old school TV's can now be picked up for free as people upgrade to digital.

- TV, video and audio stores sometimes accept trade-ins and in turn re-sell good equipment, sometimes with a short warranty.

New Electronics

The big advantage of buying new is that you're getting a warranty and the latest features. A warranty is good to have on electronics equipment. The disadvantage is that you'll pay more. If you do buy new:

- Buy from reputable retailers where possible. Stereo Steve's may give you a good deal, but they may be out of business the next day.

- If you see a great price on "the gear" at a store you have reservations about buying from, approach a more reputable store and see if they'll meet their competitor's price. They often will. It's a retail battlefield out there, and most won't turn down even a small sales victory in the war.

- Always keep your receipt and warranty card in a safe place. If you need a repair but don't have these forms, the store may not honour the warranty—meaning you pay.

- Never accept the marked price as the lowest, even if it's already on sale. Audio/video stores will usually negotiate. Ask for a further discount, or a deal, such as a free DVD with a DVD player, or protective case with the purchase of an MP3 player. I've found this almost always works.

- Boxing Day and January sales are usually the best time to buy because stores want to clear out the old stock to make room for the new. Salespeople are broke then too ("My credit card bill was how much?!?!"). Thus, commissioned salespeople are scrambling to make enough to survive in these lean months. Month-end is a particularly fruitful time to negotiate a good price, since commissioned salespeople are usually more desperate to meet their monthly sales quota.

- Many electronics superstores have come to Canada from the U.S., bringing increased competition and forcing lower prices. Don't pass up the bargains these free-market competitors bring. If dealing with one of the electronics or office superstores, play one against the other. Many of these will beat any price by as much as 5 to 10% of the difference—an incentive to shop around!

- Extended warranties: The puzzling thing about these expensive little features is this: a salesperson has just spent the last half-hour telling you how great and wonderful this DVD player is, and then once he's convinced you of this, he turns around and tries to sell you an extended warranty package since "you never know when it's going to break down." Sounds contradictory? It is. Salespeople love to sell you these warranties for one reason—they make big money on them. In fact, in some cases, they're making almost as much on the warranty as on the products themselves.

So is it worth it? The research says it best: NO! First, most defects will show up in the first year (the standard manufacturer's warranty period). Second, the extended warranties are usually offered by companies other than the manufacturer, so if they go out of business, you're out of luck. Third, some basic credit cards will automatically double your warranty up to an extra year when you use them to pay. And finally, you may still get stuck paying shipping if your equipment is sent away for repair. The bottom line: Unless you are extremely hard on equipment and/or lug it around (for example, a laptop or digital camera), don't buy them.

Guidelines for Buying Video and Audio Equipment

- Choose an established format. While no technology is immune to obsolescence, some formats seem prepared to stay for a while. Digital and wireless have taken hold, with MP3 players and streaming video pushing down sales of DVDs and CDs. Microcassettes, mini CDs, and DATs have yet to be established, and there's a good chance they never will be.

- Avoid buying new technologies. You'll pay big to be the first on your floor with the latest electronic gizmo. Even worse, because it's new, the flaws haven't been ironed out.

- Avoid the bells and whistles and lights they stick on audio and video equipment. There is no correlation between sound or picture quality and flashing lights. In fact, if you look at the very top equipment, you'll notice an absence of these gimmicks.

- Stick with well-known brands. You'll find them easier to service.

- If you want to know which brand is best, don't ask a salesperson. She'll just tell you the name of the brand she sells. Instead, ask a major electronics repair shop that handles many brands. They're the people who actually see inside these machines and they know which brands break down most.

- Be wary of U.S. deals. While some prices seem good, with duty, taxes, and exchanges the "bargain" may be less than it first appeared. Also, some U.S. warranties aren't valid here— your full three-year U.S. warranty may turn out to be only an American souvenir: worthless in Canada.

- Avoid the time-limited offer. Some pushy salespeople offer a "special" price that's only good for "today." Give them time-limited attention by promptly leaving the store.

- When buying TV or audio packages, avoid their "pre-packaged" systems. A favourite trick is putting a decent CD player, tuner, and amp with a crappy pair of speakers. Looks like a good deal but they take you on the speakers. If you are going for a package deal, make sure *you* can choose the pieces.

- Do some research ahead of time. Nothing keeps a fast-talking salesperson honest better than a customer armed with some knowledge. They realize you are not the gullible sap they mistakenly took you for. This is particularly key for students, since many salespeople realize that this may be a student's first major electronics purchase, and try to exploit this to their advantage. Become familiar with the technical terms and features of what you are buying. Magazines such as *Consumer Reports* (a non-profit and therefore pretty unbiased source) and other buying guides, found in most libraries, are a great resource—far better than a company's glossy promo material.

Things That Go Bump in the Night (and Even in Broad Daylight)

Being a student, you may not feel that you own many things of interest to a would-be thief. After all, what sort of sicko would want to steal a bookcase full of Russian literature, or a dining room table with wobbly legs? Well, students in fact are a prime target of thieves and are often left empty-handed after a ripoff. What do the thieves take?

Burglar's Student Shopping List

- Home audio/video equipment
- Personal electronics (ie: cellphones, ipods)
- Computers
- Bikes and other sports equipment
- Jewellery
- Clothing such as leather jackets
- Car audio systems

Students are a target because they disappear at predictable times like Christmas break, exam periods, Easter holidays, Thanksgiving, and Reading Week. Students also tend to be more lax about security, often adopting an "open door" policy (not to mention open windows, cars, etc.). This is particularly true in student dorms and apartments.

There is no foolproof way to keep burglars out, but there are things you can do to discourage them. After all, if your house is discouraging and your neighbour's is inviting, whose house do you think they're going to ransack?

So What Can You Do?

- Add an extra lock. Because student housing has a frequent turnover of tenants, there tend to be "spare" keys floating around. Add a deadbolt for extra security, and replace the lock cylinders in the regular lock if possible (check with the manager on this). Most importantly, regardless of your trusting nature, use the locks!

- Invest in a timer for your lights, particularly if you go away for several days or more at a time.

- Leave a radio on to create some noise while you're out of the house. I've found Yoko Ono music particularly effective in keeping all but the most audio-challenged thief away.

- Stop the press! Cancel your paper and have your mail taken in when you're away on holiday or other long periods. That pile of Victoria's Secret catalogues at the door is a dead giveaway that the guys are away! This will also help you avoid

having valuable mail swiped, including such things as credit
cards and other financial information.

- Always secure windows. Students are more likely to live in
  basement or ground-floor apartments than in penthouse
  suites, and low windows can be easily pried. Use a piece of
  wood to block sliding track windows and doors.

- Store extreme valuables in a bank safety deposit box. It will
  save you having to worry about security .

- Avoid letting it be known you live alone. If you have an answering machine, start your creative message with "We can't come
  to the phone" rather than "I can't come to the phone." A single
  person is more likely to be victimized than someone living with
  roommates.

- Use deterrents. A loud barking dog, security company stickers, or even a deranged-looking roommate who froths at the
  mouth can help ward off potential thieves.

- Limit the cold hard cash you have stashed in your house.
  Most standard insurance policies will only cover a maximum
  of $500 in cash. Speaking of which . . .

Don't Worry, Be Happy—Be Insured

Although it can sometimes be a real hassle to collect,
having contents insurance can save you from disaster
when someone walks away with the few valuables you
may have. Although you may not feel like you have very
much of value, assets such as computers, TVs, stereos,
jewellery, family antiques, bikes, and clothing can all add
up. Even if these prized possessions have seen better
years, most contents insurance policies now offer
replacement value for items stolen or damaged. That
Commodore 64 computer you are still plucking away at,
for instance, would be valued at what it would cost to
buy an equivalent new one.

Check to see if your parents' insurance covers you while
you're away at school. Most policies will cover you while you
are attending school, but check to be sure. It's worth the call.

If you need to buy your own insurance and have valuables worth a minimum of $5,000, at least purchase a basic policy. Keep it cheap by splitting it with roommates if you have them.

What Should You Be Aware of in the Insurance Game?

- Although most policies now give replacement value, check to make sure you aren't just covered for a depreciated value.

- Always check your policy to see what items are excluded from coverage. Some policies have more clauses than a downtown mall in December. If there's something you want covered that isn't, see if they'll include it. Policies in some provinces, for example, don't include bicycles.

- Check what limitations there are on items covered. Some policies may limit the amount of coverage to, say, $6,000 for jewellery or $500 for coin collections. Those heirloom diamond earrings from your cross-dressing Uncle Fred may be worth more than your policy's limit.

- Always make a list of your valuables, including the make, model, value, and serial number, and keep the list in a safe place along with receipts for major items. If your place is ransacked, it will make it easier to identify what was taken. Otherwise you may not realize that something is missing until many years later, by which time it will be tougher to collect.

- Check to see how much your contents are insured for. A minimal policy usually covers up to $25,000. You and your roommates could easily exceed this limit with a few good computers, a TV, jewellery, and a stereo system. However, you can usually increase your coverage by paying a slightly higher premium.

- If you are taking valuables such as your family jewels, coins, or art to school, you should have them appraised and insured appropriately. Additional coverage will usually cost about $13 per $1,000 above your standard policy coverage. If they are possessions you are not going to use, then a bank safety deposit box may be a far cheaper option.

- If you are going away for school, have your parents notify your insurance company of the change in circumstances and of your new address.

- Most insurance covers natural disasters such as fire and storms, whereas damage from other occurrences such as a flooded, leaky basement may not be covered. This is particularly important because students often end up living in basements or storing some of their possessions there. If you have items of value in storage (the "I don't want to see it but I don't want to part with it" room), place them on wooden skids (which can usually be obtained free from factories or companies that toss them) to keep them off the ground. Also, use plastic storage boxes. This will help protect things from uninsured damage such as damp or leaky basements and garages, a fairly common disaster story among students with basement or garage storage.

- If you want to know exactly what your policy covers, ask for a copy of the insurance company's plain-language guide.

- Take photographs of your possessions so as to remember what you own, and be sure to store these as hard copies or digitally, away from where you reside.

- Check to see that items such as laptops are insured outside your place of residence. Some policies require you to pay extra for this type of coverage on these items.

Top Excuses Why You're Broke by November

1. You got so enchanted with Spanish class that you just had to fly to Cancun to try it out.

2. The profs have all gone pay-per-view.

3. You didn't realize parking on campus was valet-style.

4. Everyone says an A paper doesn't come easy, but you found out that they don't come cheap either!

5. Since taking that course on Freud, it's been expensive trying to feed your ego, id, and super-ego on a meagre budget.

6. You accidentally ran over the school mascot. Who'd have thought it would cost so much to replace an eight-foot-tall orange budgie?

7. You were so distraught with guilt after reading Marx, that you discarded all the trappings of this capitalist society.

8. There were so many books for your history course that you had to hire a librarian just to keep them straight.

9. That delayed growth spurt has really taken its toll on your food budget.

10. You walked out of economics class so depressed by the trade deficit that you felt compelled to try to balance it through a massive spending blitz.

11. You donated to so many social causes at school that you've become one yourself.

12. Classes are so good they've been charging a cover at the door.

13. Those 1-900 charges were for your human sexuality course helpline.

14. You grew so attached to your zoology subjects that you just had to keep them—and it's not cheap keeping 15 obsessive-compulsive rabbits, six nicotine-addicted rats, three undersexed monkeys, and two salivating dogs.

15. What? You mean you don't have to tip your prof?

CHAPTER 8

Cost-Cutting Tips

Telephone: Dialling M for Money

> "Talk is cheap"
> —Unknown

You've probably seen the commercial: An emotional mother picks up the phone to be greeted by her son's voice. Tears soon follow. The dialogue continues on both ends, accompanied by intermittent laughing. Mom cries even more, even son sniffles (a real New Age, sensitive guy). As the tears continue to flow, a voiceover cuts in about the phone company strengthening the bonds between parent and offspring . . . touching, eh? What the commercial doesn't tell you is that those tears were probably brought on by the first phone bill of the term. But, alas, the phone companies are the last to be teary-eyed. Students away from family, friends, and lovers mean big bucks in long-distance calls. The phone companies are fighting to get your business. So take advantage of their battling. You can do a lot to save on basic services, options, and the biggest money-grabber of all—long-distance calls.

Access to a phone, is almost essential for a student. Not only is it a convenience but it is also becoming a valuable tool for performing tasks such as banking and accessing information. So, basic service is something that you will want to have at as cheap a price as possib.. Your choice basically comes down to a landline, cell phone, VOIP (internet phone) or a combination of these.

If you go the landline route you can lower your costs on your service:

- If you live off-campus, try splitting the cost. If you are boarding, ask to share the existing line (often that's included in your board).

If you are sharing with roommates, have one of them put the phone in her name. If there are unsettled phone charges and the accounts in your name, you will be the one responsible (no one likes to 'fess up to those 1-900 calls). Having the phone in your roommate's name is also a good way to avoid those pesky phone solicitors who work their way through the phone directory—let your roommate deal with the carpet cleaners.

- Avoid a lot of gimmicky lights and whistles on the phone you buy. Why pay for a lot of features that you will not use?

- If you live in residence, you may have a phone on your floor (with a very long, impatient lineup leading to it). If you don't mind talking in that sappy "I miss you sweetheart" voice while the rest of your floor listens in, then a shared residence phone should suffice. However, if you require access to information via the Internet or the university's network, or have some other need for a private line, then you may need to have your own phone installed.

- Prior to subscribing to local phone service, compare plan rates as many Canadian regions now have competition.

Service Options

Phone companies now offer a variety of services, and they will try their best to convince you that you need them, enticing you through a free trial period, hoping that after a month or two of relying on these features, you won't want to discontinue them. Call waiting, forwarding, and display are but a few of these extra features for which you must dig deeper. Choose from these options carefully, as extra charges add up quickly. And remember that features like call display require a phone that can handle this option (which costs you more as well). To limit your telephone expenses, keep the following suggestions in mind:

- If you don't want the options after you've had your free trial, cancel immediately. Otherwise, the phone company may automatically bill you for them.

- If you choose call waiting, set an agreement with your roommates that incoming long-distance calls have priority over in-progress local calls. This way, you won't get stuck with the expense of returning a pile of long-distance calls after your roommate gabs for hours about what to wear to tomorrow's aerobics class (you know how guys can go on about that stuff).

- If you have long-winded roommates with a habit of describing their life story to everyone who calls, you'll probably want to opt for call waiting. It will save your friends the frustration of not getting through, yet it's still cheaper than getting your own line.

The VOIP Alternative

A growing option for hanging up on your landline provider is using an internet phone (VOIP). Using your internet connection you can now have a home line through your computer at a fraction of the cost. Services such as MagicJack and Ooma are two options. The drawback is that you are dependant on a stable internet connection for it to always work. Some of these services also allow you to keep your existing landline number. Definitely an option to consider as this technology has improved significantly.

Phone Cards

Phone cards can be a great convenience, particularly when making long-distance calls from a pay phone. However, many can be costly when making local calls—try to use the correct

---

Features for the Future?

Technology moves fast! Watch for these "valuable" calling features, coming soon to a phone company near you!

Exam Display—Haven't cracked a book all term? Not even sure of the course name? No problem, with exam display. This option lets you dial into your prof's office and zero in on tomorrow's exam. A great feature for the night of the final!

Call Zapping—Bothered by those robotic-sounding phone solicitors? Annoyed by constant begging by your ex? Well, free your line and your time: zap those callers into outer space with this handy option. Solicitors and surveyors take cover!

Call Recall—A must-have for those Saturday morning amnesiacs! Your phone recalls what you can't. Eliminate those nagging questions: Where did I leave my car? (Do I even own one?) Whose clothes am I wearing anyway? Who's that stranger sleeping in my tub? Is that really a goat on my balcony? Comes with the bonus guilt-blocking feature for those things you'd rather not recall.

Fine Decline—Is your room looking like a branch library? Has the library hired a fines officer specifically for your case? Graduate from Overdue U with this little tool that eliminates those costly penalties. With one quick dial to the library records, you can close the chapter on those overdue fees.

Call Excuse—Need to get off the hook? This little feature lets you choose from a whole menu of excuses guaranteed to get you the time you need. Breaking a date with that Neanderthal linebacker? Need to explain those fractional marks to the parental units? Seeking that sympathetic extension from the dean? Sweat no more when you connect with this trusty little time-stretcher.

---

change instead. Prepaid cards can also cost you significantly more per minute than you would normally pay—so avoid.

Long Distance: The Next Most Expensive Thing to Being There

Super Saturdays, More for Less, Advantage Plus . . . you've seen the hype. All those savings on long-distance calls show us just how badly we were being gouged on phone bills prior to competition. Now the fight is on, and every company is out to tell you that you will save the most by dialing with them! If you're like most people, the slogan "more for less" has probably come to mean more annoying commercials, more junk mail, more confusing gimmicks, and less clarity about how to save the most money. However, there are some simple steps you can take to ensure that you and your money are not disconnected.

Go one month with your traditional phone carrier when you arrive at university or college. Then examine your long distance phone bill to get a picture of your calling pattern. Pay specific attention to the following things:

1. Who you call the most.
2. How much time you spend conversing with frequent chatters.
3. When you make most of your calls (evenings? weekends? after midnight?).
4. Where you are calling (regionally? provincially? nationally? U.S.? overseas?).

Once you have detected a pattern, look at the various discounts offered by the carriers and see which one is going to give you the maximum savings based on the time, duration, and frequency with which you call people.

For example, you may find you have frequent marathon conversations with your out-of-province boyfriend after night class, or with your parents on weekends (or the night before a big exam, in which case you probably wake them up sometime between 2 AM and 4 AM—parents love those calls). You don't phone anyone out of the country (you don't even know anyone out of the country) and you have classes during the day so you rarely call during prime time. Therefore, you would probably want to choose a plan that offered the biggest discounts in the evening when you talk the longest, and on weekends when you call home. You can ignore the companies that emphasize the deep discounts during weekdays or on international calls since this doesn't fit your phoning pattern.

Once you have this information, there are a number of other factors to keep in mind to help you choose the cheapest option:

- Check to see if the carrier charges you in small increments (e.g., 6 seconds) or if they round up to the next highest minute. This may not seem like a big deal, but if the number of calls you make is high, it could mean a significant increase in cost.

- Never let these companies debit your account directly. Make sure you get a chance to review the charges before you pay. (It's easier to get a statement corrected than it is to get a refund.)

- Avoid long distance companies that require you to pay an activation, signup, network fee or monthly fee for their long-distance plans. There is enough competition that you shouldn't have to pay anything to join.

- Resist signing a long-term agreement with any company (some may offer an incentive, perhaps a free month, for paying in advance for six months or a year). This may look attractive, but remember that competition is tough. The company you sign with this month may be out of business next month (some are on shaky ground now), or a competing company may offer you a much better deal a few months from now.

- Find out how easy it is to switch out of the plan if you are not happy with it. You want the flexibility to switch out without delay or financial penalty.

- Assess the situation should your long-distance pattern change. If you pulled the cord on the out-of-province boyfriend back home, a different phone carrier might now offer a cheaper option, based on your new situation.

- This is a rapidly changing industry. New products are coming out all the time. Keep an eye on what the other phone companies are offering. You may have the best deal now, but it may not be the best tomorrow.

- If you do switch to another company, check the two companies' bills for the switch-over period. You may find that you actually got a bonus: double-billed for that period! Have them correct it right away.

- If you are purchasing Internet access and/or cable service as well as phone service, ask if they will give you a better deal for subscribing to both. Some companies are now bundling these multiple services at a reduced cost.

Long-distance Networks: Phone Time in Bulk

If you've examined your long-distance calling pattern and determined that you qualify as a chronic long-distance junkie (if only this time could be credited to your communications degree), you may want to check out one of many long-distance networks that offer a specified amount of calling for a set monthly fee. These are sometimes limited to calls within a certain region (e.g., within the province or to major centres). If most or all of your long-distance calls are within this area, then you may save a considerable amount of money by going this route. Another big plus with this feature is that some plans allow other people to call you for free on this line. Therefore, you may want to split the cost with the person you talk to most, making it cheaper and allowing you both to save. It's also best to have the service put on the phone line that gets used for the most long-distance calls. Now, I know love lasts forever (or at least until Thanksgiving), but if all your long-distance calls are to one romantic interest (as opposed to numerous long-distance chatters), you are probably best to avoid locking yourself into any long-term commitment to this type of network (say, more than two or three months). If you are considering the flat fee option, keep the following points in mind:

- A generous amount of calling time is usually allowed, but there may be limitations in terms of peak and off-hour calling (which may be different from the other phone companies you've used).

- Most companies don't allow you to carry over unused time from one month to the next, so your time on the phone should be consistently high enough each month to make having this plan worthwhile.

- This feature usually only applies when you use your home phone. So if you're phoning from somewhere other than home, you'll likely rack up additional long-distance charges.

- Ensure that you can stop and start for periods such as Christmas or summer break, without repeatedly incurring any activation fees that some companies charge.

Once you have decided which long-distance plan is best for your situation, set up the account and find out what date this savings plan will take effect as orders take a few days or so to process. And remember; don't feel guilty about leaving your current phone company if you discover another one is better suited to you.

Additional Money Savers

Once you have chosen a plan, there are a number of other long-distance tips that can save you additional bucks.

- Call people who have answering machines when you know they won't be home. This way, they will call you back at their expense. This works well with businesses—phone them when they are closed and leave a message on their machine.

- Many businesses have 1-800 numbers which you should always use to save yourself the long distance expense. Most are published on their company website, however if not, try phoning collect (the worst they can do is decline your call).

- Generally avoid taking on too many different plans at once, particularly if they charge you a network fee. Many now tack this fee on which can run from $2 to $10 per month regardless of whether you actually make any long distance calls.

Cellular Phones

Wireless phones are big sellers, and the price for phones and air time has come down as mobile phone companies battle it out for the "ear waves." But they'll still cost you plenty. In fact, although prices have come down considerably, an average user in Canada (500 minutes a month) can still expect to pay significantly more than an average U.S. user. Cell phones themselves are often cheap. It's making use of them that will cost you! Charges can add up.

Your choices are basically to choose a monthly package plan or to pay as you go. A package plan usually will charge you an activation fee of around $35 along with a system access fee of around $6.95 per month (This is a uniquely Canadian fee tacked on by most of the cell phone companies and contrary to what some of these companies had propagated, not a government fee. Fortunately most providers have dropped it). There is also a monthly 911 emergency service fee. Monthly packages then start at roughly $15 to $30 per month, which will usually give you 50-200 minutes of free calling per month (some will give you weekends and evenings free). Monthly packages can however, run you as high as $50 to $100 depending on how much you love to talk. Extra local minutes will usually cost you $.20 to $.35 with outgoing text messaging, picture messaging, internet and long distance costing extra depending on where you are calling from, and your plan. And of course there are extra features such as call waiting, call display, etc that some plans will charge you extra for.

For most plans you are usually committed to a minimum 12-month contract with some plans requiring you to sign on for 2 years. The actual cost of the phone tends to range anywhere from $75 all the way up to $750 plus. The cost of the phone itself tends to be reduced (and in some cases is included "free") depending on the price and length of the contract you sign. Keep in mind that cancelling for some of these plans prior to the time that you agreed to, can set you back from $100 to $300, depending on when you cancel (Cell providers can no longer charge you a financial penalty for cancelling your plan after 2 years). Some companies now offer pay by the month pre-paid and pay as you go plans, without having to sign a contract and without the extra fees. As a way to manage what you spend on cell phone use, pay as you go may be your cheapest and most flexible option.

So is it worth it? Cost-wise, possibly, depending on your plan and usage. For example, it may be cost effective if you have low usage or a low fee plan and you use your cell to replace your landline. Competition has brought the price of some plans down to where it is now competitive with a landline. From a safety standpoint, both options have some merit, particularly if you are driving, walking, or cycling alone at night. It can certainly add some peace of mind when you are only seconds away from being in touch with parents, family, or police. However, the big drawback is that a cell phone is a lot like a credit card—once you have one, it becomes very tempting and convenient to use it for more than just emergencies. Soon the definition of emergency expands to include a social call here, a casual call home there, a call to put a hold on that dress you liked, and so on. If you are reluctant to lock yourself in long term the no contract, pay by the month or pay as you go options may be the best.

Bottom line: If it is absolutely for an emergency, the plan with the cheapest monthly rate but highest per minute charge may be better, but for high use a higher total minute package is likely your best bet.

Cell phone service can easily set you back $125–$300 before you even make a call. If you absolutely must go cellular, try the following strategies:

- If you only use the phone occasionally, see if you can share its use and expense with a roommate or family member.

- Shop around – portability has arrived. You can now take your phone number with you if you want to switch carriers in the same local area. Find out all the costs and fees then negotiate for free extras and waived fees.

- Choose the cheapest package for your needs and look into group discounts if you buy with friends or roommates.

- Use free voice and video call services such as LINE, Viber, Skype or Facetime. They are all free and allow you to also text and photo share using the app – meaning big savings to your cell phone bill when you use your WiFi connection.

- Victim of Fashion? Cell phones are continually being released about as fast as new lines of fashion. So go for last season's model or a refurbished model and save a bundle as companies clear out last season's stock. Remember with the beating that cell phones take and the frequency with which they are lost or stolen, do you want to have a lot of cash tied up in the latest high priced model?

- Ask to have the $35 activation fee waived by activating your phone on-line.

- With most of these options you are the one who pays, even when people phone you. Chatty friends could prove costly. For them, answer machine mode and a call back on a cheap phone may save you plenty.

- Buy an unlocked phone (or have it unlocked) and you will be set free of being tied to one carrier. Carriers lock phones to keep you from switching to another carrier who may just give you a better deal. You can pay to have it done (usually $10-$30) or you can do it yourself with a little digging on-line for your phone's unlock code.

Smart phone – Phone smarts

The cell phone has evolved from a device to talk to friends to a communications hub, computer, multi-media centre and more. The introduction of smartphones including the most well known Blackberry and iPhone has also greatly changed their pricing through the addition of costly data plans. Unfortunately, there's been a real lack of competition in Canada, meaning high costs for Canadians. The good news is that the CRTC, which regulates this, has finally opened up the market to new service providers, meaning long awaited competition has arrived. The exclusive providers of the most trendy of these devices know this and are trying to get you to lock into an expensive two year data plan (at a much higher cost than most other countries including the U.S.) – something that could leave you saying iBroke after a few years of use. The best option is to say no to these enslaving long term plans before checking out what no-contract options the new players have to offer. The biggest drawback to the newer entrants is quality and range of coverage – a real drawback if you travel. An alternative may be to buy these devices "unlocked" from another source and use it without a contract on a compatible network offering the best deal at the time.

On-line Calling: Can it get any better than free?

Skype (http://www.skype.com/allfeatures/skypetoskypecall/) as well as services such as voipstunt.com/en/index.html offer what can be a great moneysaver on your long distance or even local communications. With a microphone or video cam you can enjoy free voice or video calls with others that have the same setup. Many of these also offer cheap long distance calls to cell or landlines.

Email

The best and cheapest option for most students is now the trusty email, or for that instantaneous response: ICQ or messenger. Most students now have access to this option and once they do the cost is nil. No more horrible stamps to lick, no more dashes to make the mail pickup, and best of all, email doesn't whine or demand more when you use it. If you want the flexibility to choose a cheaper Internet provider without having to change your email address every time you switch (or when you graduate), you can get a free permanent address at **www.hotmail.com, gmail.com, mail.com or mail.yahoo.com.**

Television and Cable: Tuning-in to Costs

Unless you suffer from some sort of CBC fixation, you will probably opt for a cable package. (Yes, there is life after Seinfeld.) There's many types to choose from. The bad news? It can be a very expensive day in Mr. Rogers' neighbourhood. Cable prices have risen significantly, along with your channel options. But there's a few things you can do to keep your cable costs low.

- Go with the basic cable service. You'll keep your costs low but still have a broad channel selection. Ask for a free trial subscription of 1 or 2 months, but make sure the trial stops automatically upon expiry. Otherwise it's too easy to forget to cancel, meaning you'll end up paying for these extra channels. Digital and HD channels will also boost your monthly costs.

- Look for a free or reduced student hookup rate at the beginning of the school year, when companies are hungry for your business.

- HDTV for Free. If you want to tune out high monthly cable costs you can often pick up some HD channels for free. Simply purchase an antenna or make your own (**www.debtfreegrad.com/freebees/HDTV_reception**). Depending on where you live, you may not get all the HDTV channels, but still, it's free and legal.

The Satellite Option: Prices Still Out of Orbit

You and your roommates have just moved in and are admiring the dish sitting comfortably in the neighbour's backyard. "She's a beaut," one roommate exclaims. "Great pickup," cries another. "Never another lonely evening," you add. Well, it may seem that way, but your neighbour's satellite dish may not be what it seems. Although costs have come down, there's still a big price tag attached.

Mini-dish receivers have come down to around $70–$200 plus installation. You can sometimes get free installation but may have to sign a one or two year contract. You'll also shell out, on average, around $35 per month in programming fees with premium packages running as high as $60–$120 monthly. So for now, cable may not be a great deal, but it's still the cheapest option.

Channels to Avoid

More and more channels are springing up every day. The cable barons are predicting an eventual 500-channel selection. But among these channels, there are several you may just want to avoid.

The Bowling Fashion Channel—Beamed in from Hamilton, Ontario, the bowling fashion capital. From alley wear to gutter gear, learn how to knock 'em dead in the aisles. Enjoy behind-the-scenes exposés of bowling models and the myths that surround their "fast-lane existence." Participate in *Alley Aerobics*, a daily workout show that will help you regain your bowling figure and form. Host Erma Rolowski leads you through pot belly pushups, beer can calisthenics, and towel tug twists.

Neutered Animal Channel—A "must view" for pets struggling to cope with a new identity. Journey along with dogs, cats, goats, and horses as they strive to survive their lost sexuality. Includes a mail-in show, "Letters from the Litterless," and the weekly veterinary show *"It" Happened to Me*. A great postoperative bonding experience for you and your cross-dressing canine.

The Hypochondriac Network—24-hour viewing as doctors rush to save people from afflictions they don't have. Includes a one-hour phone-in show where callers can compare non-ailments. Also includes *Placebo Kitchen*, a chance to whip up your own remedies for whatever you're sure you've got.

The Sports Union Channel—Features documentaries on the plight of underpaid pro athletes as they strive to cope with strike-shortened seasons. Includes the travel survival show *Europe on $5,000 a Day* and *Rink Rap*, a phone-in help show tackling topics such as "Adjusting to a Domestic-Built Car," "Learning to Abide by the Law," and "From Illegal to Prescription Drugs—Making the Transition." On *Striking Out*, follow the hardships of baseball players who strive to survive away from their mistresses. And don't miss Alan Eagleson's prime-time financial planning show, *It's My Money*.

Escape from Reality...TV that is

Perhaps it is little wonder that cable TV subscriptions have been dropping recently. Whether it's a declining appetite for one more twisted reality TV situation, or the rising cost of cable service, many are giving up high priced packages in favour of watching TV shows, sports and movies for free. Free or lower cost streaming video sites like TV Gorge, Awooh, Fancast and Hulu (US only) and subscription sites such as Netflix, are drawing people away from traditional cable service. Are cable companies worried? Likely, as they try and recoup their lost revenue by capping internet use and charging for high usage – by those who are... well, likely streaming content rather than subscribing to their packages.

Utilities and Electricity: Avoiding Shock

Utilities are another way that students shell out big bucks, but it's easy to forget that you're paying for anything, until, all of a sudden ...BANG!... a high-voltage jolt: the hydro bill. But there are many ways you can turn down the meter and avoid those shocks to the pocketbook.

If you're paying your own hydro bill, the following tips can save you big time, even if you use only some of them. If your hydro's included in your rent, you may want to read this anyway, if just to be more environmentally friendly.

Fuelling Around

You probably will be restricted to using whichever source of heat your place has: gas, electricity, oil, or occasionally wood. If you have a choice when apartment hunting, your cheapest option by far is gas. However, while you may not be able to choose which fuel you use, you can usually choose how much you use.

Here are your best bets for cutting costs:

- Keep the heat down when your place is empty. It usually takes little time to heat a place back up. If you're away for a long period of time (a weekend) in the winter, turn the heat down or off. (But not completely off in a house—a frozen water pipe that bursts and causes damage could negate any savings on heat.)

- Keep temperatures low. Go for 65°F during the day and 60°F at night. For each one-degree drop in the thermostat setting, you'll save three percent on the fuel bill. (If you're used to 70°F, a drop to 65°F will cut your bill by 15 percent).

- Load up on mom's handknit sweaters and keep comfy blankets around the house. Self-warming is cheaper than house warming.

- If you're only heating one small room, why use the full furnace? Use a small, portable electric heater to keep warm.

- If you have a large place, shut doors and close heating vents in rooms or parts of the house you don't use.

- Use blankets, towels, or snoozing roommates to block gaps at the base of doors leading outside.

- Study the economics of snuggling: a big blanket and a snuggly couch can keep you and all of your roommates warm cheaply while watching TV or reading.

- On cool sunny days, open the blinds and drapes. It will help heat up the house. Close them in the evening to keep heat in.

Hot Water

A water heater is a huge expense, so cut your consumption and turn your hot water into cold, hard cash.

- Turn the water off while soaping and thereby cut your hot water consumption in half.

- If you can, lower the thermostat on your water heater by 10–20°F. Your gas or hydro company may do it for you for free. You'll probably notice little difference in temperature but a substantial difference in cost.

- Turn off the hot water heater if you go away for an extended period of time.

- Contact your local hydro company to find out when off-peak hours are. The advantages of this vary from city to city, but you can sometimes save money by using these off-peak times. In some places you will save only if you have a special meter that records when you use hot water and electricity.

- Don't soak yourself. Mr. Bubbles had the wrong idea. A shower can be 20–25 percent cheaper than a bath.

- Get a new head. A more energy-efficient shower head can do an amazing job of cutting down the hot water you use.

- Get rid of drips. A leaky faucet can pour a ton of money down the drain, especially if it's hot water. One drop a second means 800 litres of hot water/month.

- Give yourself a buzz. An electric razor uses much less energy than shaving with a razor and warm water.

Lights

- Turn off lights you're not using. Sounds like echoes of your parents, but you *can* save on electricity.

- Use fluorescent or halogen bulbs—they use less electricity than traditional bulbs—or buy energy-efficient light bulbs.

- Be a romantic—go for dimmer switches. It'll save you cash and maybe improve your love life.

- Turn tri-lights (lights with three settings) to low unless using them to read by.

- Rather than leaving hall lights on at night, replace with low-energy-use nightlights.

Air Conditioner

Like a car, an air conditioner is great to have but costly to run. However, by plugging into a few wise strategies, you can make using an A/C a much less chilling experience.

- Turn the air conditioner off when no one is around.

- Use it only when you really need it. Use cheaper alternatives such as fans if you can.

- Block off rooms you don't use, and keep doors and windows closed.

- Close blinds and curtains during the day to keep cool. If you still need to switch on the A/C, it'll take a lot less energy to cool your place off.

- Switch off the A/C in the evening when the temperature outside cools off.

- Avoid using hair dryers, the oven, and excess lamps during warm days. These items heat up your place and make your air conditioner work a lot harder.

Dishwasher

Despite their convenience and the time they save, dishwashers do suck up the power. If you are lucky enough to have one, here are some tips for cutting the cost:

- Run dishes through on shorter cycles. Rinse them first and they'll come out sparkling.

- Skip the dry cycle, and let them dry on their own. You can save up to 45 percent of the energy required by the dishwasher.

- Fill the dishwasher completely before doing a load.

- Wash large pots and pans by hand. You'll be able to put more plates in the dishwasher at one time, meaning fewer loads.

- Reuse glasses and mugs and you'll also cut down on the number of loads.

- Use less detergent than the box tells you. You can usually cut down by a third to a half without noticing any difference. The soap companies may not love you for it, but our lakes and rivers will.

Panhandling Your Way to Savings

Stove-Top Savers

- Put a lid on it. Cook food with the lids on (it's faster and thus much cheaper).

- Start with warm tap water when boiling food—this too will cut cooking time and energy consumption.

- Turn off electric burners several minutes before food is done. The retained heat will keep cooking the food.

- Don't drown your veggies—an overfilled pot will take more energy to boil.

- Stop the overkill. Use smaller burners for smaller pots. Things will cook just as fast but use much less energy.

- Stay on top. Cook on the stove instead of in the oven when you can. It'll use less energy.

Oven Magic

- Don't preheat your oven (unless making a time-baked item such as a cake). It's much more expensive to preheat, with little noticeable difference in the end result.

- Turn the oven down several minutes before things are cooked. They'll continue to cook with the retained heat.

- Use a microwave or toaster oven for smaller items or for heating leftovers. It's cheaper, and you'll spend less time salivating while you wait for food to cook.

Thawing Out the Chilly Climate

- Unstuff that fridge. You'll spend more to cool an overcrowded fridge, since fridges work more efficiently when half to two-thirds full.

- Set the thermostat on your fridge to a slightly warmer temperature than normal, particularly in the winter.

- Thaw frozen foods in the fridge, as it will help keep the fridge cool.

- Don't graze with the door open. Remove what you want and munch with the door closed.

Keeping It Clean: Money Savers 101

More often than not, you will find that your housecleaning schedule is determined less by a prearranged plan than by outside events. That is, you are most likely to clean when:

1. Your parents are visiting.
2. You want to impress your new date.
3. You want to find your old date.
4. You're putting off starting that dreaded essay.
5. You've lost your hot concert tickets under the mammoth paper pyramid in your room.

No matter what motivates you to attack the grime and slime, you can cut your cleaning costs drastically.

Wiping Up Without Wiping Out Your Budget

Manufacturers love to have you believe that you need a different cleaner for everything: a cleaner for fresh stains, a cleaner for old stains, a cleaner for pans, a cleaner for sinks. It's in their interest to sell you 10 specific cleaners that you end up only using a portion of, rather than peddling you one all-purpose cleaner that you'll finish entirely. You needn't fall for that trap.

Manufacturers spend millions on packaging and marketing to convince you that you must use their cleaner. But will you really be shunned on-campus if you don't use Martha Stewart's Potpourri Grime Blaster to clean your drain? Not likely. Some thrifty ways to save money on your cleaning needs:

- Use old ripped clothing or rags for cleaning. While you may not want to be swishing around the room with your most intimate apparel, old socks, T-shirts, cotton shorts, and ripped-up sheets will save you the cost of buying wipe cloths or paper towels. Cleaning can be an even more gratifying experience if you use the T-shirts left behind by your cruel and heartless ex-boyfriend to clean out the toilet bowl or kitty litter box.

- Check under the couch cushions weekly. You'll probably find a pocketful of cash (as well as a few unidentifiables that should probably stay that way).

- Instead of buying cloths or paper towels to wipe mirrors and windows, try using newspapers. They wipe well without streaking or leaving lint.

- Always buy mops with replaceable pads.

- If you frequently use specific commercial cleaners or soaps, buy refill sizes.

- If shampooing rugs, go together with other friends and rent a steam cleaner for the weekend. It'll work out to be cheaper than renting it by the hour or day.

- Avoid drape, upholstery, and carpet-cleaning solicitors. They're often overpriced and do a poor job. If you do use one, go with a reputable firm you contact yourself.

- Buy spray bottles or reuse old ones to dispense cleaners. You'll use much less liquid than if you pour it on thick.

Cleaning Formulas for the Budding Chemist

You can probably get most of your cleaning potions without leaving the kitchen. Using some of the cheapest ingredients, you can whip these up easily as you need them, without a lot of space or environmental waste.

Windows and Mirrors—Use half a cup of white vinegar with one quart of cool water (add a drop of lemon juice if you miss the "freshly cleaned" scent).

Pots and Pans—Soaking burnt-on food in baking soda (a bleach for tough things) will clean most pots and pans.

Drain Cleaner—Mix one cup of salt, one cup of baking soda, and boiling water. Pour down drain to unclog. Add one cup of vinegar for tough clogs.

Furniture—Use olive oil to clean wood furniture (or mix three parts olive oil with one part vinegar).

Upholstery—Shaving creme will lift many stains and smudges.

Carpet Stains—Use club soda to remove stains from carpet.

Wall Cleaner—For cleaning painted walls, mix one cup ammonia, one-quarter cup white vinegar, one-quarter cup washing soda, and one gallon warm water. For specific marks use soft art gum eraser and rub gently.

Bathroom Sinks, Tubs, and Toilets—Use vinegar and/or baking soda, and wipe.

All-Purpose Cleaners—Mix one-half cup vinegar, one pint rubbing alcohol, and one teaspoon liquid dishwashing detergent in a gallon jug. Fill remainder with water. Great for grimy windows, bathroom fixtures, and tiles.

Scents for Cents
Leave Garbage Around—Orange and lemon rind can be placed around the room in small bowls to give a natural scent.

Baking Soda—An open box in your fridge helps eliminate the "fumes de fromage."

Cedar Chips or Lavender—Put some of these fragrant chips or dried lavender in a cloth or mesh bag (an old stocking will work) to help keep your drawers smelling clean—a real outdoors scent. Putting a few in the clothes closet will also help protect woolens from moth damage.

Bogus Baking—Want to make your kitchen smell like you really know what you are doing? Mix one cup water, six whole cloves, and half a lemon into a dish. Microwave on high for 3–5 minutes (or 8–10 minutes in a convection oven). Then dart out to the bakery to pick up some fresh cinnamon buns in case anyone asks to see what you made.

Foot Fumes—When there are some pretty noxious fumes coming from your roommate's Nikes, don't call 911 right away. Sprinkle baking soda in shoes overnight to deodorize and then empty down the sink in the morning to help keep the drain clean. Your roommate won't even know.

Taken to the Cleaners

Laundry
Laundry can put your spending money through the financial wringer. But rather than grabbing your clothes and beating them clean by the lake (a risky venture if you live in Windsor or Toronto), you can take a few less drastic measures to keep your money from washing away with the Tide.

General Suds Savers
- Make sure you do full loads. It's much cheaper and will save you time.

- Combine your laundry with your roommate's (as long as you don't mind her Maidenforms taking a tumble with your Calvin Kleins).

- Instead of using a tumble dryer, go natural. A wooden or wire rack for hang-drying your clothes will pay for itself many times over. Some fabrics actually prefer this type of care.

- "Just half a cup please." Manufacturers want you to use as much of their product as possible, but you can cut the amount of detergent you use by half or a third per load, and you'll probably notice no difference except a slightly fuller pocket.

- Nothing's more embarrassing, particularly to guys, than when water causes shrinkage. That once bulky possession of yours is now half its original size. In fact, probably more money is wasted on damaged clothes due to shrinkage than any other cause. The simple solution: stick with cold water and avoid the dryer on delicates and shrinkable fabrics such as cotton.

- Consider using small towels rather than bulky, oversize beach towels. They take up mega-room in the washer and take much longer to tumble dry. You'll cut down on the number of loads you need to do, and your drying time.

- Wash delicates by the much-cheaper hand method. They last longer this way, too.

- Avoid bleaches and other harsh detergents, which significantly shorten the life of your clothes. Use only when absolutely necessary.

- Set aside your name-brand allegiances. Try no-name and alternative detergents. After all, this is the time in your life for experimentation.

Laundromats

Laundromats can end up removing more than just dirt from your new clothes. They will also help you use up any leftover change in your pocket with pinball, arcade games, books, etc. Many now offer coffee, meals, snacks, and even alcohol (but please don't drink and dry). To save on laundromat expenses:

- Avoid buying detergent at the laundromat, since it's usually much more expensive. Bring your own box, or zip-locked bag, of soap.

- Take something to do. You can read only so many two-year-old *People* magazines while you're waiting for your clothes. You'll avoid being bored and tempted to spend extra money there.

- Choose a warm dryer. If it's already heated up, you'll reduce your drying time and expense.

At Home

- Cut the length of wash cycles by a third, which will cut your water and electricity costs. Chances are, things will be just as clean.

- Use cold water for all your washes unless the clothes are badly stained. Even just switching the rinse cycle from hot to cold could save the equivalent of 220 hot showers a year, a big saving of energy and thus money.

- Avoid overstuffing the dryer, as things can actually take longer to dry when there's not enough room for a good tumble.

- To cut down on drying time and cost, clean the filter between drying loads.

- Hang clothes before they are completely tumbled dry—you'll cut down on drying time as well as ironing time and expense.

"Out, Damned Spot!"—*A frustrated Lady Macbeth at the campus laundromat*

Stains can be frustrating and costly in two big ways: they can wreck your favourite top, and then drain your cash trying potions, lotions, and drycleaning to remove them. But the great news is, you can often get them out with simple, low-cost solutions you already have on hand.

No Pain, No Cash-Drain Stain Removal Guide

Rather than fork over a fortune for stain removers and drycleaning, you can cut your costs with some simple tips:

- Clean things as soon as they're stained. You will have a better chance of avoiding expensive laundering.

- Use common household products. Most fabric stains, for example, can be removed by sponging them. Here are a few handy potions to try:

  - Vinegar—to remove beer, lipstick, perspiration
  - Rubbing alcohol—to remove shoe polish and ink
  - Hair shampoo—to remove ring around the collar
  - Dishwashing liquid—to remove alcohol and grass stains
  - Hydrogen peroxide—(for bleachables) to remove blood, coffee, alcohol

- Lemon juice—for rust and perspiration (rinse with water afterwards)
- To avoid damage, try cleaning a small spot on an unexposed area first.

Signs Your Apartment May Need Cleaning

- *National Geographic* wants to do a photo shoot on lost civilizations.
- Pile of paper on your desk has been condemned as an "unsafe free-standing structure."
- Your mother is in traction after failing to navigate the laundry moguls.
- Third date this week listed as MIA (missing in apartment).
- Molly Maid demanding "danger pay."
- Stephen Harper quoted as saying, "My Canada includes Québec . . . but not your apartment."
- "Rumpy" the dog hasn't been seen since you played fetch in your roommate's bedroom.
- The province's Health and Safety Act specifically mentions your place.
- The area under your bed resembles a food composter.
- Guests remove their shoes *after* they leave your place.
- Your answering machine message tells people you'll return their call when you can actually locate the phone.
- False fire alarms are traced to your fermenting laundry pile.
- Olympic climbing team arrives to attempt "Mt. Empties" in your living room.
- Once-extinct species of rodent spotted in your place.
- UN blacklists your place as a germ warfare testing site.

CHAPTER 9

Bulking Up:
A Smart Buyer's Guide

As September rolls around, grocers begin to wear an ever-growing smug smile as they proudly load up the shelves with Oreo cookies, pop, chips, ready-made pizzas, and microwave dinners. But perhaps the proudest smile of all, the one that stretches from cheek to cheek, is sported as they carefully put the finishing touches on that sacred grocery monument built in honour of students throughout the nation: the Kraft Dinner display.

One thing that grocers keep tucked under their belts is the knowledge that these students are, in many cases, making their first solo trek through the supermarket aisles—a trek marked by a lack of experience in meal planning: How much to spend? How much to buy? What to buy, and what to do with it once it is bought? Knowing that students often make food purchases that are impulsive, inefficient, and, perhaps most importantly, based on a lack of information, grocers and their colleagues can easily set their traps and tricks to take advantage of this situation.

How can students avoid the many pitfalls that grocers, restaurant owners, and convenience store owners prepare for them? By adopting a few simple tactics and techniques, you can load your cart with a mountain of delicious, good-quality food and save a bundle in the process.

Tackling the Supermarket: Taking the Bite out of Food Costs

"Superstores" stock almost every available food. From the nutritious to the decadent, from the staples to the exotic, it is there for the choosing. But shopping is like using the telephone: it's a wonderful experience . . . until it comes time to pay.

Fortunately, there are a number of simple things that you can do to make the reckoning at the checkout a less painful and much cheaper experience.

- Prepare a shopping list before you go and divide it into categories such as fruits and vegetables, meats, breads and cereals, dairy products, canned goods, and snacks. This way, you can ensure that you have a balance of food.

- Plan the menu for at least two or three meals during the week so that you can purchase all the necessary ingredients.

- If you're not feeling any culinary inspiration check for quick, easy, and cheap recipe ideas (or share your own favorites) in the Campus Kitchen at www.debtfreegrad.com/kitchen.

- Plan to buy some quick and easy (and preferably nutritious) meals to have on hand when you are tight for time. This will help you avoid the all-too-easy and more expensive habit of ordering pizza or other fast food. Examples of quick and easy meals include Kraft Dinner, and noodles with spaghetti sauce.

- Include on your list one or two delicacies for yourself, such as cheesecake or Häagen-Dazs ice cream. This way you can indulge yourself without having to pay the high price, tax, and tip at a dessert parlour.

- Include on your list any necessary items that you know are on sale at your store. Weekly flyers listing specials are delivered by most major supermarkets or posted at the entrance to the store—glance over them before shopping and make any late additions to your list.

- Most important, *stick to your list*. This helps you avoid impulse purchases and non-nutritious excesses. Make an exception for unadvertised specials that are in line with your meal plans.

- Avoid shopping on an empty stomach. A shopping trip driven by hunger can result in a doubling of your checkout bill (not to mention a cupboard full of Oreos and Twinkies—hardly a balanced menu).

- Shop in the evenings or late Saturday afternoons. Many grocery stores mark down items with a short shelf life at the end of the day or business week. This includes vegetables, pies, bread, and other baked goods. Some bakeries also mark down baked foods by as much as 50 percent towards the end of the day. (You can freeze these items to keep them fresh.)

- Check the "expiry" or "best before" date on goods as you purchase them. Stores often put goods nearing expiry at the front of the shelf to get rid of them first (many stores even refill their shelves from the back). Grab the items with distant expiry dates; they will taste fresher and will also cut down on your food spoilage.

- Stoop and save. More expensive name brands are often placed at eye level on store shelves. Look low and pay less.

Quantities

Many manufacturers and retailers entice shoppers to buy in large quantities by offering substantial savings on jumbo-size items. However, what is a student supposed to do with a two-gallon drum of mustard or a 100-pack of hamburger buns? Not only do you require your own warehouse to store these purchases, but you also require a bigger budget. In the case of perishable goods, they often go bad before they get used, thereby negating any possible savings. In this environment of super-bargain-bonus-extra-value-saver packs, how can the single student get a good deal?

- Look for weekly specials on products in smaller sizes. These are often priced as "loss leaders" (items sold by retailers at or below cost) in order to lure customers into their store.

- Buy items that can be split up and divided into smaller portions and refrigerated or frozen (e.g., cheese, margarine, meat). *Note*: It is very important that these items are wrapped carefully in freezer paper or freezer-safe plastic wrap so that they are not ruined.

- Purchase in bulk food sections whenever possible. This way you can buy the exact quantity you want at the same price as someone buying 10 times that amount. Spices, flour, cereal, and nuts are but a few examples of products sold in bulk. Incidentally, you also save money on fancy packaging, and help the environment.

- Buy large quantities *only* of items that are nonperishable and/or that you know you will use in a reasonable amount of time (e.g., peanut butter, pepper, pasta, canned goods). Things such as bananas, lettuce, and strawberries have a limited shelf life. A half-price sale on 10 pounds of ripe tomatoes is no bargain if you are only going to end up throwing most of them out.

- Go together with roommates to take advantage of bulk buying on frequently used items and necessities, such as milk, toilet paper, hand soap, laundry and dish detergent, plastic wrap, light bulbs, and multipurpose cleaners.

- Fruit in season can be bought and frozen for use during the winter months (e.g., raspberries, blueberries, tomatoes, rhubarb). In most cases, this can be done very easily by washing the fruit and freezing it in zip-lock bags. This gives you fruit year-round and is much cheaper than buying imported or greenhouse-grown fruit out of season.

- Fresh pies on sale can be bought and frozen until needed. Store them in large zip-lock bags to keep them fresh. (An even better idea is to be extra kind to your mom or grandmother during the summer months so that they'll make you fresh ones to freeze!)

- Ask for rain checks on sale items that are sold out, even if you don't need them right away. If you need them later on when the items are back in stock, you will still be able to purchase them at the sale price. Keep in mind that some rain checks are only valid for a certain period of time (e.g., 30 days).

- Stock up on the manufacturers' discount coupons that are frequently available in store aisles or on product packages, particularly if they are for items that you use a lot. The advantage of these coupons over store-issued coupons is that they can be used at almost all stores and they often have no (or at least a distant) expiry date. If you buy a certain brand of cereal and there is a stack of coupons in the store, *stock up*—they may last you the entire year.

- Find out if your grocer offers a student discount. Some markets or grocers offer discounts to students and seniors on certain days of the week. Better still, help out a senior by taking them shopping and maybe they'll give you the senior's discount.

Choosing Your Store

"All supermarkets are not created equal." That is certainly the message that grocers want you to receive. Slogans such as "Lowest Everyday Price," "Where Your Dollar Goes Further," and "Guaranteed Savings" are all used to convince you that their store is the best.

How do you choose the best place to save money on groceries? What should you look for to get the best value? There are a few factors to consider.

First of all, your choice of where to shop is largely limited by your transportation resources. Certainly you don't want to spend an hour taking a bus, transferring twice, and then walking a mile to save a dollar on the Piggly Wiggly's hamburger cut of the week. As I mentioned in chapter 6, your choice of accommodation should take into account the proximity of grocery stores, among other shops. How then do you choose your store?

Let's assume that you have already chosen your place to live. You should try to choose a store that has good selection and reasonable prices, and that is going to be open at hours that fit into your schedule.

Grocery Chain Stores or "Superstores"

As a general rule, the large superstores offer good selection and plenty of weekly specials or "loss leaders." However, the regular prices are much higher at some stores. So take a shopping trip to a couple of nearby stores and find out which one has the best day-to-day prices on the type of items that *you* will be buying (great meat prices at a store aren't much good if you're a vegetarian).

A disadvantage of superstores is that sometimes their prices are particularly high for small portions, a big disadvantage for the single shopper. They also sometimes fail to mark the price on many items, which makes it difficult to know what you are actually paying until you see the bill.

Co-ops

Co-ops have been growing in popularity during the last few years. Members of a co-op pay a small fee for a share in the business, which in turn allows them to shop there. They may also have to put in a couple of hours per month assisting at the store, or pay a small additional fee to be exempted from work. If volunteer work is required, students need to be sure that the hours are flexible and won't cut seriously into their study time. Terms and conditions of membership (if even required) vary widely. The advantage of a co-op is that the prices are often very good, since it is run as a nonprofit entity. As well, co-ops often carry natural or organic types of produce, or products that can be purchased in bulk or with little extra packaging.

There are some things to watch for if you are considering using a co-op. Some co-ops are run better than others. Check to see how long it has been in business and, equally important, how good the selection is. Some co-ops are relatively small and may not carry everything you want. If they only carry a portion of what you are shopping for and you still have to make a trip to another store, it may not be worth your while. Also, check to see whether the things you want are carried on a regular basis, so you'll know the products are there when you need them.

Perhaps more important, particularly for a student, are the hours the co-op is open. The store may not have the long hours you require if you have classes for most of the day (or if you like to round up your food at obscure hours). Check on this before joining.

Warehouse Clubs

Another option that has become increasingly popular is the "warehouse club." Members pay a small yearly fee ($25–$50 is average), and are able to purchase almost anything, including groceries, gardening supplies, auto parts, computer equipment, and CDs. These mega-stores, which resemble airport hangars, spend very little money on advertising and fancy fixtures or aesthetics, buy in huge quantities, and thus theoretically pass on huge savings.

Disadvantages sometimes include long lineups (reminiscent of course add/drop lines), a somewhat limited selection in a particular item (e.g., instead of a variety of blenders they may carry one brand, one model, one colour). Because they try to keep overhead costs low, they are often located in obscure areas of the city, making it inconvenient to get there unless you have a car. Pooling with roommates is the best way to use these industrial-quantity retailers.

Markets

An increasing number of farmer's markets are sprouting up across the country. Some operate year-round, while others operate from spring to fall. Most markets offer very fresh produce at reasonable prices, as well as fresh meat (a great place if you like your chicken with the head still on), dairy products, other natural or organic products such as honey, as well as homemade jams, peanut butter, and baked goods.

An advantage of these markets is that there are often many different vendors in one building selling the same products, resulting in competition that keeps the prices low. If you live in a culturally diverse area, you may also find a selection of some unique foods and delicacies.

A disadvantage of these markets is that, while they may offer a great selection of produce and dairy products, you may have difficulty finding that box of Cheerios, Diet Coke, and other recognizable brand names. As well, some of these markets only operate during limited hours, such as certain weekdays and Saturday mornings.

Bulk Food Stores

The name may suggest a supplier of high-calorie food for the varsity weightlifting team, but in fact, the bulk food store is another popular option for obtaining your groceries. Large bins of unpackaged food allow you to measure out the precise quantity you need, or you can purchase from the many premeasured portions on a per-pound or per-gram basis.

The big advantages include being able to buy the exact amount you need without being penalized for purchasing in small quantities (a great option if you are buying for one person), and not having to pay for fancy packaging or brand names. You can buy raw ingredients for baking, or premixed ingredients for cookies, muffins, dips, pancakes, etc. (in some cases all you have to do is add water).

Possible drawbacks include the limited selection of certain necessary items, such as fresh produce and dairy products, and a distinct absence of most brand names (perhaps you just *have* to have Mr. Christie chocolate chip cookies). However, keep in mind that many of the bulk products are made at the same places that produce the brand name products.

Convenience Stores

In addition to the handy location and extended hours, advantages often include regular low prices on items such as milk, bread, and pop.

The big disadvantages of corner stores are that the savings on a few items are quickly offset by huge markups on the other items they carry. In addition, the selection and sizes are often very limited. Also, some of these stores may not carry the freshest goods since they may not have a huge product turnover. Here it is particularly important that you check the expiry or best-before date (if there is more than a half-inch of dust on it, leave it to collect more).

"I'll Take 20 of Those" and Other Great Pick-Up Lines

Once you've chosen your store, remember the following:

- Most warehouse clubs allow you to bring another person in on your membership when you shop. You can also cut the membership cost in half by splitting it with a friend or roommate.

- Don't assume that everything at a warehouse club is a great deal simply because it comes in a big container. In some cases, it may be cheaper to buy certain items at a grocery or convenience store (e.g., milk, bread).

Bulking Up

- At markets, look around to see which vendors have the best prices and the freshest produce. If you shop there regularly, you will find that some vendors are consistently better than others. Take advantage of the competitive environment.

- Some grocery stores and co-ops operate on a BYOB basis . . . bring your own bags! Otherwise, they may charge you a nominal fee (5¢–10¢ per bag). It's a great incentive to recycle.

- When buying at bulk stores, consider the quantity needed and how long it will keep. Some products such as spices will keep for long periods of time, while others spoil quickly and/or have to be kept under certain conditions (e.g., frozen) to extend their shelf life. See the chart below on storing foods.

- At supermarket chains, consider purchasing the house-brand products instead of name-brand products. House brands are often substantially cheaper and are, in many cases, produced at the same plant as the name brands. Chances are that when you are dipping your nachos into the house-brand sour cream, you won't be able to tell it from the national name brand.

- When shopping in supermarkets (or any stores), if you find a discrepancy between the advertised price and the actual price, draw it to the clerk's attention and ask for an explanation. I have found that the store will often greatly reduce the item or even give it to you to avoid any publicity of their "error."

- When shopping at a market, go early for the best selection. Remember, the fresh pies go quickly!

- Most warehouse clubs promote their food by offering free samples throughout the food section, and they often hire part-time staff to give these out (e.g., a grandmotherly type to give out cookie samples, a retired sea captain to give out shrimp hors d'oeuvres). Time your trip around lunchtime on a Saturday and you can practically freebie your way to a full meal. (I find taking a couple of disguises helpful, as you can wheel around the aisles a couple of times for multiple helpings—the Freddy Krueger mask works particularly well for getting extra-big helpings from the elderly baking lady!)

- If you shop regularly in a supermarket that has a no-charge Savings Discount Card, take one out. If you forget yours at home, ask the cashier to ring your purchases through on their counter card. They will usually do this even though it's something they don't publicize. (If they won't, ask the person ahead or behind to borrow theirs—I've never had anyone say no.)

- Impulse buying can be a real problem, particularly in warehouse clubs. There are so many interesting things (in addition to food) at some very good prices, that it's easy to get caught up in the buying frenzy. You may find yourself wheeling home a power lawn mower . . . only to remember that you live in a highrise. So once again, stick to your list.

- Many stores, particularly the superstores, list the unit price of an item (e.g., 3.1¢/gram). Because many products come in a variety of odd sizes and prices, use these guides for a quick comparison to find the best value.

- Watch the register when your items are being rung through. By the end of the day, many register clerks seem to be staggering around in a stupor, and may miss the sale price on the cartload of broccoli that you've stocked up on.

Five Ways to Firmer Thighs and Leaner Breasts: Tips for the Meat Market

It's a meat market out there! . . . at least in one corner of the store. And even worse, it's an expensive market. But you need not fear the wild beasts that lurk there. While only a strict vegetarian can avoid them completely, you can certainly render their bite on your pocketbook less harmful. The following tips will help your dollar go a lot further.

- Buy meat in larger quantities when it is on sale and freeze it. With meat so expensive, this is one sale item that's worth a spot in the freezer.

- When making stews, soups, and stir-fries, buy a cheaper cut and marinate the meat to tenderize it before cooking. You probably won't notice a big difference.

- When buying hamburger, buy the cheaper regular ground beef and make it leaner yourself. To do this, take thawed hamburger, pour boiling water over the meat and then drain it. Repeat three times. Then brown in a frying pan and drain off any excess fat.

- Buy whole chickens, rather than separate parts. It's cheaper and you can cook it whole and freeze the leftovers for sandwiches and quick prepare dinners.

- In recipes requiring a certain amount of ground beef, reduce the amount by 25–50 percent and replace it with the less expensive tofu, or grains such as bulgur.

- Avoid prepared meats (e.g., deboned, cubed, seasoned, battered) when you can do it yourself. You'll usually save money, and the prep work can often be done in very little time.

- Buy chicken legs instead of breasts. They're almost always cheaper.

- Add different types of cooked pasta to a mixture of ground beef and tomatoes. It will make this meat dish go a lot further.

- Add any leftover vegetables, meat, etc. to soups or stews to make them last longer—they're all going down the same way anyway!

- Major supermarkets usually have a certain type of luncheon meat on sale each week. Buy extra and freeze some. Repeat this each week and you will always have a variety to choose from (which will make sandwiches for lunch more appealing). Refer to the food storage chart later in this chapter for maximum storage times of luncheon meats.

Getting Fresh, Staying Fresh: Storage Tips for the Starving Student

Although some of you will hold fast to the belief that the greatest invention ever was the twist-top beer cap, you should also consider the zip-lock bag and Tupperware-type containers as being right up there as well. They've revolutionized fresh-food storage. Proper storage means less food spoilage, and thus greater potential savings to you. A few simple suggestions will keep things fresher longer:

- Foods such as cookies, baked goods, crackers, cereals, etc. can be stored easily in zip-lock bags. Not only will things keep fresher and longer, but it will also prevent the small creatures inhabiting many student accommodations from joining your meal plan.

- Buy a variety of sizes of zip-lock bags to have on hand. The potential number of uses both inside and outside the kitchen is enormous.

- Reusable plastic airtight containers are invaluable for storing food in fridges and freezers, and for taking lunches to school. Make sure that you get ones that are safe for dishwashers, freezers, and microwaves.

- Glass airtight containers are great for storing items such as flour, sugar, and pasta long-term, without the food taking on the funny taste of some plastic containers.

- Items such as potatoes, onions, and garlic should be stored in a cool, dry place with plenty of air circulation to prevent spoilage. A hanging wire basket is ideal for this.

- When freezing baked goods, fruit, or vegetables, freeze as soon as possible to lock in fresh taste. You may want to date these to avoid freezer spoilage (identification of some of these items would stump even the most seasoned paleontology professor). Check the chart in this chapter to see the life span of frozen and other stored goods.

- Don't overdo the environmental zealousness by storing different foods all in the same container. Fruit salad never tastes the same after bedding down for a week with the fireball chilli.

Basic Rules on Cleaning Fridges

If it moves and squirms, it may have worms.
If it's grown hair, stomach beware.
If it's green like gout, toss it out.

The "Don't Waste Your Dough" Food Storage Guide

Food	Refrigerator (4°C)	Freezer (−18°C)
Meats and Poultry (uncooked)		
Roasts, steak (beef)	3 to 5 days	10 to 12 months
Roasts, chops (pork, veal)	3 to 5 days	8 to 10 months
Roasts, chops (lamb)	3 to 5 days	6 to 9 months
Ground and stew meats	1 to 2 days	2 to 3 months
Chicken, turkey pieces	2 to 3 days	6 months
	(1 to 2 days, whole)	(12 months, whole)
Meat and Poultry (cooked)		
Meat and meat dishes	3 to 4 days	2 to 3 months
Poultry	3 to 4 days	1 to 3 months
Processed Meats		
Bacon, frankfurters, ham (whole), sausage (smoked)	7 days	1 to 2 months
Luncheon meats	3 to 5 days	1 to 2 months
Fish (uncooked)		
Fat fish (e.g., salmon, mackerel)	1 to 2 days	2-3 months
Lean fish (e.g., cod, haddock)	1 to 2 days	6 months
Fish (cooked)		
Fat fish (e.g., salmon, mackerel)	3 to 4 days	4-6 months
Lean fish (e.g., cod, haddock)	3 to 4 days	4-6 months
Dairy Products and Eggs		
Eggs	3 weeks	4 months (eggs, yolks)
Hard cheese	3 to 4 months	6 months
Soft cheese	2 weeks	4 months
Ice cream	—	1 to 2 months
Margarine	1 month (opened)	6 months
Butter	3 weeks (opened)	1 year (salted)
		3 months (unsalted)
Milk	3 to 4 days (opened)	6 weeks
Miscellaneous		
Bread	1 to 2 weeks	1 month
Mayonnaise	2 months (opened)	Don't freeze
Soups and stews	3 to 4 days	2 to 3 months
TV dinners	Keep frozen	3 to 4 months
Fruits and vegetables	Varies with type	1 year

Lunches

Perhaps the most regular costly drain on a student's funds is lunch. In the haste to make that 8:00 AM class (10:00 AM for the Artsies), students will often forgo breakfast only to find themselves famished by lunchtime and shelling out $7–$10 for a prepared lunch on campus. Not only is campus food likely to leave a nutritional void, but it's also more expensive, since you are paying for overhead and preparation costs, and the meal may be taxed as well. (Finding a good, affordable meal on campus is like trying to find a sober Engineer on a weekend.) Eating on campus can mean an extra cost of $4–$5 per day ($80–$100 a month) on lunches alone! An easy solution is preparing lunches that are far more nutritional in value at a fraction of the cost. Most food you buy and prepare yourself is tax-free, and the overhead is low. Here are some suggestions:

- Buy fruit such as oranges, apples, and plums that can be easily carried around in your knapsack without being squashed (avoid pears, overripe bananas, peaches, etc.). If you really crave these softer fruits, cut them up ahead of time and carry them in a resealable container to keep them fresh and leak-proof.

- Refill plastic or glass juice bottles at home with juice from frozen concentrate. This can easily cut your costs for packaged juice by 50–70 percent.

- Premixed salad in a resealable plastic container (with the dressing in a separate container) should remain fresh for nearly a day—a much cheaper route than buying.

- Purchase large bags of chips, nuts, cookies, gummy bears, squares, bagels, etc. and divide them up into zip-lock bags. This is much cheaper than buying individual bags of these same items. Make them up at the beginning of the week and they'll be ready to take in your knapsack each day.

- When eating at fast-food chains, ask for extra packages of salt, pepper, salad dressing, jam, napkins (bibs if you're really sloppy), plastic forks, etc. (available in reasonable quantities at no extra cost and great to take for lunches).

- Many campus cafeterias have microwaves available for use at no charge. Take meat or cheese sandwiches, leftover pizza, chilli, lasagna, etc. to heat for lunch. This gives you some variety and will help avoid that dreaded "lunch-bag letdown."

- Invest in a reusable nylon lunch bag. They are light, washable, inexpensive, and will last for years. (If you really want to go all out, you can buy an insulated one.)

- Buy large containers of natural yoghurt and flavour it with fruit (frozen or fresh) and/or honey. This can be taken for lunches in small plastic containers and is much cheaper than buying small individual yoghurt cups.

- Clean and cut up vegetables such as carrots, celery, and radishes in large quantities and store in a large container of water in the fridge. They will last for weeks and can be packed in resealable bags for lunches.

Campus Meal Plans

- Try to get a meal plan that fits your eating habits.

- Most meal plans operate on a point or cash debit system. Make sure that if you buy a plan such as this you can be refunded for points not used at the end of the school year. It's usually better to underestimate your plan and add points as you go, rather than get a refund, since there may be an administration fee.

- Some meal plans may allow you to purchase alcohol at on-campus licensed establishments. Avoid ever using this option! One friend of mine who found this a great convenience, also found that he had run out of meal-plan points by January (which actually worked out OK, since he was also running equally low on grade points by that time).

- If you tend to devour anything in sight and your eating has caused the occasional food shortage, the cheapest option for you may be to purchase an all-you-can-eat meal plan, which some schools offer.

Tips for Off-campus Students

- Many campuses offer cafeteria meal plans for off-campus

students. If you spend a lot of time on campus, have only a short break for dinner, or live far from campus, it may be worth your while to purchase a meal plan for one meal a day. It is probably cheaper and more time-efficient than trying to make it home to eat. If you are not inclined to use the stove at home, then it might also be one way to ensure you have one hot meal per day.

- To maximize value and stretch your meal-plan dollars, bring your own desserts, drinks, fruits, and snacks (this is where the highest markup often occurs), and purchase only your main course on your meal plan.

The Baker's Dozen:
13 Signs to Avoid the Cafeteria Food

1. Frequent deliveries from the animal research lab.
2. Kitchen staff "brown-bags it."
3. No sign of the school mascot in over a week.
4. Having to sign a waiver clause at the bottom of your bill.
5. After-dinner mints taste surprisingly like Tums.
6. The all-you-can-eat special has never been attempted.
7. Lighting so dim that you need to feel for your food.
8. Food is often used by the football team as part of some cruel initiation ritual.
9. Reserved ambulance parking by the exit.
10. Special of the day hasn't changed since your parents went here.
11. Provincial health cards accepted instead of Visa.
12. Missing diners featured on the milk cartons.
13. Food bank frequently seen returning food.

Dining Out: Tips for the Tippers

It is obvious that you are not always going to want to eat at home. Sometimes that three-day-old meatloaf in the fridge just isn't going to make you salivate. When you do eat out, follow these strategies to ensure you get maximum food value for your money:

- Use coupons when you can. Restaurants want students' business, and they will usually offer coupons to get you there. Student newspapers and coupon mailouts are the best place to find them. The best times to find coupons in student newspapers include the beginning of school (Orientation Week kits are also often full of money-saving coupons), Homecoming weekend, and after Reading Week (they know you're broke by then).

- Take advantage of the all-you-can-eat buffet or student special. A self-confessed vacuum cleaner when it comes to food, I found these a great way to fill up. One stop here every seven days means one guaranteed good feed per week. Strap on the feedbag and enjoy.

- Take advantage of special "student nights." Many restaurants offer a particular night, such as "2 for 1 Tuesdays," when the eats are cheap. If you play it right, you can literally find a student special somewhere every night of the week.

- Alcohol is a big cash cow for restaurants: the markup is huge, taxes are high (this is the government milking the cow), and you tip on top of it all. When dining out, set a limit ahead of time on how much you'll consume. It is easy to spend two or three times the amount on beverages as on food. If you're going to drink, a better option is to have a round or two at home as a starter before you go—a much cheaper alternative!

- When ordering wine, pass on the cork sniffing and order the house wine. Most restaurants use a popular brand with wide appeal and a much lower price.

- When ordering, don't hesitate to order water. Even if you order a pop or juice the markup is huge. Cut out the beverage and you can often cut your bill by 20–30 percent!

- Especially when ordering spicy food, cut down your drink costs by ordering a pitcher of water from the start. Many restaurants love to add a little zing to their dishes to spice up the old bar sales.

- A good money-saving option is to eat with a friend and split appetizers, desserts, and, depending on the dish, even main courses. Don't hesitate to ask for an additional plate.

- Ask for a doggy bag for the food you can't finish. It can save you the cost of tomorrow's lunch.

- Consider eating out at lunch rather than dinner. Restaurants often have a lunch menu or buffet almost identical to the one they serve at dinner, only at a much lower price!

- Some eating places are divided into a restaurant part and a pub section. The food in the pub is often very similar in taste but much cheaper. Eat there and save.

- Take advantage of off-hour specials that many restaurants offer for those who dine at nonpeak hours. Big discounts are sometimes given to those who eat before 5:00 PM. This is an inconvenient time for some people but is often perfect for students, who perhaps have to catch a night class anyway.

- If you are looking for good, nutritious food at student prices, consider delis or market eateries, where you don't have to pay for service and thus avoid the tipping costs.

- Larger companies and their marketing agencies have recently discovered that the college and university market is huge—as much as $4–$5 billion in discretionary income (how did they ever miss it?). In response, advertisers have decided this is a population definitely worth targeting. Their student marketing campaigns now include travelling carnivals, where free samples and coupons are offered for everything from Pop Tarts to Tuna Topper (as well as non-food items such as deodorants, shampoos, and perfumes). So grab your knapsack, laundry bag, backpack, and suitcase and generously help yourself to these travelling Freebie Fiestas.

- Hospital cafeterias are often cheaper than the campus cafeteria. I know that's probably not the place you want to go on a first date, but you can buy a reasonably priced meal for those times when it's just your stomach that needs to be satisfied. A fair number of universities or colleges have hospitals either on campus or nearby, which makes the hospital cafeteria a convenient place to grab a cheap lunch or dinner. (You may also meet an eligible doctor, in which case you may not need this book.)

- It seems that there is always some sort of reception or ceremony on campus to celebrate somebody's big accomplishment—like some prof who found the secret to the mating ritual of the East Amazonian Barn Fly. The occasion may not be earth-shattering, but it often means free food. So when you see a crowd and someone making a speech, look impressed, clap a few times, and then make a beeline for the food.

- Specialty coffee shops have become the trend in recent years, with each one trying to outdo the others by selling a more exotic gourmet blend. Needless to say, their popularity comes at a cost. If you have become one of the converted caffeine connoisseurs, then consider buying a coffeemaker and some good beans to brew at home.

- If it is the coffee-shop atmosphere you enjoy and there is one particular café you like, then ask if they have a frequent-drinker card (coffee, that is). Many retailers want your loyalty and offer a free cup for, say, every sixth cup you buy, as an incentive to return. Not a huge bonus but nevertheless a roughly 20 percent savings to you.

- Some cafe's will give you a discount for using your own cup. Carry your own with you and save some cash.

Obviously, you will not adopt all the suggestions in this chapter for saving on food. But if you adopt the ones that fit your timetable and lifestyle, then you should save a bundle. Eat, enjoy, and keep your stomach and wallet full!

CHAPTER 10

Supplies and Demand

If you thought you'd never use the information they threw at you in Intro Economics, you might want to think again. When it comes to buying school supplies, you may end up paying lots more if you wait until everyone else is scrambling for the same books and materials you are. Avoid the supply squeeze by getting in ahead of the demand crunch. Let's look at how you can apply a little Keynesian theory to keep your money supply from dwindling too quickly.

Books

Most students have barely gotten over their tuition bills when they get sideswiped by book lists. Students can easily drop $800–$1,500 on a year's worth of books. While you can't eliminate this expense, you can reduce it plenty.

The first step is to categorize the books on your list. Start by determining which books are absolutely essential to the course and which ones are additional or optional. Then, figure out which are the most important secondary books and which ones are suggested reading only. Once you've categorized the list, you can make smarter choices about where to spend money and where to cut corners.

Main Textbooks—These are the ones you are absolutely going to need, and so it's not worth forgoing them to save cash. You'll probably want to review the readings when exams arrive, and so it's better to own these books than to rely on finding them in the library when everyone else wants them too. Many students make notes in their textbooks, which are also convenient at exam time.

Important Secondary Textbooks—You'll need these but you

may be able to get them by borrowing from the library or by going together with a friend and splitting the cost. If you know someone who took the course before, you can perhaps borrow his books. If you make good notes from these, you may not even need to have a copy around when exam time comes.

Suggested Readings—In many courses the main readings are so heavy that you'll never make it to suggested readings, so don't run out and buy all these right away. This is the best place to scrimp by borrowing from the library or even from your professor. (Some people never make it past the main textbook, so your prof will think you are really keen if you're doing the suggested readings!) With some textbooks, the only way you'll end up reading them is if you are snowed in with no date and a broken TV on a Friday night.

How to Buy Textbooks: Saving Literally

Get your reading list early so that you can get your books ahead of the stampede at the start of term. Many professors have their book lists available prior to the start of school, usually in printed form but sometimes on-line.

Before you head straight to the campus bookstore to buy a brand new copy, try instead to pick up your main texts and any supplementary reading you want from the following sources:

- Trade Online—You can now buy, sell or exchange textbooks without forking out the commission that many used bookstores charge—meaning more money in your pocket. Check out the free textbook exchange site at **www.textbooktrader.ca**

- Another option is used bookstores. Many colleges and universities operate these as a service to students, with a small commission to them taken from the selling price. Most towns have at least one, in the school vicinity. You'll pay much less than at a new bookstore.

- Talk to friends who took the course to see if they'll lend or sell you their books. They'll probably give you a good deal.

- Check "For Sale" boards, department bulletin boards, and student newspapers for used texts for sale. In addition, put up a posting advertising the books you'd like to buy.

- Talk to your professors. They sometimes have a few spare copies and will lend you one for the year (or sell to you if they're Business profs). If they wrote the book, they'll probably have plenty of autographed copies sitting on their office shelves collecting dust.

Here are some things to watch when buying used books (or even new):

- Check against the reading list carefully to see that you have the correct edition. You don't want to get stuck with an old edition when the prof is using a revised version.

- If you do get stuck with an old version, don't run out to buy the revised edition before you check with your prof to see if it matters—the change could be minor, perhaps a different picture of Einstein... on a good hair day!

- Try to get used textbooks from someone who did well in the course. That way, any highlights or notes in the margin will be more valuable than if you get the text from someone who eked out a D–.

Commercial Bookstores

While they may not regularly carry the more academic works, commercial bookstores may have reference materials such as writing handbooks, dictionaries, thesauruses, and classic literary and political works. If you need to go the new-textbook route, remember that many bookstores now offer regular reader programs (the frequent flyers of the mind), which can offer you discounts on all books, software, and pre-ordered texts. If you know your reading list ahead of time (at least 3–4 weeks ahead of time) you can usually pre-order the texts you need and save. Based on one of the largest such plans which charges a $25 annual membership fee, you would need to spend $250 or more to break even. This may be an option if you can't find many of your books used and/or if you combine with roommates on one of these cards.

Bookstores in September are a lot like Charlie Sheen on a rant: some unbelievable lines! So why not play it safe and avoid them both? By exploring these other avenues, you'll have fewer books to buy new at full price. With textbooks, keep in mind:

- Unless you intend to use your textbooks after your course is through, sell them as soon as you've finished with them. If you wait a few years to sell, your edition may be too outdated to sell for top dollar.

- Some books you may want to keep for future reference or general appeal. For instance, you may want to hang onto your copy of Marx's *Das Kapital* so you can have it prominently displayed when the Campus Socialists have their next gathering at your place.

- Your best place to unload books is usually through posting boards, particularly the free on-line posting boards, such as **www.textbooktrader.ca**, friends in the same faculty, and campus used-book stores. Used-book stores will usually charge you a small percentage of the proceeds from your books, but it saves you the trouble of advertising them.

Getting Your Supplies Cheap

Okay, you are going to need supplies for school. After all, you need paper on which to compose those masterpieces, binders to organize the pages of notes you'll make, and pens, pencils, staplers, and folders to create those thought-provoking dissertations you'll be handing in. These little things here and there add up to some serious cash. But here, too, you can cut your costs by shopping wisely.

Freebies

There are lots of creative ways to get some of your supplies absolutely FREE.

Pens, Pencils, Rulers, Post-it Notes, etc.—Visit campus job fairs, business shows, marketing fairs, and other corporate-sponsored events. You'll get more office freebies than you know what to do with. Don't let a rejection letter be the only thing you get from these companies.

Folders for Notes, Pens, Notepads—These items abound at tourist and convention centres. Many companies also toss out older binders and folders, and they'd be happy to have you help them remove their clutter.

Paperless Society . . . What's That?—Offices, printing places, and other businesses generate a lot of wasted paper. Why not save a tree by recycling? Ask if you can have some of their standard-size scrap paper to run off rough drafts of essays, assignments, labs, etc. You'll save plenty on paper costs. Printing places are also frequently a good source of giveaway notepads made from leftover paper. Ask the next time you're having an essay printed.

Diary of a Dayplanner—Almost every student trades in her paper scraps for a real dayplanner when she trundles off to college or university. These pocket calendars can cost as much or as little as you want. Freebies abound at banks or insurance companies—just ask your agent or bank teller. Many schools also now put out their own as a service to students (complete with school events and plenty of advertising). They're usually free and run for the school year rather than the calendar year.

Buying a Dayplanner

If you want to spring for your own bound dayplanner, you can save a bit by waiting till mid-to-late-January to get a discount. If you want to go looseleaf, there are a few more options:

- Decide on the size and style of pages that you want, then buy the refill pages from specialty daytimer companies but *not* the binders they peddle with them. They gouge big time on these.

- Buy a binder at an office supply store. You can get leather or good synthetics at these places and pay $1/3$ to $1/5$ the price you'd pay at a dayplanner or leather store.

- You can also download planner pages for free at **diyplanner.com/templates/index** to print yourself, or if you are feeling creative, design your own for printing.

- The better your dayplanner binder looks, the more likely it is to get stolen. If your expensive leather binder is stolen, the biggest loss may be the information contained inside. A solid synthetic is durable yet less appealing to thieves.

- With many students having mobile devices, an electronic day planner may be your best and cheapest option. There are plenty available for free, many of which you can customize and print out, if necessary. Check out **www.debtfreegrad.com/pages/freeres&tools/freestuff.html**

for some free options.

Places to Shop for Supplies

Obviously, you are not going to get all your supplies for free. So here's how you can cut your costs on the supplies you've got to buy:

Office Warehouse Stores—Many warehouse-style stores have cropped up in the last few years, and there are more to come. The bottom line is big savings for you. Some of the items they sell come in large multipacks. So figure out your supplies for the year, or split with a friend, and buy everything at once. These stores sometimes have membership cards—yes, I know, another membership card—but they're usually free and will entitle you to further discounts.

Warehouse Clubs—If you can't hook into an office warehouse store, you'll find many of the other warehouse clubs have large office and stationery supply sections. With these you usually have to pay for a yearly membership card, so it may not be worth the expense, unless you split it with a friend.

Back-to-School Sales—If you buy your school supplies at the end of August, you should also be able to take advantage of back-to-school sales. Stock up then at discount retailers, where you'll probably get the best deals.

Corner and Convenience Stores—Avoid these places when buying stationery, as they often charge a much higher price for supplies. If you stock up ahead of time, you can avoid an expensive late-night paper run at these places.

Used Office Supply Stores—If you want to go the used route, these may be a good option. While they mainly carry furniture, you may find smaller supplies as well.

Bankruptcy Sales and Auctions—Pretty well every company has an office. If they go belly up, you may find some of the office supplies you're looking for.

Last-Minute Supply Saving Tips

- Buy a multiple photocopy card at your school. Usually you can make copies for 4¢–6¢ apiece, a better rate than if you pay with cash. Avoid copy machines in places like drug and convenience stores, and public libraries which sometimes charge you two or three times that amount.

- If you have a Smartphone, avoid paying to send long distance faxes. Instead use an app and your Smartphone camera to scan and send during free evening and weekend calling times.

High-Tech, Low-Price Computer Sense

It's pretty obvious that computers are now a huge part of our life, for everything from banking and work to entertainment. I can picture us someday standing over the toaster talking into it as we recite a list of tasks for it and the rest of the appliances to do.

In 1994, for the first time, there were more personal computers sold in North America than there were television sets—and the trend continues. Ten years ago a computer was an asset to a student—now it's become a necessity. But we're not talking a $20 toaster here. Computers can set you back thousands of dollars. And the frustrating thing is that it seems like by the time you get it from the store to the parking lot, it's obsolete.

If you rarely use a computer, you may be better off using those in the computer labs on campus. Most are available free or at a nominal cost. On the other hand, it may be worth the price to avoid the crowded labs.

How do you sort through the technobabble to make a smart purchase rather than a purchase that smarts? You needn't have a computer science degree, nor do you need to drop a bundle to keep up. Some simple strategies will keep your PC from standing for "Pretty Costly."

Become Computer Literate—You don't need to become an overnight expert: simply learn the basics of a computer and its main parts. This will help you know what to buy and the right questions to ask. Great resources include library books and magazines, computer fairs, or a friend who's a genuine computer geek (if you can pry him away from his terminal).

Learn What Is Available—I'd suggest going to reputable computer stores where the sales staff are knowledgeable. This is probably better than some department store where you may end up with a guy from sporting goods who thinks a "hard drive" is a long golf shot.

Determine What Your Needs Will Be—Will you be doing advanced spreadsheets and graphics or using it strictly as a word processor? Your subject area or major will probably help determine this.

What's current today will seem obsolete tomorrow. When it comes to computer equipment, newer, faster models are constantly coming onto the market. Generally, increased speed and/or larger memory and storage capacity will equal increased cost. This leads to two common problems: underbuying and overbuying.

You want to buy a good cheap machine but you don't want to buy something that won't be able to run any of the programs coming out in the next couple of years. Often the prices and deals are amazing, almost too good to be true . . . which they might just be. Are they selling equipment so cheaply because it's fast becoming an archaic model with little use?

An equally common mistake is buying more equipment than you need or can afford. You should assess your needs over the next two to three years, not on what you hope to be doing eight or ten years from now. If you look too far ahead, you'll pay top dollar just to have the fastest machine in your dorm. A couple of years from now, that machine will probably be worth half of what you paid.

Select Your Software—Before you buy a computer, check out the programs that you may be using. Most colleges and universities (and some high schools) have facilities where you can try out or see demonstrations of various software. If that's not the case, go into a good computer store and act like you have a pocketful of money you want to get rid of. Ask about the advantages of different programs, when these programs came out, and when the next version is expected to be released. Find out how much computer power and memory they require, and how much space they'll take up on your hard drive. Most importantly, *try* them to see if they are user-friendly. Computer magazines and online blogs and review sites are constantly testing software and publishing comparative studies. Spend a few hours in the library reading unbiased reports (i.e., not published by the software company itself) to find out which programs give the best performance for the lowest price.

Select Your Hardware—Once you've selected the software programs you want to run, you'll want to choose the computer system that is able to run them. Also, decide whether you want a brand name or a cheaper "clone." Clones often use the same parts inside with a different name outside.

Buy Smart—Computer outlets often resemble a Toys 'R' Us stores for adults. Grown-ups running around pressing buttons, blasting away on the newest game, cranking up the volume for the sound effects. . . . It's easy to get caught up in all the high-tech wizardry that's at your fingertips, but try to keep a level head while those around you are losing theirs. Buy what you need and can afford, not what you think would be cool.

Care For Your Tech Tools—When you spend that much, go the extra mile to purchase accessories like an electricity surge protector, dust covers, and so on to ensure you're not forking over more cash later for expensive repairs.

Where to Buy a New Computer

As computers continue to grow in popularity (yes, even Granny surfs the Net), more and more stores and retailers are cropping up to grab a piece of the action. Not only do you have a confusing selection of brands, but also different ways you can buy.

Specialty Stores—The specialty computer store emphasizes knowledgeable staff, personal service, and technical support. However, you'll sometimes pay a significantly higher price (up to 15–25 percent more) than at discount stores.

Custom Builders—These are techno-whizzes turned entrepreneurs who assemble computers to your liking . . . sort of like designer computers. Sound expensive? Well, not necessarily. Some of these people are hobbyists—they often work out of their own home or apartment, meaning low overhead, some great prices, and you can get some personalized service. The only drawback is that because it's a hobby or part-time business, they may not have the business two or three years from now.

Office Superstores—They often have excellent prices and good warranties. The only problem is you usually don't get the support of knowledgeable staff—a real drawback if you're just entering the computer age.

Computer Superstores—A gift from our friends south of the border, these stores give great prices and have excellent selection, although the staff can tend to lack knowledge. Ask for a department manager to serve you in this situation, since they probably have a better knowledge, or bring a computer-whiz friend to the store with you.

Warehouse Clubs—These places thrive on low prices. However, selection is limited, which makes comparison-shopping difficult. You'll probably get the least knowledgeable staff here, so short of pointing out the power switch, don't expect much from them. They do, however, tend to have liberal return policies and may offer longer warranties. For some purchases these stores are great, but for a computer you might want to focus on the other retail options.

Direct Order and On-line Retailers—Although direct order houses don't give you that hands-on feeling, they can give you some great prices. These places are particularly good when you already know what you want to buy. If you consider these options, keep the following points in mind:

- Make sure they have 24-hour service to assist you with technical problems (usually a toll-free number).

- Find out whether they will send a service person to your house if something breaks down, or whether you have to ship the computer back to the manufacturer. Shipping can be expensive and time-consuming. If there is a major technical problem will they send a free replacement machine while they fix yours? Profs may not buy the "technical difficulties" line as an excuse for a missed deadline.

- Pay by credit card rather than cheque. If there's a problem, you can stop payment through a "charge back" by the card company.

- Order only from established, reputable companies. There are plenty of fly-by-night companies which will disappear long before the warranty expires.

- If you are ordering from a U.S. or overseas company, check on delivery time in Canada. Delays at customs are common. Also, check on who pays the shipping charges, the validity of the warranty in Canada and whether there are additional duties charged.

Shopping Savvy

- Shop around and compare carefully. Some retailers will beat a competitor's price by as much as 5-10%.

- Many systems have very subtle but important differences. Write down particulars to help you compare.

- If service and support are your top concerns, but you see a much better price at a superstore, see if the store with the service you want will meet the superstore price. Some will, just to get your business.

- Don't be afraid to negotiate. Just because the sign says "Lowest Price" doesn't mean it can't be lower. Also, ask them to throw in some free software, a protective case, etc.

- Try to keep your options open. Some computers can be upgraded without spending a fortune to do it. This could mean big savings in the future.

- When buying any computer equipment or accessories, *ask* what the price is rather than assuming it is still the advertised price. The industry is releasing newer models so rapidly that the price on the slightly older model you've chosen may be cheaper than the price marked or advertised the previous day.

Slightly Driven Drives—The Used Option

Another, even cheaper, option is to go the used route, particularly if you'll only be using your computer for basic applications such as word processing. Computers, like cars, lose most of their value in the first 1 or 2 years. By choosing the used option, you may be able to cut your cost by as much as 80 percent, a potential saving of thousands of dollars. The amount you save will depend on your quest for speed and memory. Generally, used computer systems range from $300–$800, while new systems commonly run from $400–$2,200 (laptops, $400–$2300)—with netbook models under $300 now widely available. The best time to look for a used computer is either January (you can purchase from a student who got a new system for Christmas) or the end of the school year, when many students are broke and have the travel itch.

Where to Buy a Used Computer

- Your best bet is to buy from a student who is upgrading to a new system. So keep your eyes and ears open for friends who are doing just that. Not only will you save big on the basic price, it's unlikely you'll be charged sales tax—potentially a savings of $100–$150 or more.

- Scour the usual campus bulletin boards and newspapers for the best deals, along with local newspapers and community bulletin boards, and free on-line sites such as **www.craigslist.org**.

- Stick up a want ad outside the campus computer store stating that you want to buy a used system. Someone coming out of the store with their brand-new system may be happy to unload their older machine.

- Check at stores that take trade-ins, sell company surplus systems, or deal specifically in used or factory-refurbished equipment. This is usually a bit more expensive than private, but you may get some form of warranty.

- Check with parents and relatives to see if there is any used equipment being sold where they work.

Printer

If you need something printed, you can get your campus computer centre, or sometimes the local copy shop, to print it out for you quite inexpensively. If your roommate has a printer and you don't, work out an arrangement whereby you use his printer in return for buying paper or an ink cartridge. You both benefit. If you want to print your own copies of essays, résumés, assignments, and so on, buying a printer may be a good idea. New, you'll pay $30–$600 or more, depending on what type you get. Inkjet printers have fallen in price and thus virtually pushed out dot matrix printers at the low end of the range, while laser printers have fallen below $100 for basic models. Even basic ink jet All-In-1 machines (scans, copies, prints) have fallen to the $50–$200 range. If cash is your boss, your cheapest option may be a mid level ink jet (usually found new in the $100–$150 range or used or refurbished for under $50). Some low end ink jets can be had for as little as $30, however you may find they are ink guzzlers, meaning frequent replacement of costly cartridges quickly eliminates any initial savings. Keep in mind that for black and white printing, laser and dot-matrix printers cost about 3¢–6¢ per page to run, compared with inkjets that cost around 4¢–11¢.

Regardless of the type, you'll generally pay more for speed, graphics quality—usually measured in dots per inch (dpi), and features such as multiple trays. Unless you'll use or need these to crank those last minute essays, stick with a basic model and take résumés and other important documents to a campus copy or computer service to be laser-printed.

Speakers, Joysticks, Fax Machines, and Other Fun Toys

If you're looking to keep your expenses low, then stay away from these items. Paying for accessories you may rarely use isn't worth it. Hold off on these toys until you work for a company that buys them for you.

Software in Hard Times

OK, so you've had your computer running for the first month and you've decided you're tired of looking at a blank screen. Time to buy some software! You'll need to shell out some cash for computer programs. Software runs anywhere from free to several hundred dollars, but here are a few tips to help keep your expenses low:

- Try a friend's copy or demonstration lab software to see what programs are worth purchasing. Rental libraries usually only charge a couple of bucks.

- Ask for an educational discount when you buy software, which usually means a 40–60 percent saving. The vendor may ask to see valid student ID.

- Shareware can be obtained from friends and copied (legally). While you won't find Windows 8 on shareware, you can get some useful programs and a hoard of games. If you like the program, then you are encouraged to register your copy and send a small payment to the software developer—usually in the range of $5–$40. Some programs, called freeware, cost nothing.

- Download sites will often let you download free software, trial versions, or scaled down versions. Some excellent sites for freebies: **www.snapfiles.com/freeware** and **www.majorgeeks.com**

- When you buy software, shop around. Electronics superstores and warehouse clubs offer some great deals and frequent "door crasher" specials just to lure you into their techie pleasure palace. They often offer a cheaper introductory price when the software first hits the shelves.

- Check for free alternatives to costly software. **Openoffice.org**, for example, offers a free office suite version that's compatible with the more costly software offered by the software behemoths.

Modems: Your First "Surf Board"

Virtually all computers now come with a modem, ethernet or WiFi card to allow you to get on line. If your computer doesn't have one you'll want to decide how you want to hook up to the internet before you run out to buy one. If you connect through a network such as in residence you'll likely need an ethernet or wireless network card ($20–$60). If you are off campus and have a high speed connection such as cable or ADSL through the phone line, the rental of a high speed modem will likely be a part of your monthly charge. You would thus just need a network card to connect.

Riding the Information Highway

If you haven't already taken a spin on the information highway, get your wallet ready . . . or maybe not. You may be able to travel a lot cheaper than you thought you could.

For dial up access through your phone line there are still some low or now free internet access providers to link you to the cyber world. Some free services may limit your time on-line, but if you mainly use your connection for email this option may do the trick.

If you go with a cable or ADSL connection you will pay more – around $50 to $90 per month. Your speed and monthly bandwidth usage, will often determine how much you pay. However, you can usually tap into a student deal in the $25 to $50 per month range. If you are in residence, you may pay a set monthly or term rate.

Highway safety tips: Cutting the costs on your cyber travel.

• Try for a trial offer. You may be able to get a free month and/or free installation. If you are hooking up either phone or cable at the same time, you may be able to negotiate only one hook up fee. If you can get a bundled package (i.e. cable TV, phone and high speed internet), you may also be able to save a few bucks.

• Read the fine print – What you see, may not be what you get. You may find the low rate only applies for 3 or 6 months and then almost doubles, or that mandatory hidden fees make it impossible to actually get the low price you see advertised. In fact, two of Canada's largest communications companies have previously been slapped with $10 million fines for false claims and advertising prices that were not available to customers.

• Get a router to share the internet with your roommates through setting up a network. A high speed connection shared with two roommates all of a sudden becomes much more affordable. Most routers are fairly easy to set up (they act almost like a cable splitter) and they will help you avoid the phone line tie ups that come with dial up access.

• When buying a router, be careful to not let them sell you more equipment than you need. Some routers support the highest speed connection, which your computer may or may not be able to make use of. Take a pseudo techie friend to help you choose.

• If you are charged by the time spent on-line, download what you need to work on (i.e. emails), go off-line and then reconnect when you need to send it. A faster modem will also save

Supplies and Demand

Double Meanings

Word	Techno-Speak	Student-Speak
Motherboard	The main circuit board inside the computer, into which every part connects.	A rather derogatory term used to describe the panel of deans discussing your probation appeal: "They're tough . . . a real motherboard."
Multiuser	The ability to let two or more people use a computer simultaneously.	A term used to describe the dorm bathrooms prior to that 9:00 AM class.
Multitasking	The ability to run more than one program simultaneously.	A broad description of your work habits the night before your mid-terms.
Serial Port	A connector used to plug in serial devices such as a modem or mouse.	The couch where roommates park to watch the soaps and conduct the exchange of gossip and fashion tips.
Shareware	Programs you can legally copy and use. If you like the program and use it, you are legally bound to send in a registration fee. In return for this fee you get a printed manual, the latest version of the program, and telephone support.	The name given to the Donna Karan miniskirt that has been borrowed by every one of your roommates, including Ed and Tom.
Spreadsheet	A program used for calculating numeric results. Common spreadsheets include Lotus 1-2-3, Microsoft Excel, and Quattro Pro.	A term used to describe the chaotic state of your desk prior to essay due dates.

WORD	TECHNO-SPEAK	STUDENT-SPEAK
Response Time	The interval between the input of a request or a command and the return of the required response.	The interval between when your alarm clock goes off and when you show any signs of movement. Usually increases exponentially as the term progresses.
Single Density	A low data density for floppy disks, used only on 8" diskettes.	The appropriate term used for your mental faculties the morning after Homecoming celebrations.
RAM Disk	Memory set aside to act like a floppy disk where you can store files.	The action taken when you discover your computer just erased your entire thesis.
Megabyte	Over one million bytes, or 1,024K. A megabyte is unit of measurement of data storage.	What you do on your first visit home when you see mom's cooking.
Information Highway	A vast communication network which connects computers to each other, allowing for the transfer and exchange of information.	The corridor leading to the professor's office the day before the final.

you on-line time spent wait for uploading and downloading of information.

Finally, perhaps the most important thing to remember when buying computer equipment is: don't rush into it. This is one time where it may pay to procrastinate. If you wait a month or so, chances are a better version will be available at an even lower price.

CHAPTER 11

Looking and Feeling Good: Getting the Look, Fashionably Priced

Unless you plan to follow the lead of "naked man"—the California scholar who adopted an *au naturel* approach to campus wear—you'll probably be shelling out some serious cash to stay in fashion. For one thing, this ain't California. And besides, where would you clip your iPod? (I don't even want to think.)

One thing you know already is that being trendy or fashionable often means being out of pocket. The fashion industry knows that, and they also know that people between the ages of 17 and 24 spend a greater proportion of their budget on wardrobe than any other age group. But you can cut your clothing costs down plenty without committing any fashion faux pas.

Where You Buy = How Much You Spend

Clothes shopping has changed dramatically as consumers have become smarter about what they buy and how much they pay. Wise shoppers have learned to recognize clues that tell them immediately how much extra they'll pay for buying at a particular store:

- A British accent probably means you'll pay 25 percent more.

- A Parisian accent with a gender indifference will add 30 percent.

- More salespeople than customers, add 20 percent.

- Copies of *Details* and *Vogue* on the counter, add another 20 percent.

- Items chained to the rack, add 25 percent. (If it's Toronto, you've probably just stumbled into some sort of kinky clothing boutique.)

- Price tags well hidden, add 20 percent.

- Short European guy with a tape measure around his neck, add 15 percent.

It can all add up. However, you can save a lot simply by carefully choosing where to drop that wad of cash.

Outlet Stores and Malls

Outlet stores and malls are popular now and can mean big savings for you. More manufacturers are opening minimally staffed warehouse-style stores that offer little personal attention in exchange for discounted prices. The quality of these outlet stores varies greatly—some offer topnotch merchandise at low prices, while others sell clothes that look like rejects from an out-of-season flea market. Here are a few words of advice:

- Try to shop at places that receive new stock frequently. Some places may be trying to unload the same picked-over merchandise that they had six months ago.

- Some outlets do get daily shipments. Shop early in the day for the best selection.

- Watch carefully for items marked as "imperfect" or "seconds." These are almost always unreturnable, so it is up to you to find the flaw and decide if it's still worth buying. So check for the third cup on that bra or the sewn-up fly on those pants—it may save you some embarrassment later.

- Sometimes the sheer magnitude of merchandise induces a rush of adrenaline that sends even the most rational consumer into an uncontrollable shopping frenzy. So before you even start to shop, decide on what you need and what you can spend. If you catch yourself about to drop a huge mound of cash on unplanned purchases, take a deep breath and give yourself some time to think. Most stores will hold items for a couple of hours or even a couple of days.

Army Surplus Stores
Great for interesting, unique items, and prices are usually pretty good. You don't have to be a paintball enthusiast or army brat to shop here. T-shirts, underwear, socks, mitts, scarves, coats, boots, etc. can all be picked up cheap.

Discount Retailers
These retailers carry out-of-season merchandise or overruns from manufacturers. (Oops, I guess we made too many!) They may also carry merchandise from bankrupt companies.

Campus T-Shirt Suppliers
It seems every student has a collection of clothing with her university logo, team insignia, residence name, student organization motto, etc. Printing these items is big business. But certain suppliers often print too many Homecoming T-shirts or other apparel for special campus events, and you may be able to get these surplus shirts, caps, shorts, jackets, etc. well below cost (they're of no use to the supplier after the event is over). Suppliers also often have seconds they'd be happy to sell you for next to nothing. Approach any custom campus clothing supplier for these deals.

Campus Athletics
Many campus team and recreation departments have a year-end sale of new and used athletic wear and uniforms. They don't have the room to store them, so you can usually pick things up very cheap.

On-line or Mail Order Catalogues
These have become an increasingly popular way to buy almost anything, including clothing. Some offer very good prices and quality, while others are questionable. The biggest problem is that you can't actually see or try anything on

before you buy. The largest companies operate out of the U.S., which means you have to consider whether it's worth the currency exchange, taxes, and shipping costs, not to mention the customs delays. Equally frustrating is the experience of needing to return something. Having to ship it back, and filling out government forms to get some of your tax payments back, can be a royal pain. Who ever thought shopping from home could be so draining?

General Clothing Tips

When it comes to fashion, the reassuring thing is that you never have to worry about being the worst-dressed person on campus, since chances are your professor will already have that honour wrapped up. Some simple strategies will keep you in style but not out of money.

- Buy clothes that fit now, not "when I shed the 'Frosh 15.'" By the time you make it to that ideal weight, you may not want to be caught dead in that outfit.

- Go with classic looks for your basics. You can avoid the boring label by adding your own accessories.

- Before you buy, figure out your cost per wearing. If you're paying $50 for something you'll only wear a couple of times, it may not be such a good deal. However, if you're spending $100 on a pair of boots you'll wear almost every day throughout the winter, the cost per wearing will be minimal.

- Buy clothes you can wear year-round. Why buy a pile of clothes you can only wear in the summer—which in Canada must be all of about four or five weeks? For instance, a heavy sweater can only be worn in the winter months, whereas T-shirts, cotton jerseys, and light sweaters can be worn alone in the spring and summer and layered together in the fall and winter. A versatile wardrobe will be a lot cheaper in the long run.

- Turn down that walking billboard job—it won't help your résumé! You'll pay extra for doing designers' advertising for them. So avoid the embroidered logos of men doing weird things to ponies and save a lot.

- Buy easy-care clothing. Anything that needs drycleaning will suck more cash from your pockets.

- A clothing money-saving rule: If buying conservative, go quality. If buying trendy, go cheap.

- Choose fabrics that are durable and offer you the best value for your money. Some examples are cotton and ramie blends, tightly knit cotton, acrylic, some wools, and denim.

Shopping Strategies

- Look carefully for flaws such as loose stitching, material flaws, and sewn-up pant legs. If it's fixable or minor, ask for a discount. Almost all places will give you at least some sort of saving.

- Time your purchases so they are end-of-season or out-of-season. This could save you 40, 50, 60 percent or more.

- Stock up big on necessities when they are on sale (socks, underwear, hosiery, etc.). They'll stay in style and you'll have them on hand when you just can't seem to find the time for laundry.

- Buy seconds if flaws are negligible or on items where it won't show, such as bras, underwear, socks. If anybody can see the flaws, they're probably too close (or so your mom would think).

- Clothing fashions are trendy and purchases are often impulsive—a deadly combination for blowing cash! Always know what the refund policy is: unlimited refund, refund within seven days, exchange only, or all sales final. If it's final, you could be shocked when you see that what you bought looks like something from an ABBA reunion tour once you see it in natural light.

Fancy Footwork

- Buy winter footwear towards the latter part of January or February. Prices are much cheaper and fortunately a classic-style boot will usually stay in fashion for years.

- Shoe stores love to peddle a variety of potions, lotions, sprays, and gels. They'll try to convince you that you need at least one or two to take proper care of your footwear, but your best bet is to avoid the commission-hungry sales clerk's pitch and ask for advice at a good shoe repair shop. Inexpensive vinegar, for example, can be used to remove salt stains from leather footwear, thus prolonging its wear.

- When shopping for running shoes, don't be an athletic supporter. Because striking doesn't pay well, these days much of the money you pay for running shoes goes to huge superstar endorsements. Consider whether their name on the high-profile logo is worth the extra money.

- There's a shoe for every sport and someone who will convince you that you better have the most expensive one. Don't run out immediately to buy a new pair of shoes every time you roll off the couch and decide you'd better take up a new activity. If you play a little of many sports, go for cross-trainers. You'll find they'll do for most sports.

Let's Be Formal: The Rental Option

For guys, in most cases that old classic navy blazer will be your cheapest way to dress up for formal functions. However, during the course of your studies, you may end up making a few appearances at formals, weddings, banquets, etc. where the tux is the ticket. This could set you back for as much or more than a wedding gift itself. But you can save considerably.

For Men

- If renting a penguin suit, ask for a student discount. Formal rental places want your business, since they figure you'll be dropping like flies in the marriage circuit once you graduate. Some stores even offer special discount packages for specific campus events.

- If you think you'll be the up-and-coming socialite on campus, you may want to purchase a tux. Formal places often sell off some of their tuxedos at a 40–60 percent discount, so it may be financially worth it if you know you'll be attending numerous formal functions. The best time to buy is November, when tuxes return from the wedding circuit.

- If you go to rental places, bring your teammates, frat brothers, and any others who are renting, and ask for a volume discount.

For Women

- If buying a formal dress, try for something that has practicality for other occasions. You want to avoid buying a dress that cost hundreds and can only be worn once.

- If you want to cut down your costs for a formal dress, check out one of the growing number of consignment shops. Some offer great prices on nearly new designer gowns and dresses.

Once you've outgrown your suits, jackets, dresses, sweaters, etc. (was I really that thin once?), try taking them to a consignment shop. They'll try to sell them and give you about 50 percent of the proceeds.

Signs You May Have a Shopping Problem

1. Have yet to emerge from Eaton's bankruptcy sale.
2. Have a private line to the Home Shopping Network.
3. Find J. Crew catalogues being faxed to your house.
4. Still think "Bay Days" are statutory holidays.
5. Have your PVR programmed to catch the late-night infomercials.
6. Thought a plastic surgeon was someone who repaired worn-out credit cards.
7. Have accumulated frequent flyer miles for riding department-store escalators.
8. Are on a first-name basis with the Wal-Mart greeters.
9. Even have a bank account for your Canadian Tire money.
10. You, not Microsoft, claim victory in browser wars.
11. Are now invited to The Gap staff parties.
12. Your economics prof has named a demand curve after you.
13. Thought a "store credit" could be put towards your degree.
14. Have started to quote Victoria's Secret models in your major term papers.
15. Thought your GPA stood for "Goods Put Away."
16. Nike sponsorship: "Just Spend It."

Beauty and the Bucks: Purchasing Personal Care Products

Unless you plan to walk around campus looking like a complete troll, you'll probably shell out at least a few dollars on personal care and health products. In fact, if you listened to TV commercials and beauty mags, you'd almost believe you're a complete failure without a certain scent, a bounce to your hair, and a glow to your skin. In actuality, if there's a time to try out a ponytail, play the bohemian artist role, or adopt the "beauty *au naturel*" granola look, it's at school. Go this route and your barber will hate you, your wallet will love you, and your parents won't know you. Here are some tips to help you greatly reduce your costs:

- Avoid expensive salons in the trendy areas of town. Do you really need a French stylist with an alternative lifestyle to get a chic cut?

- If you want to get a cut-rate cut, try a beauty or barber school. They'll often lop off your locks for a fraction of the cost of professionals.

- Some places will charge an extra $2–$5 for shampooing your hair. Avoid this financial follicle folly and wash your hair at home.

- Do something shady. Despite the hype about skin wrinkles and aging, and how special formulas can prevent them, the number one enemy of skin is still the sun. If you are going to buy any lotion, buy a good-quality sunblock.

- If you stock up on free samples of shampoo, perfumes, and colognes, you'll cut down on what you need to buy.

- An Obsession on the rocks! Keep your fragrance chilled and it will last longer. In the fridge, it can keep up to two years without spoiling—if your roommates don't get to it first!

- Refill liquid soap and lotion containers when possible. Some stores will give you a cheaper price when you do this.

- Go electric. You'll save in the long run by using an electric razor. Not only will you save on blades, shaving cream, and tonics, but it also takes less energy to run an electric razor than it does for the hot water used with a hand razor.

Health

Health is one area where it doesn't pay to skimp. Fortunately, in Canada we have universal health coverage . . . for now, anyway. But there's a lot you can do to cut down on the extra related costs.

I know it sounds like a cliché, but eat nutritionally, get plenty of exercise, and get enough rest. You'll help to cut your expenses on everything from cold remedies and pain relievers to lost employment wages.

You can often pick up guidebooks on nutritional requirements and fitness suggestions at your campus student health centre or by phoning your nearest Health Canada office. They're absolutely free!

Fitness

When it comes to fitness, your bank account usually gets the biggest workout. Millions are spent annually on attempts to stay slim and trim. Your best bet is to take advantage of your own campus recreation facilities, which are usually included as part of your tuition fees and are the least expensive version of a health club you'll ever enjoy. If you venture off campus, check out facilities at some outside institutions such as high schools and service clubs, which may offer memberships. They're usually cheap, especially if you are a student.

If you're interested in commercial clubs, take advantage of free trials at more than one club (this could last for months!) and don't be afraid to negotiate the price by insisting on a student rate. Avoid pressure sales tactics, too, especially if someone tries to sell you a long-term membership (anything over a year). Most provinces have a five to ten day cooling off period during which time you can cancel your membership contract. Fitness clubs are notorious for changing ownership or closing and reopening; meaning you could get stuck with a worthless membership.

Prescriptions: An Expensive Pill to Swallow

If you're fortunate enough to be covered by your parents' health plan, you may not have to shell out for prescriptions. If you're not covered that way, you may be covered by your school's plan (you may pay a fee as part of your tuition costs). If so, make sure you're getting the best coverage:

- If you have your own coverage, you may have to "opt out" of your school's plan by a certain date to get a refund. Don't miss the deadline or you'll miss that always-welcome cheque; sometimes as much as a hundred dollars or more!

- Check to see what's covered by your plan. This will help you plan for expenses not covered. For example, some plans don't cover birth control or other specific medications. Others only pay a percentage of your prescription costs.

- Some parents' plans cover your prescriptions, orthodontics, eyewear, dentist (yes, there's a financial reason for being afraid of the dentist), and other nonmedical procedures *only* while you are a student. Take advantage of this coverage prior to graduation from college or university (or your 18th or 25th birthday, depending on the plan) so you won't be shelling out more of your own cash later.

- If you use an over-the-counter medication (you pay) that's also sold by prescription (they may pay), ask your doctor to put it on prescription so it's covered by your plan. Check first to make sure your plan does in fact cover that specific medication.

- Ask how much a pharmacy's dispensing fee is, as it can vary considerably (by as much as $6). Some plans will only pay up to a certain amount of this fee.

- Your province may have a pharmacy program for low income residents, which as a starving student, you will often qualify for. This can mean full or partial funding of many prescriptions and health care expenses not covered by your standard health care coverage.

If you are not covered by a plan, there are a few options you can take to avoid the bitter costs of medicine.

- Ask doctors for samples. Plead your non-covered student situation and they may be able to help out with samples (drug dealers . . . er, I mean sales reps love to give these away to doctors). Medications sometimes need to be switched due to side effects or other reasons. You can avoid the expense of paying for a full prescription of which you only use a small amount by asking for free samples for the first few days.

- Just say no to expensive drugs. Ask if any prescribed medicine is available in generic form, which is usually much cheaper (ask your doctor ahead of time if there is any disadvantage to going generic).

- If you're on a long-term medication, one option is to get a large prescription, as this will cut down on frequent dispensing fees.

Dentists

Open wide . . . your wallet, that is! Some dental work may be covered by your parents' plan or through an extra option that you can purchase on your school health plan. Otherwise, it's coming out of your wallet. If you're not covered by a plan, cut your costs by taking the following steps:

- Find out if there is a dental school or dental hygienist program near your home or at your school. Dental work is done by dental students at a cheaper rate, and supervised by a trained dentist. Some schools will film you having your teeth drilled for instructional videos. It's a good way to get a free filling (better rehearse that spitting scene).

- Always ask for your free toothbrush or floss, which many dentists give as parting gifts till your next appointment.

- If you need your wisdom teeth out (ouch!), try to get this done at the hospital. The procedure's sometimes partially covered by health insurance there, whereas it's not always covered if it's done in a dental surgeon's private office.

- If your dentist is taking an upgrading course, volunteer to be their subject for the program, which can mean free dental work.

Alternative Care

While some provinces and health plans will cover part of the expense of a chiropractor, massage therapist, or other forms of health care, you may have to pay part yourself. Unfortunatley, a growing list of items such as massage, routine eye exams, physicals, and some medical supplies are no longer covered on provincial or private plans. Check ahead rather than assume it's covered. Ask alternative practitioners whether they have a student rate.

CHAPTER 12

Planes, Trains, and Automobiles

Unless you stay in your room for the year, you'll probably spend plenty of time getting to and from school, the grocery store, pub, work, laundromat, and so on. Unfortunately, that can be costly. Looking ahead at your alternatives will help you choose the route best for you.

The Automobile

The North American love affair with the car is something that we have all grown up with. From the time we are little, we are bombarded with commercials that show us the many things that come with cars: power, prestige, admiration, and, of course, beautiful people, who are falling all over our new car. Perhaps the thing that is touted most by the car companies is the freedom a car provides. But don't believe it! When you are a student, the freedom that you'll enjoy the *least* with a car is financial freedom. The average yearly cost of driving and maintaining a car will run you two or three times the tuition you will pay at any Canadian university. It doesn't come cheap.

The average cost to own and operate a typical car for one year is estimated to be over $8,300. The cost could have been even more for you, since students are likely to pay more for insurance. What's worse, that price doesn't include such things as parking, car washes, fuzzy dice, Garfield ornaments, parking tickets, and towing fees. The question then becomes: Do you own the car or does the car own you?

Needless to say, owning a car has become a way of life for many of us, and I'm not suggesting that we can all easily do without one. However, if there is one expense that will certainly add to your debt load and literally keep you paying down the road, it is an automobile.

Having said this, there are many things you can do to lower your car operating and maintenance costs, sometimes by as much as $2,000–$3,000 per year. These strategies include everything from what you buy, how you buy it, and where you drive it to how you insure it and how you treat it.

Car Cost-Cutting Strategies

- *Buy Used*—Without a doubt, you'll save big if you forgo the desire for that new car. Buy from friends or from classified ads for the best deals. Rarely will you find a great bargain at a car dealer. A good Canadian consumer guide to consult if you're buying a car is the *Lemon-Aid Used Car Guide* by Phil Edmonston. It's published annually, and there are *Lemon-Aid* guides for new cars and trucks as well.

- *Go Economy*—Leave the gas guzzlers behind in favour of models that are easy on fuel consumption. Not only will you do a huge favour to the environment, but you'll also avoid being vulnerable to price hikes.

- *Share with Family Members*—You may not want to share that car with sis, but splitting the costs on a vehicle could save you a ton on insurance, maintenance, licensing, etc.

- *Drive "the Bomber" Till It Drops*—You're usually better off to drive a car into the ground than to keep switching cars. Even accounting for repairs, you'll probably find this works out to a much cheaper strategy.

- *Take Out the Minimum Insurance Possible*—If you have a lower-value car, cancel the collision entirely if possible (would you pay $1,000 to fix a car worth only $400 anyway?). You can also raise the deductible (e.g., from $250–$500) and lower your rates a bit.

- *Everybody into the Pool*—Jamming the car with students not only helps to keep you warm while driving in the winter, it can also warm your wallet. Arrange for others to take turns springing for the gas. Avoid making a formal payment arrangement for rides lest you have to pay the insurance company to add a rider on your policy.

- *Keep Your Car Tuned*—As with people, preventive maintenance is the cheaper way to car health. So oil and tune your car regularly, which will cut down on gas expenses and costly repairs, and guard against rust.

Insurance Savers

If you're fortunate enough to tap into the family set of wheels from time to time, you'll save big-time over running your own car. Okay, so that '87 family wagon with the eclectic mix of bumper stickers may not be the sportiest of vehicles, but it will probably do the trick. Auto insurance varies significantly from province to province so the following tips may apply.

- It's not worth a sex change, but if you're female you'll get a huge break on insurance if you're insured as an occasional driver. Companies will often cover females on their parents' car as an occasional driver for $75 a year, and sometimes even for free. If you're a guy, you mayl get clubbed for around $700–$800 (ouch!). If you are on your parents' insurance and 25 or older, you can probably have the occasional driver insurance fee you pay completely eliminated (if, of course, you have a good driving record).

- If you're a student living away from home and are insured as an occasional driver on your parents' policy, then you could fall into some big savings. Insurance companies don't like to publicize this (I guess it just slips their minds), but some companies will cut your rate in half! Generally, you can get this saving no matter how far away from home you are, as long as you're not in the same city as your parents. Thus you'd still be insured to drive when home on weekends. If you're male, this could save you $350–$400 or more. Ask your insurance company if they will give you this lower rate.

- Before you rush out to buy your own car, in which case you'd be insured as a primary driver, remember that insurance will shoot up on average to around $3,000–$6,000-plus per year for men and roughly $2,000–$3,000 for women.

- If you're over 25 and have a good driving record, make sure you receive a reduced insurance rate. The amount you pay decreases significantly, by as much as 50 percent. (I guess that's just the first sign that you're getting old and mellow.)

- If you make the move from your little town to the big city in the same province, you could end up paying more for insurance, sometimes as much as 25 percent. So if you're leaving the town of Nanaimo for school in Vancouver, buy your insurance at the lower small-town rate before you go. Keep your licence address from home rather than your big-city address and you'll still be considered a small-town resident.

Motorcycles

Motorcycles are a cheaper option than a car, even though you'll probably pay more for insurance. Accessories might also set you back (e.g., helmet, gloves, leather clothing if that's your style, good rain suit). Safety, as I'm sure your mother has told you, is also a factor (which explains why some of the insurance costs are often steep). As with cars, it pays to consider used bikes and to try to keep insurance costs low.

The end of the school year or the fall are often good times to get a deal on a used pair of wheels. Many boomers snap out of their midlife crises (or have their spouse snap them out of it) and end up selling their "toy" after a summer of recapturing their youth.

To keep your insurance costs low, one option is to not take out collision. Collision could add roughly another 50 percent to your policy costs. As well, you can take out the limited liability policy rather than the more expensive comprehensive, which covers such things as theft and vandalism, but can add around 25 percent to what you pay. Of course, you take a risk since bikes are frequently stolen or vandalized, so assess whether the risk justifies the expense.

Cabs

Cabs are generally expensive. However, even using a cab two or three times a week would still be a much cheaper option than owning and operating a car. Sure, you may spend most of the ride clinging to the door handle as the cabby recounts his numerous licence violations and close calls with inanimate objects. But cabs are particularly great when you are with a bunch of friends and when copious amounts of alcohol have been consumed.

Avoid taking cabs when you are by yourself unless you feel safety is a factor or you have too many pieces of luggage to carry to and from the bus stop. You'll pay for the convenience and feel obliged to tip. At rush hour a cab will cost you even more as the meter ticks away in traffic. You'll no doubt use cabs at one time or another, whether to make that exam when you overslept, or catch that last-minute flight. But keep your pockets full by using them sparingly.

Psuedo-Cabs

If you are stuck for a ride but a cab weighs heavily on your budget, there's a service out to break the taxi cab monopoly. Uber.com (now available in Canadian cities such as Montreal, Toronto and Halifax) and Lyft (US only) allow you to access enlisted non-cab drivers through a smartphone app. You pay for your ride through a credit card maintained by the service – generally at a lower price than cabs.

Buses, Subways, and Other Mass Transit

Mass transit is usually one of students' best options. It's fairly cheap and in most cases reliable. You'll find that trains and buses are pretty packed at peak hours. People are crammed in like sardines, and after a couple of weeks, you'll know who showers and who doesn't, who has the garlic breath, who drank too much the night before—and you'll position yourself accordingly.

Buses are probably the most common form of transit, while the subway is also a popular choice in large city centres such as Montreal (where it's known as the Metro) and Toronto. The subway provides not only cheap transportation but also complementary entertainment via the strange assortment of people—so sit back and enjoy the circus!

- Look into transit prices where you live. Some transit companies, particularly buses, give a discount to students, while some even let students ride *free!* (Who says there's no such thing as a free ride?)

- Public transit got a little bit better as you may now claim a tax credit for transit passes purchased - just make sure to hang on to your receipts.

- If you rely on mass transit for daily transportation, consider a monthly or yearly pass. It's often cheaper and less hassle than always having to buy tickets. Stopovers to visit friends or pick up groceries are also easier because you don't have to shell out the money for yet another ticket.

- A pass may only save you money in certain months. Avoid buying for months when you may be in town for only part of the time, such as December or April.

- Some cities, like Vancouver, charge you more to ride the bus at peak times such as rush hour. You might consider planning your classes so you don't need to travel at those more expensive times.

- Check whether your school offers subsidized transit to and from campus, or a negotiated bus pass included in your student fees.

- Some campuses offer a "late-night bus run" (which describes what you'll need to do if you miss it) to bring everyone home that helped close up the bar. These deals are often subsidized and are thus usually cheaper than taking a cab.

- If the bus doesn't go down your street and you are worried about safety at night, ask the driver if they'll go down your street or stop closer to your home. Some transit companies, at the driver's discretion, will do this at night as a safety service. A much cheaper option than a cab.

- Many campuses now offer free escort services (no, I'm not talking about a free date) to walk you to your class and back, usually at night. Many also offer shuttle and safety bus services to areas around campus. Check to see if your school has such a service, and use it. It will save you big bucks in cab or bus fares in the evening hours, not to mention giving you peace of mind.

Bicycles

Everyone wins with what is by far the most efficient form of transportation. Cycling uses five times less energy than walking, and bikes are one of the cheapest forms of transportation, with no extra cost for insurance, operator's licence, etc. They can even be an inexpensive way to entertain yourself, especially if you live in an area with scenic cycling routes or steep hills. In some Canadian climates, you can ride most, if not all, of the year. Not only is it cheap, but it also gives you exercise. And finally, it just plain makes sense, more sense than busing for an hour to a fitness club to get on the stationary cycling machines.

Buying a Bike

- Buy for your practical needs. If you think you'll be ploughing your way down the bike path year-round, go for a mountain bike or hybrid with more traction and stability.

- Remember, the better your bike, the more appeal it has to thieves. Invest in a lock, and don't abandon your bike for long periods like overnight stays.

- Go for off-season or end-of-season sales. If you can forgo the newest spring colour, you can usually get a good deal.

Check out used bikes (the fitness kick gone sour). The best bets for finding great deals are on-line, the campus bulletin boards, campus and local papers, as well as garage sales, particularly in the spring. Both campus and city police may auction off stolen bikes that were recovered but unclaimed. You can frequently get great deals at campus auctions, but since they aren't well publicized, drop into the campus doughnut shop and ask your local constable when the auction is held. At any auction, check out the merchandise thoroughly before you bid.

Protecting Your "Melon": Helmets

Bike shops will try to sell you all sorts of accessories to decorate both you and your bike. But before you have yourself looking like an overdone Christmas tree, consider whether you really need the shorts, goggles, racing shoes, and gloves to pick up milk from the corner store. Keep your accessories to what's required by law in some places: a helmet, light, reflectors, and perhaps a horn. While you want to get the best deal, buying a helmet is one area you don't want to skimp at the expense of safety. Make sure the helmet is safety-approved and that it fits properly.

Short of theft, your bike should last for years. Wipe it

off in wet weather and oil it occasionally, and it should last as long as you keep pedalling it. Local cycling clubs often host free tune-up clinics in the spring to keep you moving.

Walk 'n' Roll

Walking—What can be said? Cheap, healthy, and relaxing. If you're not in a hurry, this may be just the money-saver for you.

Another way to roll into class is on in-line skates. They're a relatively cheap way to go ($80–$250 for skates, $50–$100 for protective equipment) and quicker than walking. If you go this route, bulletin boards, skate swaps, and "repeat" sports stores offer good used skates and accessories, while late summer/early fall sales offer savings if you buy new. Watch for bylaws that may limit your savings by limiting where you can use in-line skates.

The Trip Home

In most cases, you'll make the trek home at least once or twice through the year. Usually, it's to raid a well-stocked fridge, perform the ritual "meet the parents thing" with your new-found romance, or merely to brace them for the shock of your mid-term marks. Whatever motivates you, there are ways to cut your costs drastically—25–50 percent in some cases.

Train
You can now get discounts on VIA Rail fares, provided you are between the ages of 12 and 25. Always book far in advance (preferably a month or so), particularly for peak periods (e.g., holidays and end of exams) to ensure a seat is available. You are better off to buy a ticket ahead of time even if you are not sure whether you'll use it, since you can normally get a full refund or exchange up to a full year from when you bought the ticket.

Bus

Bus companies such as Greyhound also offer discounts for students, with some routes discounted as much as 45%. U.S. upstart Megabus, also offers steep discounts on their routes, particularly for advance bookings, (although routes in Canada are quite limited). Like the train, peak times book up, although the companies sometimes add extra buses. Bus fare is usually very cheap, and you get free food samples on your seat—oh, those crumbs aren't for eating?

Car

If you have your own car, you can cut your costs by taking others with you. Cram a half a dozen people into that Honda Civic and you'll save a bundle if your passengers cover the gas.

If you want to find a ride home, you're bound to get an even better deal. Usually you'll just split the cost of gas. Post a notice on ride boards and check around for people travelling the same way. Someone in your last weekly class is often a good bet, as they will be done class and ready to go at the same time as you.

If you commute daily from home, you can save a lot by going the ride-share route. Some students spend as much as an hour-and-a-half commuting one-way. The best way to line up rides is still through word of mouth (mind everybody else's business) or a notice on campus bulletin or ride boards, which many campuses now have on-line to assist with ride sharing. Find out who's going where and when.

If you need a reliable set of wheels for the trip home, you may go the rental route. For occasional trips, this may be a good option, particularly if you split with friends. (See chapter 14 on travel, for information on how to get the best rental deals.)

Plane

For those of you who *really* got away from home, your return ticket may be by plane. Look for seat sales and book early, as these are often time-limited. Also, take advantage of frequent-flyer points (especially if you ever travel for student council, etc.—they may pay but let you keep the frequent-flyer points). This is one time when credit card gimmicks may be worth something. See travel chapter for further flight savings.

A final option: students occasionally advertise plane tickets for sale that they no longer need. (That Engineering boyfriend of hers back home may have changed—he may now be History!)

CHAPTER 13

Eat, Drink, and Be Merry—But Still Be Well Off!

Unlike the government, which deals with a cash squeeze by axing its social programs, you don't have to cut out yours. By adopting some simple strategies and creative solutions, you can remain the social animal you've always been. In fact, rather than limiting your social life, you will probably discover there are more money-smart activities than you could ever make time for.

A Distinct Society

Student life is different. There is a different culture, a different language, a different outlook, and often there's a different price. Take advantage of your student status—make sure you're paying that great price reserved for students.

- Always ask if there's a student discount. Many places won't let you know unless you ask. Ask before they ring up your purchase or they may not give you the discount.

- Carry student ID with you all the time. Even though you look like Sophomore Sam garbed in your school paraphernalia, some places won't recognize your student status without you flashing a valid ID.

- Find out whether any other student discount cards are available. They are often distributed free on campus.

- Find out ways to entertain along with other ways to save and make money through the free on-line magazine, *The MoneyRunner* at **www.moneyrunner.ca**.

Out on the Town

Movies

- Check your on-campus theatre or film society for upcoming shows.

- Take advantage of mid-week cheap nights or matinees at commercial theatres, when tickets are often half-price.

- If a movie's a dog, ask for your money back. Most theatres will give you a refund, as long as you leave within the first half-hour of the movie.

- Check out second-run theatres, which usually charge several dollars less for movies that have been out for a couple of months.

- If you're sick of that same old formula—car chase + shoot-out + bare breasts = movie—try the repertory cinemas. Often these theatres have great movies, including limited-run films, international films, and cult classics. You'll usually pay less than at regular theatres. In addition, they frequently offer an annual membership, usually under $10, which will give you discounts on admission prices (and maybe even munchies!).

- Go for films that are especially good on the big screen. Save others, such as comedies which will look just as good on TV, for when you can stream them on-line or rent them from your local video store.

Munching at the Movies

If you think going to movies means getting robbed at the ticket booth, then you know that you'll also get mugged at the food counter. Movie theatres actually generate more profits from their refreshment booth than they do from admissions. To save your cents once inside the theatre, try the following strategies:

- Bring your own snacks to the cinema. You'll get a better selection at a fraction of the cost by bringing your own peanuts, chocolate bars, etc. While theatres don't promote this practice, it is normally allowed as long as you do not bring in any glass containers (unless otherwise posted).

- If you buy beverages, order one large drink and an extra cup. You and your friend will have plenty to split, at a fraction of the cost.

- Would you like pop with your ice? Ask them to hold off on the filler and give you more of the real stuff.

Broadway on a Budget

Live theatre is taking on a whole new popularity as people decide they'd like to do something in life other than gaze at TV and computer screens. But theatre can cost you big, with ticket prices on the major productions running from $75–$100 or more. The following tips should help you avoid these hefty prices.

- Volunteer at a local community theatre. You will get to see some great shows, as well as pump up the résumé with volunteer experience.

- Take advantage of free or low-cost shows on campus. Drama departments and campus theatre groups offer some great productions at bare-bones prices.

- Take advantage of preview nights. Tickets are usually a lot cheaper for these shows, which run before the official opening night. So what if Romeo forgets Juliet's name a couple of times during the performance, it's still a great deal.

- Check out "underground" or "alternative" theatres in your community, which are often both inexpensive and interesting.

If you're sampling professional or big-stage productions, try these tricks to avoid big-ticket prices:

- Ask about group discounts, usually available for groups of 10 or more. The savings are often significant. You and the other members of the campus mud-wrestling team might find it cheap to get cultured after all.

- Ask for student rates and packages. The future of theatre depends on getting young people interested in this medium. Thus, discounts offered to students are often "dramatic."

- "Rush" seats—last-minute no-shows or unsold seats—are usually sold off cheaply just prior to the performance. If you're prepared to go a bit early and take a chance, it's a good way to scoop up some savings. Some larger cities even have an outlet that just sells rush tickets for the various performances.

- Avoid Friday and Saturday evenings, which are usually more expensive.

- If you love the theatre but can't quite afford a season ticket, consider splitting a season ticket with friends. You can get the package discount but not have to fork over for the whole bill of plays. Some theatres may even offer a discount "flex pass" which allows you to purchase tickets to a limited number of shows, say four of the eight shows offered, and to choose the plays you want to see.

- If your entertainment funds for the month come down to a fistful of change, you may still be able to mingle with the theatre crowd. Some theatres, art galleries and symphonies have a pay-what-you-can performance. Proceeds sometimes go to a local charity.

Comedy

If your roommates have lost their sense of humour, and even the class clown has lost his touch, you may be able to eke out a few yuks down at the comedy clubs. Stand-up comedy is popular, but the cost may wipe the smile right off your face. For cheap laughs, try the following tips:

- Take advantage of special student nights, which are some-times half-price.

- Some campus bars offer comedy that is so cheap it's a joke . . . or even free.

- If you find *watching* stand-up humour too passive, remember there's always the chance to participate in amateur night when the cost is on them and the joke's on you.

Concerts

It's always great to fork over $100 to hear some rebel band denounce the capitalism and materialism in our society and then watch them leave in a limo bound for their suite at the Ritz Carlton. However, you can often pay a "song" for these concerts by choosing from the following strategies:

- If it's a show that's not sold out, you can sometimes pick up last-minute seats from the box office or from scalpers who are scrambling to cut their losses on the pile of unsold tickets they are holding. Caveat emptor with scalpers, however, since counterfeit tickets can be common. These guys aren't exactly members of the Better Business Bureau.

- If you think the average fan often gets shafted when it comes to obtaining good seats, you're not alone. Many of the prime tickets are held for radio stations and sponsoring companies. If you want front-row seats for the big show, your best bet may be through radio show promotions or connections to big business. So, turn on the radio and stick by the phone, or check with your parents, relatives, and friends to see if there are any spare box seats or front-row tickets floating around their companies.

- Some larger cities have ticket clearance outlets, which are a central box office for selling unsold last-minute seats. You can often get good seats at great prices here.

- Some ticket agencies tack costly service charges on top of regular ticket prices. You know the fees:
    - $4 service charge
    - $3 tax
    - $2.50 handling fee
    - $3 for the privilege of standing in line overnight
    - $4 for the luxury of sitting behind a post because all the good seats went to the scalpers
    - $2 because it's Friday and we don't like working

The list is endless. While you can't always do a lot, you may be able to cut down on these charges by buying from places like campus ticket outlets or directly from the theatre or concert hall box office. Other concert cost-cutters:

- If you can, hold off on buying the Green Day halter top, or the Bon Jovi belt buckle. The markup is huge on concert merchandise, and you'll probably find it cheaper in a retail store.

- If you buy food at concerts or other events at large concert halls and stadiums, you'll pay a fortune. Can you say McRipoff? Stock up on snacks before you go. While bringing potato chips may not win you many friends at the opera, packing a lunch for open-air concerts and sporting events saves you a bundle. Note that security at most concert halls and stadiums won't let you bring in alcohol or hard containers.

Free-for-Alls

- Look for free concerts, particularly during holidays and the warmer months. Often they are promos sponsored by the beverage companies and local radio stations. Some good Canadian talent here, along with a smattering of dried-out, rehabbed musicians trying to make a comeback.

- There's free entertainment and it's loose in the streets! You can take in some amazing free festivals in towns and cities around the country, from the Busker Festival in Halifax, the Jazz Festival in Montreal, and the Home County Folk Festival in London, to Winterlude in Ottawa, Caribana in Toronto, and Celebration of Light in Vancouver. Most of these festivals offer all or much of the entertainment for free. Drop by your local tourist bureau to get the scoop and enjoy.

- Check out the campus concert scene, where you'll find some great up-and-coming bands who haven't quite made the big time—sort of like the triple-A teams of the music world.

- If your school has a Faculty of Music, you may dig up some free concerts. While you're more likely to find classical or jazz than techno punk, the quality is usually very good. And, if you really want to mellow out, you may just want to saunter into a piano recital now and then.

Alcohol

"Another round" can be the most expensive phrase to come out of a student's mouth. In fact, alcohol drains enormous quantities of student cash. Despite grudging Saturday morning pledges never to partake again, many students continue to sop up the suds in a big way.

Studies show that, on average, student drinkers consume roughly six and a half drinks per week. If a typical drink costs $5.00, then the average student drinker would spend roughly $33 per week on alcohol, or over $1,700 per year.

This figure doesn't even account for money spent on tipping, cab rides (an essential cost), misplaced clothes, hangover remedies, unwanted dates and other incidentals. As you can see, drinking is no minor expense.

The best way to save $1,700 is to avoid alcohol entirely. You'd have enough for a great stereo, a Caribbean vacation, or a closet full of new clothes—however you want to break it down. While this is the cheapest option, it may not be the one chosen by the 86 percent of students who drink at least occasionally.

If you do drink, it's going to cost you. The good news is that you can drink and still cut your costs dramatically.

Drinking Out: The "Don't Get Soaked" Strategy

- Forgo the label peeling ritual. Drink draft rather than expensive bottled beers. I once overheard a campus bar manager boasting about the profit he made off first-year students who were more easily drawn to the brand-name bottles than the on-tap suds.

- Timing's important. When you drink can affect what you pay. Some bars have happy hours with cheap drinks, sometimes even half-price. Some provinces don't allow happy hours, but if they do, enjoy.

- Alternate alcohol with nonalcoholic drinks. It will cut your costs significantly, and still leave you something to hold in your hand.

- Order house wine rather than that expensive bottle of Chardonnay off the wine list.

- Pay as you play. A tab is much too convenient. Pay by cash as you drink, and you'll avoid the shock of a full evening's bill.

- Leave the car at home. This may not seem like a cost saver, but you'll spend far less on a cab, bus, or subway ticket than on a parking fine, towing fee, or, worse still, an impaired driving charge and the accompanying increased insurance costs.

Drinking In

A far cheaper option when it comes to alcohol is drinking in. You'll save on markup, tips, and extra taxes which ring up your bar or restaurant bill. When getting spirited at home, follow these guidelines:

- Buy domestic wines if possible. You'll save on tariff and transportation costs built into the price of imported wines.

- If you do buy imported, buy wines, beers, and spirits from countries that have a low-valued currency. You'll pay less for a Romanian or Bulgarian wine than an Austrian or German wine, for example.

- If you plan to make mixed drinks, go for the lower-priced brands of alcohol. You'll probably never notice the difference.

- If you drink wine regularly, buy it in larger sizes, as it is usually cheaper. If you're a sporadic wine taster, buy smaller bottles, since it will only keep seven to 10 days well-corked in the fridge (after that, don't toss it; use it for cooking or marinating meats).

- Pre-mixed drinks are popular, particularly summer coolers. However, you'll pay more for the convenience. You can experiment with wine, carbonated water, and fruit juices to make your own equally refreshing yet far less expensive versions.

- "When duty calls": Whenever you travel, always obtain your allotted amount of duty-free alcohol. You'll save plenty in government taxes and tariffs. Even if you don't drink yourself, a nice bottle of wine or spirits can make a good gift for dinner parties or the holidays.

- Expensive liquors, such as Irish Cream or Kahlúa, can leave a bitter financial aftertaste. However, these drinks can often be made more cheaply on your own. Here's one on the house:

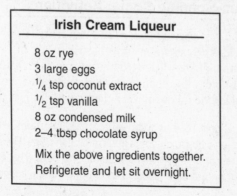

Irish Cream Liqueur

8 oz rye
3 large eggs
$1/4$ tsp coconut extract
$1/2$ tsp vanilla
8 oz condensed milk
2–4 tbsp chocolate syrup

Mix the above ingredients together.
Refrigerate and let sit overnight.

Taxing Matters

If you think your money's going to pay the grape pickers in California or a beer meister tucked away in some medieval German castle, think again. In fact, most of it is going to our hard-labouring bureaucrats in government. When you buy alcohol, an average of 40–50 percent of the retail price may go to taxes. That equals $16–$20 when you buy a case of 24 beer, or $3–$6 on an average bottle of wine. Below are a few tax-cutting tips.

Homemade Beer and Wine

Self-brewing is one of the fastest growing areas in the brewing industry. Any self-respecting beer connoisseur can tell you why: it's cheaper and often better! How much cheaper? A 50-litre batch of beer (about six 24s) costs you around $100–$130, compared to a retail price of $210–$250. That's roughly a 100–130 percent difference for a couple of hours of your time.

How much can you save by making your own wine? Well, at a do-it-yourself winery store with less than an hour of your time your cost per 750-millilitre bottle will average approximately $4–6, a far cry from the $8–$14 or more you'd pay in the store. You can further reduce the cost by buying a kit for around $60–$90. But, do you have the room, do you want the mess, and can you handle the resulting swarm of instant wine conoisseurs traipsing through your place?

Campus-Specific Social Activities

One of the best parts of college and university is what you gain outside the classroom (not that you can't, of course, be a fountain of knowledge from what you learn *inside* the classroom). For more good times than you could ever imagine, consider the following very cheap opportunities:

- Most schools have a wide variety of clubs, from ski and investment clubs to outdoors and Caribbean clubs. These are often free or charge minimal membership fees. The events they put on are often subsidized and therefore inexpensive.

Probably one of the absolute cheapest ways to meet people, have a good time, and even learn something in the process.

- Student councils also offer a smorgasbord of programs, ranging from spirit weeks and Homecoming days to charity events. You've already paid for many of these activities through your student fees, so get your money's worth by participating.

For more academic entertainment freebies, consider the following suggestions:

- If you've had enough of reading, let someone else do it for you. A variety of best-selling novelists and poets give readings on the campus circuit, hoping you'll be inspired enough to buy their books.

- Just what you needed, one more lecture. But special lectures on campus are good and almost always free. Many renowned speakers, including entertainment and athletic figures, politicians (always looking for an audience), business leaders, social leaders, humanitarians, scientists, media figures, and so on, give lectures on campuses around the country. Your campus provides a venue for them—and cheap entertainment and information for you.

- If you love to learn but not the stress of term papers and exams, your campus may offer a great option. Universities either through their students' council or continuing education department, offer non-credit workshops and courses on a variety of topics. Ranging from digital photography, calligraphy and modern dance to improv, bicycle maintenance and Thai cooking, they are usually offered at a nominal cost and sometimes even free! A great way to explore an interest, meet people and in the case of cooking courses, satisfy your palate.

Signs that guy in your Psychology class may be Rob Ford

- Bolts for classroom exit when he nervously mistakes surprise quiz for random testing.

- Video emerges of him and three inebriated lab monkeys in campus pub conga line.

- Lobbying the Prof to televise class debates.

- Repeated shouts from back of the class asking "What? This isn't Mixology 101?"

- Stripped of class presidential powers by classmates mid-term.

- Has exams rescheduled due to late night talk show circuit conflict.

- Study group raided for third time this term.

- Passes off campus paper photo of him with questionable object in mouth, as kazoo from football pep rally.

- Brother keeps showing up to publicly defend his classroom tirades.

- Addictions term paper cites only primary sources.

- Class yearbook mug strangely accompanied by numbers underneath photo.

- Angrily declares failing grade attributable to academic left wing conspiracy.

The Sporting Life

Playing Sports

If entertainment to you means straying away from the couch and venturing into some sort of sports complex, campus can offer the discount route.

- You can usually learn and enjoy a sport through the recreation or physical education department, or campus athletic clubs, at a huge discount compared to what it would cost at a commercial facility. Fencing, scuba, and kayaking are just a few good examples.

- In some cases, if they don't offer or teach a particular sport on campus, your school may have an arrangement with an off campus community club or organization that does. These are frequently offered at a significant discount to what the general public would pay. Check with your campus recreation services to see what's available.

- For athletic equipment, consider buying at equipment swaps on campus. Campus clubs, such as the ski club, often set up swaps and sales where you can pick up equipment at a fraction of the retail cost.

- Campus athletic clubs often arrange deals with certain companies, who offer cut-rate prices on athletic equipment. For example, squash racquets might be available at a 20–30 percent discount for squash club members. You may have to pay a few bucks to join the club, but the savings could be worth it.

- Save money by purchasing your equipment at community sales or "second play" sports stores. If you have old equipment you don't use anymore, ask whether you can trade it in.

Armchair Athletics: A Sporting Gesture

If participation is not a word in your vocabulary, but watching others work up a sweat is something you do enjoy, you can take in some cheap sporting entertainment.

- Campus athletics offer great ways to see some topnotch athletics. Campus activities are often free or minimally priced for students.

- If your campus has good recreation facilities, your school may end up actually hosting national or even international meets by pro or Olympic teams. As a student, you can often get much cheaper tickets for these events.

- If there is a particular event or competition coming to your campus that you want to see, ask about volunteering at it. In many cases you will get to see it for free, as well as the added benefit of a volunteer experience for your resume. In some cases you may even get paid a wage or honorarium.

- Join the thousands who have rediscovered sports played by people who want to play. Many cities have triple-A and minor league teams, and tickets to see them compete are a fraction of the cost of professional sports. And guess what? They'll actually play the *whole* season!

Entertaining at Home

Video (DVD and Video Tape)

If you like the "opulence" of home when doing your movie viewing—the comfortable couch an arm's reach from the fridge, and the power of the pause button locked in your hand—videos are a cheap way to go. While many video rental places have closed, as content moves on-line, there are still some places to rent your favorite flick. When renting, a few tips to make it even cheaper:

- Take advantage of special nights. Video stores sometimes try to compete with theatres by offering deals such as Two-for-One Tuesdays.

- Many video places offer promos, such as every 10th movie free, or a free movie on your birthday. Take advantage of these if you can.

- Avoid places that charge a membership fee unless it means guaranteed major savings.

- New releases sometimes cost more on weekends than during the week. You may want to rent these during the week and save older movies for the weekend.

- Try classics for a change. They're usually the cheapest to rent, and there is a great selection, as other customers clamour after the latest releases.

- You're usually better off to go to a place where the selection's consistently good. That corner store may save you a buck or two, but if the selection's poor and you end up renting movies you wouldn't normally watch *for free* you're really not saving.

- Avoid *buying* videos unless they're absolute classics (e.g., "I've watched this 27 times and I still get choked up when she falls in love with the werewolf"). Most bought movies end their run sitting idly on your shelf.

Video Freebies

- Rather than renting videos at rental stores, borrow them from the library. They're free and the late charges are much cheaper.

Compact Discs

- "Any six CDs for one cent." CD and DVD clubs, which used to lure you with the promise of cheap music, have been shutting their doors. The once popular CDs have been losing ground as digital music surges in popularity, however they still have some popularity due to their higher sound quality versus downloaded music.

- If you're buying new CDs or videos, the cheapest places are on-line sites, warehouse clubs (good prices, limited selection), electronic superstores (good prices, better selection), and music and video warehouse superstores (good prices, great selection). If you buy used, CD exchange and resale stores offer some very good savings. Because CDs tend to stay in good condition, buying used is usually a safe option.

- If some of your favourite CD's or DVD's have now dropped off your personal favourites list, organize a swap with friends and roommates. Chances are they are up for a change of music too.

- For single songs, downloads are probably your cheapest bet. Some web sites allow you to download for free, while others will charge you per song or a flat monthly fee.

- Streaming music sites such as Songza and soon to be available in Canada, Spotify, offer a great selection of music genres. You can choose from different playlists to suit your mood and occasion. Best of all is a price that is easy to listen to; Free!

Reading Riches

Books

Entertainment may also include the calm relaxation of curling up with a good book—something that is not assigned for a change. Fortunately, there are some cheap options:

- The library is one of your cheapest bets. If they don't have it, they can probably get it for you, free, from another library.

- If you've breezed through all your books and crave more, trade with roommates and friends. You'll get a taste of what other people read. If your roommates haven't yet graduated past the *Archie* comic stage, you may want to check out a community book exchange.

- A great time to buy new books, including bestsellers, is January. Some books are half-price, while many stores offer 15–20 percent off all selections. Stock up at this time.

- If you patronize one store, they may give you a frequent-reader card, which entitles you to further discounts (while others will sell you the card).

- Warehouse stores can give some great deals on current bestsellers—sometimes up to 50 percent off the cover price.

- For a cheap, recycled read, a garage sale may be the ticket. Who knows what other people's libraries will provide?

Magazines

Whether you're rushing down to the corner store to see if you made *People*'s "Most Beautiful People Issue" or checking out the latest fish centrefold in *Field and Stream*, you can drop a lot of cash on magazines. You can cut your costs significantly by adhering to the following advice:

- If you buy a particular magazine regularly, go for a subscription. You'll pay a fraction of the newsstand cost.

- Take advantage of student subscription rates, which are even cheaper than the everyday subscription rate.

- If you have roommates, you may want to go together on subscriptions. Two of you might be big *Rolling Stone* readers, while your other business wanna-be roommates may be clamouring for their copy of the *Wall Street Journal*. Some distributors will cut you a deal on multiple subscriptions.

- Swap magazines on your residence floor or in your house. Just don't forget to cover up your answers in the *Cosmo* "Is He Right for Me?" survey.

Potluck Pleasures

Even on those cold February nights when you're singing those end-of-cash-flow blues, you can still keep the entertainment ball rolling.

Hosting a potluck dinner is one of the cheapest ways to entertain. Having each friend make one dish for dinner offers three big advantages: it's quick, it's cost-efficient, and it's filling.

Potlucks take eating to the level of social entertainment, but with no pushy waiters, no expensive menus, and no annoying waits—just great company. And best of all, they're cheap! (I find setting your bathroom scales up 10 pounds is a great strategy. Your guests will weigh in prior to the feed, be alarmed by their apparent weight gain, and thus cut their consumption accordingly. Do I smell *leftovers*?)

Frugal Feasts From the Top: Celebrity College Favourites

Conrad's "Black Bean Soup"—Assemble cronies and other makeshift cooks for a lavish cooking feast. Although seasoned French chefs are preferred, gathering Canadian chefs and having them renounce their citizenship to pretend they're French will do. Gather a big pot or even pork barrel to load up the ingredients. Fill with black beans and the finest ingredients you can buy including truffles and champagne (as this can be costly, insure you have a company credit card handy). Let sit for days. Set timer for a couple of hours but be sure that you pull from the stove well ahead of time so things are half cooked. Simmer and serve. As this makes a lot, load up any excesses in boxes and remove at night so as not to be observed (or so you hope). Note: Although things should cook up nicely be careful in case recipe turns sour, as you never know when the other cooks may turn on you when the heat is on.

Bill Clinton: "Saucy Bill's Big Cheese Lasagna"— Pick up intern for some spice. Stop by grocery store to get some frozen lasagna and cheap wine. Return home and give lasagna to White House staff. Leave with intern in adjoining room to allow things to heat up. After things have really got cooking return and devour lasagna and wine. Three weeks later deny you've ever had lasagna and claim only to have heard of the dish. Dismiss these links to you and lasagna as a half-baked right wing plot by the kitchen staff. Help intern find job in other cities so that they can sample lasagna in other parts of the country. Repeat daily.

Ross Rebagliati: "Gold Medal Ice Cream"—Mix ice, milk, homegrown herbs and other coastal flavour enhancers. Blend in big bucket. "Veg" for an hour and then just "chill." Invite friends over to indulge. Prepare and eat daily. When you start to gain weight, claim to have only sampled the ice cream a few years ago, and attribute the extra pounds to hanging around dessert addicts who devour the stuff regularly. Phone Bill Clinton for an alibi.

Alan Eagleson: "Prime Rib of Beef"—Get classmates, housemates, and friends together—asking them to bring the roast potatoes and other ingredients. Hand roommates the recipe and make them prepare the roast. When they have finished, have them retire to the lounge where you can boast about how *you* have furthered the art of cooking. Sneak back into the kitchen. Grease palm continuously and skim off all you can from the finished dinner except for one bowl. Place bowl on table and invite everybody back for a small sample. Carefully stickhandle your way around any questions about the whereabouts of the rest of the meal. Repeat often and live off what you've hidden for you and your family.

Tiger Woods' "Club House Sandwich"—Put aside, a perfectly good dish. Grab multiple bread slices (one can never satisfy) along with numerous ingredients, and a large stash of cash. Pile all ingredients between slices. Let hot and spicy be your measure, as no ingredient is too high priced, or out of bounds. Indisciminately invite "hungry" guests over to sample your concoction. Indulge yourself now, as this dish is likely to be much costlier later. If recipe experience leaves guests with a bad aftertaste, split, divide and garnish them generously with parting cash. Share recipe with less critical pro golfers, as they too most certainly tried a few side dishes that didn't turn out. Warning, consumption of this recipe may affect driving judgment!

Jerry Springer: "Tainted Meat Tarts"—Assemble the most eclectic group of acidic fruits, wild nuts, fowl, hams and caustic sauces available. Spice it up. Prod, provoke, and manipulate and bring to a high boil. Let it flow (not worrying about the pans). Remember, with this recipe it's the dough that is crucial . . . so get as much as you can, whatever the cost! Serve. When people complain about the poor taste, deliver a rhetorical commentary on the worthiness of the process. Recycle ingredients by sending to other show hosts with similarly tasteless recipes.

> ***Britney Spears: "Raunch Dressing"***—Take mediocre ingredients. Progressively whip together to a beat. Add colour and fluff. Add odd dressings for flavour. Cook until very overdone. Pour on thick but spread thin everywhere for maximum exposure. Serve, serve, and serve again—until your guests can't stand it anymore! Presentation is crucial on this basically bland dish. So repackage constantly to prevent staleness and prolong shelf life. Even if you like this recipe, save face—don't admit it!

Dating and Romance

When relationships start to intensify and feelings begin to grow stronger, the next thing that inevitably comes up is the big "C" word . . . yes, cash flow (or lack thereof). But dating needn't mean a crash for your cash. In fact, there's lots you can do to keep love glowing and money growing:

- Try new and interesting things that don't cost money.

- Try simple things. Advertisers love to convince us that we need to spend lots of money to show our love and affection for someone. Imagine some commercials are now actually telling people how much they should spend on a diamond ring! However, the simple (and inexpensive) things are often the most appreciated and remembered.

- Go for fun activities that will keep the laughter flowing.

- Be spontaneous. Sometimes the sudden or surprise things you do can be the most fun.

- Two is better than one. Take advantage of discounts for couples.

Twelve Great Student Dates

- Go to a local beach or park and have a picnic. If you want to spice it up, bring some wine glasses and a nice bottle of wine (be careful where you are; some provinces disallow alcohol in public places).

- Rent a favourite movie together and make your favourite munchies and exotic blender drinks.

- Take a trip to the local pet store and name all the animals, or identify which celebrity they resemble.

- Go tobogganing or cross-country skiing together and pack a thermos of hot chocolate and Bailey's.

- Have a Christmas wrapping party with the appropriate foods and beverages. Of course, you should save any alcoholic beverages for after the wrapping or your animal-rights activist Uncle Ted may end up with Cousin Melanie's *Guide to Hunting in the Great White North*. Make the party complete with Christmas music and a holiday video such as *How the Grinch Stole Christmas*.

- Make a big deal of other holidays, too. For example, create a spooky scene for Halloween, complete with carved pumpkins and costumes, or plan a celebration of the Chinese New Year.

- Take a fun class or course together and discover a new passion. Some things to try: Tai Chi, ballroom dancing (guys, your girlfriends will love it if you suggest this), photography, fitness classes, massage courses, etc.

- Volunteer to do some community work together. Everybody wins with this type of date.

- If you're in the middle of mid-terms, turn an afternoon of hitting the books into a pleasurable experience. Study in the park and bring a favourite game or frisbee to take fun breaks.

- Try cooking an exotic meal together, perhaps a dish from a different country once a month. Candles and a few flowers can add to the romance.

- Borrow a dog to take for a long walk. (Don't forget to check with the owner before making off with Bowzer.) You should *definitely* do this if you're single.

- Do a *New York Times* crossword together.

Holidays and Special Occasions

Gift Giving
Gift giving is great. It's great to give gifts and it's great to receive them. But it also takes its toll on a student budget. In

fact, it seems to get worse as the years progress. First, you get the traditional occasions: birthdays, Christmas, Chanukah, Valentine's Day. Then the weddings start: a marriage here, another one over there, and another one that falls soon after—basically adhering to the domino theory. Then the baby gifts start to kick in: first one, then another, oops there's twins. Gift giving can take its toll on even the fittest budget. But remember that when you are a student, those close to you will understand you not breaking the budget in search of that "perfect gift." You can give generously to others without giving up everything else in your budget.

- Plan early for birthday and holiday gifts and take advantage of sales as you see them. The retail markup is high on many items, but if you buy after the holiday for the next year, you'll sometimes get 30–60 percent off.

- Save money by creating homemade gifts. Not only is it much less expensive than buying from the store, it's also more personal. If you're artistic, do a painting, create a carving or ceramic bowl, make a photo or flower arrangement, knit a sweater, design jewellery, or even create a memorable video.

- Try making cookies, cakes, homemade liquors (see "Alcohol" above) or grant someone a coupon for one home-cooked meal or chore such as painting the deck. You'll be surprised how well appreciated a gift like this will be.

- Some people celebrate a holiday such as Christmas on the day of, but do the gift exchange a few days later. This allows them to do their gift buying at the Boxing Day sales and save a fortune. (How disheartening it can be to see that $80 sweater you gave dad, on sale for $40 a week later.) Not only does postponing save on the gifts, but also on wrapping paper, cards, tags, bows, etc.

- Be efficient. Many families, in order to duck the conspicuous consumption and the January credit crunch, organize Christmas gift draws where everyone picks a name and buys for only one family member. They also set a spending limit.

- Gift draws also work well among friends, floormates, and roommates. Your bank account is going to love you.

- Exercise the right side of your brain—try a gift exchange where everybody has to create a gift.

- Go together with friends or family when buying a gift. You'll save money on the wrapping and card, and by pooling your resources you will probably be able to buy a much nicer gift than you could afford alone.

Wrapping: The Big Cover-Up

The card and gift wrapping sometimes cost as much as the gift itself. You can cut your expenses here as well, and be environmentally friendly in the process. Improvise by decorating boxes with artwork and markers instead of wrapping paper, or save money by reusing wrapping paper and bows. Buy all-occasion paper rather than occasion-specific paper (this way, you can avoid wrapping your mom's birthday gift in paper adorned with a million prancing reindeer).

Gift Getting

Of course, it's always nice to have a few gifts come your way as well: that great calculator you've always wanted, that book of Spanish love sonnets you pined for. But how many other well-intentioned gifts lie quietly in a closet six months later, untouched since the time you opened them: that bulky waffle iron, the wild necktie, those psychedelic PJs from your nearsighted Auntie May? There *are* some strategic ways to get useful gifts and spare the agony for those who give them.

- Always give suggestions of things you really need or want.

- Give suggestions for a few practical things you know you need (e.g., running shoes), as well as for one or two less practical things you'd like to have or will buy anyway (e.g., if you plan to go to that U2 concert, perhaps suggest a ticket as your birthday gift).

- Money is always a great gift for the starving student. It allows you to pick just the right purchase, and you can wait to buy things when they're on sale (for example, after Christmas). An excellent option may be to ask for a Canada Savings Bond or RESP contribution to put towards your education.

- Some people hate giving cash, so suggest gift certificates (ask for certificates without an expiry date). Be sure to mention stores you really like (a certificate for The Bay or The Body Shop will probably be easier to use than one for McDuff's House of Kilts). Ask for a certificate at an established store to lessen the chance it will be bankrupt before you ever get there.

- Ask for things that aren't likely to go on sale later. This means avoiding seasonal items such as clothing and sports equipment. You're better off having Uncle Alex spend $70 on your four favourite CDs than on a pair of snowshoes you can get for $40 a few months later at Sammy's Sports Spring Sale Extravaganza.

Holiday Decorating

No matter what the holiday, decorations are expensive, and once the occasion's over they sit dormant for nearly a year. Instead of shelling out for these once-a-year wonders, seek leftover decorations from home or improvise with decorations you make yourself.

CHAPTER 14

Gee, I Gotta Get Out of Here!
Travelling on the Cheap

Escape from Alcatraz. Well, school may not be quite that bad, but as the year wears on, you can see the commonalities: only bread and water to eat (or worse, cafeteria food), prison guards abound (well, overzealous campus security), lots of time behind bars (or, rather, inside them), long days and nights of solitary confinement (actually, endless hours isolated in your room, churning out papers), feeling ashamed for the past crimes you've committed (feeling guilty about the wild weekends that have left you panic-stricken about homework), wondering about the possibilities of early parole (assessing the chances you'll become a Christmas graduate), biding time till your release papers (counting the days till your graduation diploma). The similarities go on.

So, how do you break out? If you're like most students, you'll probably want to get away for some R & R. But how much fun and adventure can you get for $17.63? Well, not a lot. But with some careful and creative planning you may be able to bring your travel costs down to the affordable range. Let's look at some great escape possibilities.

Where to Go from Here

You can pull out the map and toss a dart to find out where

that road trip's going, or you can be strategic and choose a great place that's going to cost you little.

- Consider off-season vacations. You can travel at a time when everyone else isn't jamming the place and the staff are actually glad to see you. You may also save 50 percent or more.

- Explore your own country. Frequently, people travel thousands of miles to see sights not nearly as spectacular as what's next door. It's often cheaper to travel within your own borders and you avoid exchanges, visas, passports, border hassles, tropical shots and medications, and additional health insurance.

- If you leave the country, try places where the cost of living is low and where the currency exchange is favourable. A trip to Cuba or Mexico will cost you far less than Bermuda or Switzerland.

- I've always felt it's a good idea to stay away from places caught in the grip of civil war. While you may get a rush of adrenaline from the sound of artillery or be entertained by the military's complimentary air show, you may not find the cost of emergency airlifts to your liking. Save the hassle and potential expense by checking out your destination ahead of time.

- Avoid large cities and touristy spots. You'll save a ton by avoiding these places, where you pay more to eat, drink, sleep, and travel. If you do decide to visit a big city, consider accommodations in a smaller town close by. Not only are such places more affordable, less crowded, quieter, less polluted, and safer, but the people also tend to be friendlier, since they're not "touristed-out."

- Be extremely wary of the do-it-yourself travel agent (including student entrepreneurs). A hastily arranged bus trip to Florida organized by the get-rich-quick artist could mean 15 hours on a school bus, heading for the Cockroach Inn and Truck Stop, somewhere in the heart of Swampsville.

- Consider visiting friends and relatives who live in other places. It'll be much cheaper and you will probably someday be able to return the favour for them. While you might be more inclined to visit your friends in P.E.I. than Cold Lake, Alberta, remember that how well you get along with your hosts may be just as important as location.

What's in That Package?

This is a good question to ask when you want to get away. Some tour packages are great deals, while others are poorly put together ripoffs.

- If you know you'll be inhaling large quantities of food and beverages, an all-inclusive deal may be the way to go. It's amazing how fast the drinks flow when you're sopping up those UV rays, which could lead to quite a tab. You'll also save the risk of carrying cash and losing it or having it stolen.

- Ask to talk to someone who's been to that resort. Often, travel agents themselves have been there to check these places out. So get a feel for whether it was worth the money: Was the water clean? Did they have plenty of activities? Did the masseuse have good hands?

- Choose your travel company carefully and watch what you're charged for, even on all-inclusive packages. I booked a tour with one well-known agency and was mistakenly charged by both the tour company and the hotel staff. It took over 10 months and many long-distance phone calls and letters before I was finally reimbursed.

Shaving Your Costs
If you're going to be using a package tour, there are ways to shave hundreds of dollars off your cost.

- *Tour Wholesalers*—Pick a tour, any tour, from travel brochures, and wholesale agents will often give you 10–15 percent or more off the package price. It's the same tour as you would get from a regular agent—only you're getting the discount price. A great option if you know the trip you want ahead of time.

- *Travel Specials*—Travel companies will frequently have specials for particular destinations—sometimes at a great price. Ask a trusty travel agent to keep you posted.

Work/Travel Programs

If you want to travel, but the cash is absent, you may want to consider combining a little work and a little play. Many organizations are available to pay or at least subsidize your trip in exchange for various types of labour, such as community work, language instruction, or research. Some will even pay you a small wage on top. You will find that some programs are country-specific, whereas others, such as the long-established Student Work Abroad Program (SWAP), have approximately 12 different countries to choose from. Keep the following points in mind when investigating work/travel programs:

- Find out exactly what things the program provides and what you must pay for yourself. Know this before you commit yourself.

- Find out whether they pay up front for your expenses or reimburse you later.

- Know exactly what financial provisions are made in case you can't fulfil your work requirements (due to illness, political circumstances, etc.). I knew one friend, for example, who was teaching when up popped a revolution; needless to say, it was a case of "class dismissed." Find out who pays for an emergency evacuation and other occurrences.

- Find out ahead of time how much you'll be working and how much free time you'll have. If your goal is primarily to travel, you may not want to be toiling away for 12 hours a day in some dingy sweatshop.

- Keep in mind that the length of term will vary depending on the program. Some only require a commitment of a few months, so it can easily fit in with your summer break, whereas other programs may require you to commit for a year or two.

- Check on how you're taxed on your earnings and compensation. Some countries will tax you heavily (yes, even more heavily than Canada), while others give you full exemption from paying tax.

- Ask for references from any organization you get involved with and check them out. Speaking to others that have participated with that organization will give you insight straight from the traveller's mouth. Also, check with your college or university placement office to see if they have heard good or bad comments about a particular program. Some programs are terrific, while others are completely disorganized and/or underhanded (they're not all in this game to promote world peace and harmony). Checking them out thoroughly ahead of time could save you from wasting a huge chunk of your money.

There are numerous places to find out about such programs:

- Check your college or university placement office for information booklets and addresses. Many have a binder or data base with information on these numerous programs.

- Contact the government, particularly Foreign Affairs and International Trade Canada.

- Check with foreign government embassies to see what programs they know about.

- If you are in a particular area of study, check with your faculty for information on programs that are specifically geared to students in that discipline.

Here are a few good additional working holiday references:

Jean-Marc Hachey. *The BIG Guide to Working and Living Overseas*. www.workingoverseas.com. University of Toronto Press, 2004.

Susan Griffith. *Work Your Way Around the World: The Globetrotter's Bible*. Crimson Publishing, 16th Edition, 2014.

Susan Griffith. *Summer Jobs Worldwide 2012: Make the Most of the Summer Break*. Crimson Publishing 2012.

Jeffrey Maltzman. *Jobs in Paradise: The Definitive Guide to Exotic Jobs Everywhere*. Rev. ed. New York: HarperCollins, 1993.

Getting There and Back: Transportation

One of the greatest expenses for any trip is, of course, getting there and back. Whether you want to hide away in a shack in the woods or find yourself on the trails of Europe, the good news is that it may cost a lot less than you thought. First of all, consider your options: Plane? Train? Bus? Car? Boat? A combination of these? How many people you are travelling with, when you are travelling, how much time you have, and where you are going will all help determine the option that's cheapest for you.

Air Travel
The friendly skies are often downright cruel to your wallet. Plane fares can leave you gagging into that bag under your seat. But there are some ways to fly you to your destination cheaply, very cheaply, and occasionally even free.

- Check on student discount fares offered through travel agents and services such as Travel Cuts (which is owned by the Canadian Federation of Students). Your student status and age will determine whether you're eligible for these low prices.

- Watch for seat sales, which are a great deal if you can get them when they're announced. They're usually limited and disappear quickly. Two free on-line fare trackers will monitor the airlines to find the cheapest deal and regularly email you with the results. They're at **www.travelocity.ca** or **www.expedia.ca.**

- Charters are often much cheaper than regular excursions. These can be a particularly good option if you are travelling between larger centres.

- Consolidators are a great way to get cheap flights. These are seats that are bought up cheaply in large blocks from airlines and then resold at discount prices. (They often don't include frills, so you may have to serve your own snacks, maybe even take a turn in the cockpit.) Savings on international flights, particularly at peak travel times, may be staggering, perhaps even hundreds of dollars—about enough for one of those delectable airport meals.

- Watch for last-minute deals. Rather than pay the fee for a last-minute travel club, check with the many discount travel agents who also offer these last-minute sell-offs. This strategy can be particularly effective if you are flexible about your destination.

- Be a human courier. Toronto to Hong Kong for $45? New York to Paris for $375? Sound too good to be true? Well, it's not! A very cheap option for light travellers flying internationally, this could be the budget ticket you've been waiting for. All you do is accompany a package or documents from one place to another. It sounds intriguing, almost illegal, but it's not. You give up your check-in luggage space for the parcel, while you get to bring carry-on luggage and receive a discount of, get this, a whopping 30–95 percent! Once you have claimed the parcel from the luggage carousel and handed it over to the waiting company representative, it's mission accomplished. It's a no-frills way to go. There are several conditions to be aware of:

- Flights are usually to larger centres.
- Trips are often for a limited time (e.g., a two-week return ticket).
- Some courier companies will charge you a membership to have access to these deals ($25–$75 on average).
- Usually you need to dress in business attire.
- Often you must be 18 or over.
- Your luggage is often limited to carry-on baggage, but ask ahead.
- Most human courier flights are run out of U.S. centres, however it may still be cheaper to get to these U.S. departure points and fly from there.

Here are a few flying tips:

- "Go ahead, bump me." While you may not want to say this in a biker bar, it can save you bucks in an airport. Airlines are notorious for overbooking, sometimes meaning there are more anxious travellers than seats. If you're not in a hurry to get somewhere, inform the airline that you are willing to be "bumped" (i.e., willing to give up your seat on a scheduled flight for one with a later departure). If they need to bump you, it could mean a free flight voucher, just for agreeing to take a later flight.

- Register for frequent-flyer points—you may eventually get a free flight out of it. However, don't let this alone determine your choice of airlines for future flights. Generally, go with the airline that offers you the cheapest air fare. Some airlines also honour "parent" or "sister" airline companies' travel points.

- Student standby used to be a way of saving through a last-minute cheap flight. While there are still some deals available, primarily on smaller or uncommon routes, there are now many better bargains to be had without the risk of being left behind. Generally, use this option only as a last resort.

- Bring snacks or lunch when travelling by air, especially if your meal is not included in the price.

- Look for Tuesday and Wednesday flights which are usually cheaper, as are red eye flights.

Car

Whenever you use a car for vacation travel, shop around and compare rental prices because the differences could be significant. Here are some tips to keep costs low:

- Rent on weekends if possible—it's cheaper.

- Ask about special weekly rates. It may be cheaper to rent for the whole week than for only three days.

- If you or your travel companion are fortunate enough to have a gold credit card, ask about paying with that. You can often have the collision insurance covered, which can be a significant saving to you.

- If you're comparing prices, be sure to add up all the hidden costs. Some rental places will charge a day rate plus mileage, while others will have a flat rate. Figure out which is best for your situation.

- Fill up the gas tank before returning the vehicle. If you leave it for the rental agency to refill, you could end up paying a higher rate for gas.

- Car rental agencies located inside the airport are usually the most expensive. It may pay to rent a car away from the airport.

- Check on the age limit. Some companies may not rent unless you're over a certain age, sometimes as old as 25.

- You can sometimes get a free trip by car through drive-aways (returning rental cars to their original location). They will frequently charge you only for gas. Inquire at car or truck rental agencies.

- Split the costs. Driving with four people in that Neon may be cramped, but the price is right.

Getting Hitched, Without a Hitch

If you're travelling on a budget, one of the cheapest ways to go is by hitchhiking. The biggest drawback, of course, is the lack of safety. Where and when you thumb a ride will make a differ-ence to your security; night travel in deserted regions is probably riskier than daytime hitching. Travelling in pairs is highly recom-mended, although this might deter some drivers who have little space or are worried for their own safety. If you choose this option, your best bet for these cheap rides is to hitch in coed pairs, which tend to look less intimidating to potential drivers.

Trains

Follow those tracks—they probably lead to one of the best forms of student transportation, particularly when travel-ling abroad: the train. Contrary to our North American experience, many trains in Western Europe, Japan, Hong Kong, and elsewhere are on time and travel fast. Here are your best bets for keeping train costs as low as possible:

- Look into youth rail passes. They often go by age and can mean big savings. Decide on the countries you're travelling to and find out if a rail pass is valid there. If half the countries you're visiting don't accept the pass, it may not be worth pur-chasing a full one.

- Purchase rail passes in Canada as they are usually cheaper, or in the case of Japan, unavailable once you are within that country.

- Whenever possible, travel at night. This is one of the best money savers, because you can crash for the night and wake up at your destination refreshed and ready to go, while spar-ing yourself the cost of accommodation. By getting to your destination early, you also have a better chance of finding a great place to stay before they're all taken. Then you can store your belongings, instead of paying for a train station locker, and you'll have a full day to explore, relax, and enjoy.

Two caveats: When travelling at night, ask another trav-eller or the conductor to wake you up when you near your destination (or set your alarm!). If not, you may take an expensive and time-consuming side trip to an unplanned destination. Also, it's best to travel this way in pairs, as safety may be a concern.

Accommodation

If you think it's a shock to the wallet to pay rent while at school, you'll be doubly shocked by the price of hotel rooms. Along with transportation and food, this bill can leave your finances homesick.

The great news is that you don't have to pay top dollar for a place with monogrammed towels, individually wrapped glasses, or pay-per-view movie channels. Fortunately, being a student allows you the flexibility to consider many alternatives that are available at a fraction of the cost of a hotel.

Hostels

If there's one form of travel that's accepted by students around the globe, it's hostelling. There are more than 4,000 hostels worldwide offering cheap accommodation in more than 90 countries. Hostels may offer modern facilities or something more rustic, and they may be located in anything from a castle to a contemporary high-rise, but they all have one thing in common: low prices. You get a place to sleep—sometimes in a shared room or bunkhouse (usually with members of the same sex)—and shower facilities. Some hostels will include a small breakfast before you hit the road. Sure, you'll sacrifice the pool, TV, and other amenities of a hotel, but when you're surrounded by the elegance and charm of downtown Vienna, who needs Oprah? The best part of hostelling, I've found, is that you meet people from literally everywhere.

If hostelling's for you, contact Hostelling International at 1-800-663-5777 or **www.hihostels.ca**. A two year membership costs around $35, (free if you're under 18) plus taxes, and usually gets you a room for $20–$40 a night. Non-members will usually pay $4–6 extra per night. All in all, a great deal.

YMCAs

Although you probably won't run into those crazy Village People who like to sing about the Y, you will run into a lot of thrifty students like yourself having a great time travelling—plus, you'll usually get a good, basic room at a rock-bottom price. Check the worldwide directory at any local YMCA/YWCA for locations and prices around the world, or call and ask them to send you free Y accommodation information on the places you're visiting.

Residence Life, Revisited

So, you miss residence . . . ? Well, you're in luck if you like to travel cheap. In the summer, many school residences around the world offer good cheap places to stay for travelling students. (Some cooperative schools offer rooms at other times, too.) Some places include a small breakfast, while others may give you use of the recreation facilities, which could cost you plenty at a hotel. Imagine, you can actually sleep in, without the usual I-should-be-at-class guilt.

Back to Nature

If you miss those summer days at camp, you can relive them through one of the cheapest ways to travel—camping. Aside from your basic camping supplies, the cost is minimal. In some areas, you can "pitch your pup" for free. To obtain information on worldwide camping, contact Kampgrounds of America (KOA) or Hostelling International (see above), which also runs campgrounds.

Bed and Breakfasts

That doesn't mean breakfast in bed, but it's a great way to travel. Costs will usually run you more than a hostel or dorm, but less than a hotel. The big bonus is that you usually get a superb breakfast, depending on the culinary capacity of your host. Some places are operated as a sole-income business, others more as a hobby. Prices, comforts, and service will therefore vary from place to place. If you are hundreds of miles from home, that smiling lady cooking breakfast may just give you the taste of home that you've been missing.

Creative Solutions

There are other options that are often forgotten in the haste to get away. Check out the following money-saving possibilities:

- *Paid to "Sit"*—Offer to house-sit in a novel or exotic place. Apply through a bonded house-sitting service and be ready to provide references. This route can provide great accommodation, and it helps out those that you sit for.

- *Trading Places*—If you and your roommates want to get away, but the vacation funds are sparse, consider this: Throughout the world, there are probably numerous other students sitting glumly, sharing those same feelings. Why not trade for a week or two—during Reading Week or Christmas break, perhaps? Place an ad in a school paper in the place you want to go (University of Hawaii, for instance). Promote your own milieu. (If you live in Halifax: "Beautiful coastal town nestled by the sea." If you're in Toronto: "Urban downtown studio minutes from theatres, sports, museums." If you're in Winnipeg . . . er, ah . . . : "Place with lots of pretty, white cold stuff flying around.") You may find a couple of Hawaii coeds just longing to experience –20° weather, while you have cravings for coconuts and a lei. If you go the swap route, always ask for references and check with all your roommates.

- *Always Remember a Condominium!*—If you're travelling with a group of friends, then renting a condominium, a cottage, or a house may be your best bet. Check with travel bureaus or rental agencies in the places you are travelling to. This option usually works best if you're staying a week or more in one place. A big advantage is that you can do your own barbecuing and cooking—a much cheaper way to feast.

- *The Cottage Route.* Most people tend to underuse their cottages, so they may be willing to rent it to you—check with friends and relatives. They might even give you a great rate—perhaps even free in exchange for cutting the grass, watering the plants, painting the deck, etc. Get the word out early.

- *Thrift on the Couch.* A new twist to crashing on your friend's couch is surfing your way around the world via a stranger's couch. **www.couchsurfing.org** lets you hook up for free with vacant couches in the places you want to go. After all, who wouldn't want a Canuck snoozing on their couch?

- *A Step Up from the Couch.* Okay, so it's not free. But the price may fit in with your travel budget to see the world. Airbnb (**Aribnb.ca**) lists rooms, apartments, cabins, lofts and even entire houses around the world that people are renting out. Prices vary (along with the quality), as the person renting sets the price. Generally there are some excellent places at great prices.

Hotels, If You REALLY Must

There may be times that you want the comforts and pampering of a hotel—beds that are actually big enough, water that's actually hot. If money's a concern, however, use them as you would chilli peppers—very sparingly.

Many student travellers use a variety of accommodation rather than just one type. A hotel, for instance, might be used once a week, along with hostels or camping. You may want to consider this flexible option.

To keep your hotel costs low, consider the following:

- *Make Sure You RATE*—Hotels often have about as many rates as they do rooms. Travel club rates, student rates, business rates, government rates (sometimes includes colleges and universities), weekend rates, specials, etc. Ask what the best rate is and negotiate further. The emptier the hotel looks, the more likely you are to get a cut rate. The one thing they won't charge you for is trying. After all, they'd rather fill the room for fewer bucks than have it empty. A card is usually all you have to flash to get business discounts. So take your business cards, even for a part-time or summer business (e.g., Tom's Tutoring Inc., or Laurie Enterprises Inc.—Established 1993).

- *Group Travel*—If you're travelling in a pack, avoid having to pay for a couple of rooms. Ask for one room with extra cots.

- *Ask to See the Cheapest Room First*—Hotels love to push the more expensive rooms unless you ask otherwise.

- *Check Your Hotel Bill Carefully*—This is one place you frequently find errors. You may discover your neighbour's adult movie rentals are on your bill. Check carefully for any other charges, such as phone calls, messages, or food charges, that may mysteriously be included in your tally. Hotels are increasingly charging for goods and services that formerly were free. Check as well to make sure that the rate you're charged matches the rate you were quoted.

Food

When travelling, you'll want to experience fine foods throughout the world. The fresh pasta of Italy, the amazing chocolate of Belgium, the cholesterol-packed junk food of the U.S.A.—it's all there to sample. However, you need not let your food expenses devour all your cash. Here are some smart food strategies:

- *When in Rome . . .*—Eat where the locals do, not where the tourists eat. Who's going to have a better idea of where reasonably priced food can be found: someone who's lived there all their life, or someone who's been there a few days?

- *Ask Other Students*—Local students from the campus in the place that you are visiting have already sniffed out the best spots that offer good value meals. In places like Germany, they'll let you gobble away with the rest of the students at residence eateries.

- *Eat the Food of the Region*—If you're visiting the Atlantic coast, eat seafood (way cheaper in Halifax than in Toronto). If in Calgary, go for that steak. (Your desire for steak in Japan, however, may leave you with little "yen" for sushi). If in Saskatchewan, pile up those wheat pancakes.

- *Don't Get Dinged in the Diner*—Beware of extra charges in some restaurants. For example, bread on the table is almost always included with the meal if you're eating in Canada, but some restaurants in places such as Italy will charge you extra if you actually start to eat the bread that is sitting there.

- *This Little Food-Saver Went to Market*—Buying at markets, delis, and food stands is considerably less expensive than eating in a restaurant. Fruits, vegetables, and baking are especially cheap by comparison.

- *Axe the Meat*—When travelling abroad, become a vacation vegetarian and you'll save big. Just make sure you obtain enough protein from cheaper non-meat sources. In some countries, you can also save on medical expenses by avoiding dairy and meat products, which are more prone to bacteria.

Phone Calls

Reaching out and touching someone could be painful when you're travelling. With extra charges, taxes, and so on in different countries, you may be paying many times more than you would at home. To mute your costs, follow these guidelines:

- Phone from a post office or phone office, where there's usually no service charge. Hotel phone calls can cost you 300–400 percent *above* normal long-distance rates in the host country.

- Use Canada Direct service. This money-saver lets you dial a local number to be connected to a long-distance operator in Canada. You'll pay the usually lower Canadian operator-assisted overseas rate. call 1-800-561-8868 or create a customized access sheet at **http://www.infocanadadirect.com**

- Free to Roam. Roaming charges can be expensive. If you're out of your local calling area and have an unlocked phone (meaning you can use it with any compatible network carrier), buy a local pre-paid SIM card – particularly if you'll frequently be using your cell phone. You'll avoid the roaming charges which can be skyhigh – particularly when you are out of the country, where charges range from $1.45 to $4.00 per minute.

Shopping

Whether you succumb to Midnight Madness in Milan or to Russia's Revolutionary Red Tag Sale, you'll probably end up dropping some Deutschmarks somewhere. But you can prevent the killing of your shillings through some simple shopping strategies.

- Avoid airport and hotel gift shops, where the souvenirs are usually more expensive and of poorer quality.

- If you plan to make major purchases abroad, check local prices before you go. You may end up hauling that Indonesian rug around for weeks, only to return home and find the exact item in Canada at a price 10 percent lower. The festival atmosphere often overcomes even the most rational shopper

- Follow that local! Cities commonly have multiple marketplaces—some where tourists shop, others where locals go.... with much better prices of course. Go early.

- Let's make a deal. Don't be afraid to barter with merchants wherever you go. Canadians are used to accepting the marked price as final. Very rarely will we stand half an hour bartering with the Gap girl for a better price on the chinos. However, abroad it's a different story. It doesn't hurt to try. If they do get offended, apologize profusely and excuse yourself as a somewhat naive, but humble, American.

- When shopping, always take a small calculator with you to figure the price out in Canadian dollars. You may discover that the converted price is no bargain. I had a rain-soaked friend who bought an umbrella in Vienna only to discover later that she paid $60 Canadian for it—quite a drenching.

- Always figure in any tax and tariffs on your purchases. This may lessen its bargain appeal. Canadian government travel info can provide this information.

- Check to see how much you can bring back into Canada duty free. You can now bring up to $200 duty-free after an absence of 24 hours or more, and up to $800 after an absence of 48 hours or more. Items such as alcohol, tobacco, plants, and firearms (so much for the souvenir shot-guns from New York), are limited or prohibited.

- I smell refund! Value-added taxes are charged in many countries. However, tourists are not required to pay them and can receive refunds when returning home. Check with customs beforehand.

- Always check for student discounts. They're often available throughout the world. You just need to ask and usually show an International Student Identity Card (see next page).

Secure Yourself

- Always check to see that you're covered by travel health insurance. A must outside Canada! Your parents' insurance may cover you, but often you'll need to purchase extra coverage. If you get sick, health care is expensive. I got food poisoning in Italy, and without insurance, I'd probably still be flipping pizzas trying to pay it off.

- Trip cancellation insurance may be worth it on expensive trips. It's usually only redeemable in the case of sickness or family tragedy, but may just save you the cost of a flight.

- You may save yourself some huge medical expenses and hassles by finding out where English-speaking doctors are located in places you are travelling to. A great way to find this information (along with guides on immunization and reducing the risks of disease) is through the Canadian-based International Association of Medical Assistance to Traveller (IAMAT). The great news is that the information they provide is free (a donation is appreciated, but not required). For more information contact IAMAT, 1262 Gordon Street, Guelph, Ontario N1L 1G6, (519) 836-0102. (**www.IAMAT.org**)

- If you think you might need any medication while travelling, take it with you. Don't assume you can drop into a store in Nepal to pick up some Tylenol when you need it. Medication is also likely to be more expensive there. Take a few of the basics: aspirin, disinfectant, bandages, and a real essential—Immodium—for when nature calls . . . and calls . . .and calls . . .

Roads to Riches: Other Travel Savers

- The International Student Identity Card can save you cash throughout the world on such things as museums, hostels and hotels, travel fares, insurance, retail, theatres, entertainment, and restaurants. It'll cost you $20 (or sometimes nothing, if your school belongs to the Canadian Federation of Students), but with continued travel it usually pays for itself fairly quickly. To take advantage of this program, you need to be a full-time student (as defined by your institution). Applications are available from Travel Cuts (**www.travelcuts.com**), VIA Rail stations, student council offices, or the Canadian Federation of Student Services, 338C Somerset Street West, Ottawa, Ont., K2P 0J9. 613-232-7394.

- Take a credit card as a backup but use it only if absolutely necessary. Some cards charge higher exchange rates and tack on extra fees. A cash advance should only be used as a last resort, since you start paying interest on it the minute you take it out.

- Smile! You're saving. Stock up on film, memory cards and batteries before you travel. Buying these elsewhere can cost two or three times what it does here.

- Check out budget travel books for more tips on student travel. Two good bets for the student traveller are the "Let's Go" series and the "Lonely Planet" series. Both offer student-oriented travel information for specific locations around the world.

CHAPTER 15

Income Tax: Avoiding the Government Panhandlers

Figuring out income tax can be about as interesting as watching chess in slow motion. It's tedious, frustrating, annoying, stressful, and painful . . . and that's just trying to phone through to the Canada Revenue Agency to request your forms. The real pain begins once you actually sit down to figure it all out.

Perhaps one of the most puzzling things about income tax is that a good number of students never even bother to fill out a form, despite the fact that in many cases hundreds of dollars would be coming their way. Think about it. If a student walked by a the Canada Revenue Agency building on the way home and $50 fell out of her pocket, she'd be peeved once she realized it was missing. She might make the effort to retrace her steps, and even check with the hard-working attendant at the door to see if it was turned in. Yet, in many cases, a student will lose hundreds in income tax that they should *not* be paying, just because they don't bother to fill out a form and mail it in.

So let's look at how you can pay the least and get the most, a strategy adopted by the majority of people who deal with government. Some of the tax measures referred to are budget proposals and have not yet been passed into law. They are thus subject to change.

Pre-tax Planning

For most people, tax planning often starts late—like 24 hours prior to the filing deadline. However, by planning early and strategically, you can reduce the amount of tax you owe and thereby increase the size of your refund cheque. Here are some ideas for the overtaxed student:

- *No Interest in Government!*—If you are a student working part-time, fill out a federal government form (yet another one) called a TD1, which allows you to have the deductions from your paycheque kept to a minimum when your estimated annual income is below a set amount. Always fill out and submit this form to your employer, even if you think there's a chance you'll make more than the maximum set amount. There's no penalty for guessing wrong. Bank the money you would otherwise have had deducted. This way, if you have to pay income tax at year's end, you'll have the money in your account, along with the accumulated interest (something the number crunchers in Ottawa wouldn't have given you). If you don't have to pay, you'll have a nice bonus saved up.

- *Put It Off*—If you think that you are going to be making more money next year than you did this year, try to put off using tax credits, such as charitable donations, until then. This will assist you in bringing down your taxable income next year, when you need the extra help. The higher your income, the higher your tax bracket. When you are a student, you often don't need these tax credits, but if you wait until you're making money, you'll be glad to have them then.

- *Check Before You Cash*—Consider how your investments will affect your tax. For example, if you cash in a mutual fund or an RRSP, will that bring your earnings up to a taxable level? Although you may need to withdraw, it is best to take out only what you need. If, for example, you need $2,000, it is not wise to cash in a $5,000 certificate, because your investment earnings on the full amount you withdraw will be added to your taxable income. It's best to have five $1,000 bonds rather than one $5,000 bond so that the money is easy to withdraw in smaller amounts.

- *Receipts*—Obtain the necessary receipts (e.g., rent, moving expense receipts) immediately. Store them safely—you will likely be charged for reissued receipts.

Filing: Contract Out or Do It Yourself?

In most cases, student income tax is fairly straightforward. Very rarely do you have stock options, film royalties, depreciation write-downs, or other complicated financial considerations. What this means is that even the most mathematically challenged student can get by doing their tax return on their own. However, if you do want to find someone else to take on the task, here are a few options to consider:

- If you're fortunate, your tax return will be handled by your very own makeshift accountant: mom or dad. Try to convince them to tackle yours when they do their own (after all, you can trust your own parents, can't you?).

- If your parents have their tax return prepared by an accountant, it may be very cheap and easy to get yours done at the same time.

- If you don't have the parental option, schools sometimes offer tax clinics to assist students with their tax returns. These clinics are usually offered at a low cost or for free. Also, some business and accounting students do taxes, often at a reasonable rate.

- When tax time calls, there are plenty of instant tax "experts" willing to take your money. Your choices range from fly-by-night scam operators to reputable accountants. Be careful: there's often a hefty charge attached and some organizations rely on hastily trained workers. A referral from someone you trust may be your best bet.

- If your tax situation is really complex, take your return to a qualified accountant. Since you are a student, you'll probably get a break (unless, of course, you're bringing in more income than they are).

Even if you get someone else to prepare your return, don't close this chapter yet. You still need to be aware of the basic claims and deductions, so that you know what to check for. Even professionals make mistakes. Remember, you are still ultimately responsible for any errors.

What You Must Claim

You are required to claim the following types of income:
- Salary or wages, including tips or gratuities (T4 slips)
- Investments, such as interest on accounts, mutual funds, and stocks (T5 slips)
- Research grants (T4A slips)
- Training allowances
- Registered Education Savings Plan (RESP) income from programs that have been set up by your parents or family for you (T4A slips)
- Self-employment earnings
- Social assistance payments, including unemployment benefits

You don't need to claim:
- Loans
- Your goods and services tax (GST/HST) credit
- Lottery winnings
- An inheritance
- Your Child Tax Benefit payments
- Scholarship, fellowship and bursary money received (up to the amount that was intended to support your enrolment in the program.)

What You Can Claim As Tuition Fees

Eligible tuition fees include the following:
- Admission fees
- Charges for the use of library or laboratory facilities
- Exemption fees
- Examination fees

- Application fees (if you later enroll at the institution)
- Charges for a certificate, diploma, or degree
- Mandatory computer service fees and/or lab fees
- Academic fees
- Textbooks (if included in total correspondence fees)
- Mandatory fees such as health and athletic service fees

You can't claim as tuition fees:

- Student association fees
- Medical expenses
- Transportation and parking
- Board and lodging
- Goods of lasting value that you will keep, such as a computer, calculator, microscope, uniform, or an academic gown
- Initiation fees or entrance fees to a professional organization
- books (unless included in total correspondence course fees). However, you may be able to claim textbook tax credit (see page 277)

In addition to tuition fees, there are other tax credits that students can use, such as an education tax credit, and deductions such as expenses for required safety equipment bought for a summer or part-time job, which are described under "Specific Tax-Saving Strategies."

How Credits and Deductions Work: A Primer

With income tax, your ultimate goal is to bring your taxable earnings down to zero. For example, if you had earnings in 2014 of $10,240 from your summer construction job, $4,050 from a part-time job and $1,525 from investment income your total income would be $15,815 (Your $3,400 scholarship is now tax free under the 2006 budget changes (Addendum 1). You would be able to reduce this further by using a variety of tax deductions and tax credits. A tax deduction of $225 in union dues, along with $75 for out of pocket safety equipment would bring your taxable income down to $15,515.

Credits: You could then use different tax credits to further reduce the tax you pay. You would start by subtracting the 2014 basic personal tax credit of $11,138, which would give you $4,377 of taxable income; an amount that you would want to further reduce, using tax credits. You would, for example subtract your $400 per month education tax credit for each of the eight months that you were in school as well as the $65 textbook credit for each month you were in full-time post secondary studies. After subtracting this $3,720 amount you would have taxable income left of $657 (almost there!). You would therefore only need to use $657 of your possible $6,253 tuition tax credit to lower your taxable income to zero. The remaining $5,596 of your tuition tax credit could be transferred to a parent or grandparent (or spouse or common-law partner) for 2014 (maximum $5,000) to lower their taxable income. Alternatively, all (or the remainder after transfer), could be carried forward to a year when you are actually making some serious money and need the tax credits.

Other Non-allowable Income Tax Deductions

1. Your gluttonous roommate, who has gained 20 pounds this term and become a permanent fixture on the couch, cannot be claimed as a depreciating asset.

2. Agreeing to ask out your roommate's shy, but nice, friend cannot be written off as a charitable donation.

3. The fungus and mildew burgeoning in the corner of the bathroom does not qualify for an agricultural tax credit.

4. Cramming around the clock in that library study carrel does not qualify you for an isolation pay subsidy.

5. The gases emitted after last weekend's drinking binge do not qualify under the alternative energy source tax credit.

6. Your multiple-personality roommate cannot take advantage of income splitting.

7. The family of cockroaches that you've grown attached to cannot be claimed as dependants.

8. Your large purchase of Mexican beer over the term does not qualify as a foreign investment.

9. Hosting your frat brothers' out-of-control parties does not qualify your apartment as a wildlife preserve.

10. Dating the stunning foreign exchange student from Guatemala cannot be claimed as foreign aid.

11. Just because you have to entertain your boyfriend's silly friends, you cannot claim your place as a certified daycare centre.

12. The cost of your beer-packed bar fridge cannot be deducted as a safety deposit box expense.

13. The entry fee for your fraternity's Annual Belching Contest cannot be considered a "gross" income deduction.

14. The money you lost in this year's hockey pool cannot be claimed as a "net" income expense.

Tax Tips

General Rules to Remember

- Always get receipts for all earnings, expenses, transactions, rent or residence fees that you'll be claiming on your income tax. Have one envelope to keep them in so you don't have to go rifling through drawers, wallets, knapsacks, and cabinets the night before the filing deadline. You will have to submit some receipts with your tax form; others you must hang on to in case you're given an "A"—an audit, that is.

- Technically, you need to hang on to all receipts for six years from the end of the tax year they apply to. But they can't audit you more than three years after your assessment notice, so you can toss them after three years.

- Keep informed about changes to tax regulations and how they affect you. Tax credits and deductions are a lot like secluded wilderness getaways: once everybody finds out about them and starts to use them, they suddenly disappear. You can get tax booklets from your local tax office, download them on-line at **www.cra-arc.gc.ca/formspubs/** or at postal outlets (early February). In addition, a particularly good pamphlet for students called "Students and Income Tax" is available from your local tax office.

- If it is nearing tax time and you haven't received your necessary receipts, such as interest income (T5), employment income (T4), and tuition fees (T2202A), contact the relevant bank, institution, or school to receive one. All forms are required to be sent to you by the end of February.

- If you have the option, e-file your return (that is, file it electronically, rather than by mail) and you'll get your refund quicker. Having the government deposit your refund directly into your bank account will also speed up the process; the form requesting a direct deposit is attached to the regular tax package.

Specific Tax-Saving Strategies

- *The Only Good Thing About High Tuition*—When claiming tuition fees on your return, you can even claim extra courses that aren't part of your degree. As long as they are taken at a recognized postsecondary institution and cost more than $100. If you take two courses at the same institution that cost

$100 or less each, you can claim the tuition if the combined cost is more than $100. For example, that $60 Tibetan dance course and the $70 hog-calling course added together would qualify as a $130 deduction.

- *The Scoundrels Made Me Do It!*—If you paid mandatory fees such as health service, athletic, lab fees, etc., you can claim these (except for student activity fees) just as you would tuition. Keep in mind that this does not apply to optional fees.

- *Send Your Parents Back to School!*—If you don't need to use your tuition, education or text book tax credits to reduce your taxable income to zero, you can transfer all or part of this amount (to a maximum of $5,000) to one of your parents (or even your grand-parents). It'll give them that back-to-school feeling. You need to fill out a form to transfer the amount you want (form T2202A). You can also now carry this over for personal use in future years.

- *Your Transfer Has Expired!* You can carry over your education tax credits to future years. Therefore if it's more beneficial to transfer them to a parent, guardian or spouse do it now (a trans-fer must be done in the year it was incurred). Otherwise carry it over and use it when you need it (when you are in the money).

- *Taking Credit*—You can also claim a $400 education tax cred-it for each month you were in school full-time. If you are attend-ing part-time and receive the disability amount (completion of form T2201 by a registered practitioner) you can claim the $400. Even if you can't claim the disability amount, but you are attending part-time because of a physical or mental impair-ment, you can still claim the $400 amount by submitting a let-ter from a medical doctor, optometrist, audiologist, occupation-al therapist, psychologist, physiotherapist, or speech language pathologist to certify your impairment. Part-time students can claim a $120 per month education tax credit.

- *Catching Your Interest*—You can now claim the interest that you pay on your government sponsored student loans. Better still, you can carry this credit over for up to five years if you don't need to use it now.

- *Settle for a Bad Job*—When it comes to meeting the tax-filing deadline, doing a bad job on your return is better than no job at all. If it looks like you're going to owe money, do the best you can, even if you can only fill in some of the amounts—just send your return in on time. You can always amend it and mail in additional information later. Even if it's a mess, you'll avoid paying late penalties, which initially are about 5 percent on the amount owing, plus an additional 1 percent per month. These guys are like the "prof from hell"—no mercy for lateness.

- *Your Kids Could Amount to Something . . . a Deduction!* Students (full and part-time) can claim child care expenses.

- *Better Late than Never*—If you miss the deadline and you should be getting a refund, don't despair! You have four years to file and get a refund (actually 10 years, but the government has the discretion to refuse anything after four years).

- *GST Cheques*—If you have little or no income to claim, *file anyway*. Once you're 19 years old, whether you have an income or not, you are eligible for a GST refund . . . you know, that stuff they've been grabbing from you every time you spend. The refund could be a few hundred dollars per year.

- *If You're Leaving Town, Go Far! (or at Least 40 Kilometres)*— You can claim moving expenses as a deduction against the taxable portion of your income from scholarships, fellowships, bursaries, certain prizes and research grants, when you go away to school full time. This includes vehicle rental, gas, meals, accommodation en route, and temporary living expenses of up to 15 days. You can also claim expenses against your new-found income if you move to a job for the summer or when you graduate. Be sure to save *all* your receipts as proof.

- *Safety and Saving*—If you had to buy safety equipment for a summer job (e.g., steel-toed boots for a construction job), you can deduct the expense against your income. Have your employer sign a Form T2200 to verify the expense. (Sorry, the Ray Bans and sunscreen for your lifeguarding job don't qualify.)

- *Your Dues*—If you had to shell out union dues for your summer or part-time job, you can deduct these on your tax form. Make sure these deductions show up on your T4 slip.

- *Lessen the Rent Dent*—In some provinces if you rented accommodations while going to school, you may be able to claim your share of the rent, in some provinces, to receive a provincial tax credit. Say you lived in a house with two roommates and you had the monster bedroom, so you paid $300 while they paid $200 each. The important thing here is to make sure your receipt shows how much you paid individually. Otherwise, the government will assume you split the total rent equally. If you were in residence, a very nominal standard amount is allowed. Always, always, always ask for a receipt before you move. You may not be able to find your landlord a few months later (elusive creatures, you know).

- *Membership Has Its Privileges*—If you are graduating and need to join a professional organization, you cannot claim the initial joining fee. However, keep your receipt for the annual membership fee, since this fee can be deducted. Accounting and law students are likely to be in this situation.

- *If You Get Away, Make It Pay*—For example, if you attend school in the U.S., you can deduct the whole amount it costs you to attend, including living expenses. If you don't need to use the full amount, you can transfer some of it (up to $5,000) to a parent.

- *Charitable Donations: The Waiting Game*—If you make donations, always ask for a receipt. As a student, your charitable donations probably won't be very high (you may even feel like a struggling charity yourself sometimes), and you may think that ten dollars here and there isn't worth the trouble of asking for a record. But keep in mind that you can save them up for five years.

  Because of other credits, chances are you won't need to claim donations to reduce your tax to zero. Tax-wise, however, your best strategy is to save receipts until you're making real cash. The tax guys only allow a 15% percent credit on amounts up to $200 but 29% percent on amounts over that. Therefore, it's better to save them (for up to five years) and claim more at the higher rate.

- *Solo*—If you anticipate being self-employed when you graduate, say as an accountant or psychologist with a private practice, you should save receipts for books and documents that pertain to your profession. You will be able to write off depreciation on these items when you begin your self-employment. (Books to build a library can be written off, but that pipe carved in the shape of Freud wouldn't pass.)

- *Your Accountant's a Write-off*—If you have investment income (including bank-account interest) and pay to have someone calculate it (in effect, hiring someone to do your return), you can claim that expense on next year's form. Just remember to ask for a receipt.

- *A Bigger Windfall Than Ever*—If you are a full-time student and receive a scholarship, bursary, or fellowship it is now tax free. Prior to 2006 amounts over $3,000 were taxable, but now it's all good!. (See Addendum 1) Part-time students are eligible for the basic scholarship exemption of $500.

- *Appreciate Depreciation*—If you run a summer business or are self-employed during the school year, you can write off depreciation on your equipment. For instance, if you have a small lawn-mowing business, you could write off the depreciation of a computer used for promotions and accounting purposes (usually at the rate of 15 percent in the first year and 30 percent a year thereafter), even though you may in fact use it more for school. Other business expenses such as software are 100 percent deductible. In the 2009 Federal Budget, a change was made allowing a 100% write off, (for the year in which it was purchased), on computer and related peripherals bought between January 27, 2009 and January 31, 2011.

- *Take Two Credits and Claim Them in the Morning*—If you had an out-of-pocket health or medical expense not covered by your health insurance plan, you may claim it as a tax credit. Out of pocket medical expenses are claimed for a 12 month period which may mean they stretch over two tax years. Because the credit amount is calculated as a percentage of your income, you should claim these in the year when your income will be the lowest.

- *What's in a Name?*—Another self-employment strategy is to buy any business-related equipment in your own name. For example, if your parents are going to buy you a computer that you will use in your business, you'd be better off if they gave you the money and then you bought the computer. That way, you could write off the depreciation against your business earnings, since the computer would be in your name.

- *Another Reason to Read*—You may now claim a textbook tax credit based on your full-time ($65/month) or part-time ($20/month) status. The amount is based on the months you are in attendance at a post-secondary institution.

- *The Happy Bus*—There's a new reason to be all smiley when riding public transit to that 8:00 am class. You can now claim a non-refundable tax credit for your purchases of transit passes. You can calculate your estimated tax credit at **www.transitpass.ca/**.

Filing your tax return is a little like going to the dentist—a little painful at the time but a whole lot better when it's over. Nonetheless, it's a process that is usually worth it for a student. Good luck and many happy returns.

Signs You've Been in School Too Long

- You actually recognize the marching band's songs.
- Classmates begin to ask you, "What was Freud really like?"
- You've spent more time in the lab than "Rodney" the research rabbit.
- You begin to pick up fashion tips from your professors.
- It's looking more and more like your midlife crisis is going to occur on campus.
- Friends' wedding invitations start to outnumber your keg party invites.
- Your demented roommate has actually amounted to something.
- Kids you babysat are showing up in your classes . . . as TAs.
- The only "heavy metal action" you're still into is in the engineering lab.
- Even the football players you started school with are beginning to graduate.
- Your dating pool starts to include faculty.
- The subjects you originally studied in political science are now a part of the history curriculum.
- Philosophy professors are actually starting to make sense.
- It's the third time this week a student has stopped you in the hall to ask for an extension.
- The lot attendant welcomes you to parents' day.
- You're the only student on campus with tenure.
- You have less hair left than your over-zapped lab rat.
- Parent care packages now include Viagra.

CHAPTER 16

Goodbye Debt, Hello Freedom: Paying It Off

If You Have Debts

Finding yourself in debt can be like starting to write your final exam only to realize you're in the wrong hall writing the wrong exam—all you can think of is the quickest and least painful way out! With large debt, your first priority should be to ward off the money collectors. Not only will this preserve the money you have to live on, but it will also reduce your stress. Here are some tips on how to defer the bill:

- For Canada Student Loans you are not required to begin repayment until six months after graduation. Even though interest is charged immediately upon graduation, those wonderful people in Ottawa allow you a six-month grace period. So tackle your other debts during this time.

- If you cannot pay your student loan because of financial hardship, ask the government to grant you repayment assistance which can be obtained on Canada Student Loans when your income is low. If you end up qualifying you will make loan payments based on a percentage of your income - which in some cases may even work out to nothing while your income is low. Contact the National Loans Service Centre at 1-888-815-4514. While you'll need to complete an application and provide supporting documentation - it may give you the temporary relief that you are looking for.

- If you have a regular bank loan, check with your financial institution to see if you can have your loan payments postponed—just think of it as asking for one big essay extension . . . in your finance course. Not to be outdone by governmental acts of mercy, many banks will also allow you to defer the start of principal repayments for six to twelve months after you graduate. You can also ask for a further repayment deferral of up to one year. Remember that even though you can postpone principal repayment with these bank loans, you still have to continue with the monthly interest payments. If you don't have the money and simply ignore your payments, you may find the bank scribbling nasty notes on your credit rating. However, if you are in this situation, your best bet is to be open and honest with your bank loans-officer. If they know your full situation, they may be more compassionate.

- If you are in a tight financial squeeze, such as not having a steady job, you may want to pay your minimum loan payment each month but avoid rushing to pay down extra. Allow a cushion of cash to cover future payments should you run into a few lean months. Searching for a job unfortunately costs money. Therefore, it is better to have extra cash on hand for job-search expenses such as resumé printing, travel to and from interviews, and interview wardrobe purchases (that $100 pair of jeans wouldn't qualify).

- If you decide to return to school, make sure you submit a confirmation of enrolment form from your school's registrar's office to the National Student Loans Service Centre, bank, or other office holding your student loans, to verify your continuing student status. Otherwise, you may find yourself paying sooner than you thought.

Paying Off Your Loans: Who Do I Pay First?

When it comes to paying off debts, it's sometimes hard to know where to begin: The Bay credit card? Mastercard? Student loan? The $20 you owe your roommate? Generally, it's best to pay off the highest-interest loans first. Hopefully, you will have taken the advice in chapter 5 and paid off and cut up those specialty credit cards. You're also best to pay off any balances still owing on your other cards.

Credit card companies will probably be charging you more interest than your student loan. If you don't have the cash to pay off your cards, you could try to take out a bank loan to consolidate your debts.

Another option, if possible, is to make that ever-familiar trip to the Bank of Mom and Dad, to see if they'll assume the loan. In other words, if you have $5,000 worth of loans and you're paying 8 1/2 percent interest on it, and your parents have $5,000 in a cashable investment that's earning 4 percent, why not see if they'll pay off your $5,000 loan? This way, they become the lender. You will make your loan payments to them and could pay them the same rate of interest as they were getting before—4 percent (or even 4 1/2 percent, since they've been such a loyal bank for you for many years). You'll end up saving 4 to 4 1/2 percent on the interest you pay—quite a bit, considering that in a year you'll save more than $200 on a $5,000 loan for this maneuver. Parents may also be a little more flexible in terms of payment schedules. This is particularly beneficial on non-government sponsored loans where you can't claim the interest deduction.

Here are the most important things to remember about paying off loans:

- Always make your loan payments on time. It'll help you establish a good credit rating (meaning it will be easier to get a loan at a reasonable interest rate in the future). If, over a 3-year period, you make 34 payments on time, but miss two, it's the two that you missed that will be looked at and negatively affect your rating.

- Consolidate your non-government-approved loans and credit card debts. Making payments on one loan will usually be cheaper and less hassle. You'll save on service charges and be less likely to miss a payment. Don't, however, combine your federal and provincial loans with your bank loans: you might lose the Repayment Assistance Plan provisions and tax deductions that government-sponsored loans offer.

- If your situation is such that you can't possibly make your payments at all, find out what your options are. Check with your bank or government loans officer: there may be some flexibility in payment schedules.

- Pay off your highest-interest loans first. You may, for example, have a Canada Student Loan charging 7 percent and a regular bank loan charging 10 percent. Pay the minimum on both, but put any extra cash toward the regular bank loan.

Since the government has finally decided to allow interest paid on government-sponsored loans to be tax deductible, it makes it even more important that you pay off credit card balances, since the interest you pay on these is not deductible.

Canada Student Loans

As mentioned, the government seems to be getting more forgiving—perhaps softening in its old age. Start by seeking repayment assistance for your loans. A reduced, or in some cases no payment scenario, may go a long way toward helping you stay afloat, since the government pays the loan interest during this time while your payments go to the loan principle (for up to 5 years). After 5 years if you still qualify, the government may still cover your interest payments as well as beginning to cover some of the principal - for up to an additional 10 years meaning that after 15 years your loan will be gone. The main determinants of your qualifying for this repayment assistance will be your income, as well as your level of re-population over the years.

Bank Student Loans
or Credit Lines

Even the banks may be willing to bend a bit when it comes to debt repayment. They may work with you to come up with manageable repayment terms. The criteria may differ from bank to bank but are generally considered on a case-by-case basis. You'll still incur interest charges (you didn't think the bank was going to get that generous, did you?). You should contact your lending bank directly to discuss this option.

Credit Cards and Other High-Interest Debt

Other debt such as credit cards should be consolidated and collapsed into a loan, or if the balance is large, switched to a low-interest-charging card to significantly reduce the interest you pay. Some of these low-interest cards charge a fee so if you are not sure which option is best you can use a free calculating tool to help you compare at **www.fcac-acfc.gc.ca/ Eng/resources/toolsCalculators/Pages/CreditCa-OutilsIn.aspx**. At the same time tear, cut, burn, mutilate, grind, shave, chew up and spit out the credit cards to avoid charging more!

With each of these debtors, you should work out a payment schedule that is manageable. The 1998 federal budget extended the time period for loan repayment from 10 to 15 years. Great deal, right? Well it may make the monthly payments smaller and more manageable, however it will also mean you pay significantly more in interest. For example paying off a $20,000 loan at 10 percent over 15 years would cost you almost $7,000 more in interest than if you were to pay it off in 10 years. As a general rule, the sooner you can pay it down the better.

Debt: Surviving the Flood

Okay, let's say that your situation is a bit worse than a stream of debt . . . it's a rushing waterfall! If you've just graduated and are adrift in your tattered financial rowboat —fighting against a torrent of debt larger than you ever dreamed possible—there are some steps you can take.

While some people may have a few leaks in their financial boat, others may be struggling just to keep their craft afloat. Sometimes getting rid of debt can feel like trying to bail water out of your leaky boat with a teacup. But consider your options before you bail out and abandon ship! Refuge, on the increasingly populated island of bankruptcy, may not be your best bet.

Option 1: Facing the Monster Yourself

To start with, go through the following exercise to get a picture of where you're at and what you're facing.

Measure the Monster

You can't tame the debt monster if you don't know how big it is. Figure your total debt from all sources—government-sponsored loans, bank loans, credit lines, credit cards, loans to family or friends, etc. Write down what your monthly payments are from each source and what the interest rate is that you are paying.

Take stock of your taming tools

What money do you have coming in to ward off the beast? Calculate your resources from employment, government assistance, investments (if you have them), assets, etc.

Calculate your costs

Now that you have completed school, what do you need to live on, i.e. housing, food, utilities, transportation? Also figure in the cost of performing your job or searching for a job if you are at that stage. Unlike at school you probably can't get away with showing up each day in faded sweats. If you are in the job search stage you'll have costs such as résumé printing, mail-outs, outfits for interviews, transportation to interviews, etc.—it all adds up. Allow something for entertainment costs even if it's a minimal amount.

Subtract your monthly costs from your monthly resources to see what you have to tackle the debt payments. What does it look like? . . . That bad, eh? Okay, not to panic yet. What can you do to reduce your expenses? Cheaper accommodation? Another roommate? Dump the car (if you have one)? Or what other money savers can you use from the previous chapters to cut your expenses? At the same time, are there any things you can do to increase the money you have? If you are in a job that is not making ends meet you may be already trying to do this by searching out other jobs. Is there a part-time job that would bring in some extra cash? Any assets you can sell? Does this give you any more money to pay off the debts?

Buying time

You may be doing all you can to make your payments but the numbers just don't add up. Where to next? Start with the list of debts that you have. Which ones can you get some relief on? Canada and Provincial Student Loans? Bank Loans? Credit Cards?

If you find that you still can't come up with a payment schedule that is workable, it may be time for . . .

Option 2: Teaming up to Tame the Monster

A credit counselling service. These counsellors will help you to shrink your debt. Unfortunately they don't have a license to print money but they can do a number of things that you couldn't accomplish on your own. They are, in effect, budgeting coaches and intermediaries between you and those who want your money.

To start with they may help you work out a budget and repayment plan, and assist you in implementing it. Where they're particularly valuable is in helping you work with creditors. (The creditors usually start licking their chops after you have fallen three months behind in debt payment.) Counsellors may, for example, get the card companies to chill out on the interest payments so you can attack the principal while you are on a debt-repayment schedule. They may also help you keep the salivating wolves (collection agencies) at bay, so they don't constantly hound you as you try to get back on your financial feet.

Credit Counselling Services

Are they all altruistic? . . . not a chance! Some of them are the ambulance chasers of the financial world—when you are down on your financial fortune they want to come and scrape off whatever you have left. Some may counsel you (making a small profit off you) and then steer you to bankruptcy with a bankruptcy trustee with whom they are actually affiliated—thus reaping more of a profit from you. (Hmm . . . smells like conflict of interest to me.)

However, there are some credit counselling services that are really out to help people. They include some that are non-profit, and/or government funded. These are your best bet. Some will charge you while others are free. Check with the Office of Consumer Affairs, Better Business Bureau or **www.creditcounsellingcanada.ca** for a non-profit listing. Some counselling services will charge you a slight fee since many are only partially funded. Regardless of where you go, your first consultation should be free. While commercial services may also give you a free consultation, once you start the counselling and repayment process they will often require $300–$500 up front.

Other animals lurk in the financial jungle waiting to pounce on your cash. If you are having trouble paying your loans and fall far enough behind in your payments, a debtor may turn the job of getting money from you to the wolves at the collection agency. These seem to be about the office equivalent of the guys who tow and impound your car as soon as your meter expires. They may well harass, insult, threaten, belittle, and bully . . . somewhat like an Opposition member in Parliament. Very intimidating, to say the least, as they walk a fine line with what is actually legal. You do have rights, however, and the credit office can inform you of them, as well as defending you from those carnivores.

In working with you, good credit counsellors will keep your best interests in mind. For example, they may assess your situation again based not only on your assets, income, and debt level, but also on what factors got you there, your earning potential, and whether budgeting can turn things around. They'll then go over the options with you. If they feel that the situation looks fixable, they may put you on a debt repayment plan in which case you'll likely get some relief from things such as interest on your credit cards, etc. If they think your situation is beyond repair they may recommend . . .

Option 3: Bankruptcy: Seeking Protection from the Monster

While probably not the route of choice for most people, in some cases this may be the preferable option. But what does it mean? Basically in bankruptcy you give up all but a few of your assets to a bankruptcy trustee except for some personal effects, a modest car if it is needed for work, (and, of course, your lucky hockey jersey). Which assets you are allowed to keep may vary from province to province. Thus you may be left with more in some provinces than in others, depending on where you file. The trustee acts to liquidate the assets and with the proceeds pays off the creditors. By doing this you gain protection from creditors as the assets that you have are surrendered and the proceeds are divided among those that you owe money to. Not only do you lose most of your personal assets, but you also have the record of your bankruptcy on your financial report card: your credit rating. Perhaps you've brought home other bad report cards in your life and got a reprimand from the folks, but this one will punish you for seven years . . . even my chemistry mark didn't get me that! It will label you a poor credit risk—of which the biggest effect may be your future ability to acquire loans, mortgages, credit cards, etc. There is also the negative social aspect of declaring bankruptcy, which you should consider.

What you gain however, is a limit to your liability for your loans. If, for example, you have a $40,000 loan that will take 15 or more years of struggle to pay off, bankruptcy would limit your repayment to the amount made by the sale of your assets. Since most students usually don't have a lot of assets in the first place, you may not have that much to surrender (a real case of "when you don't have nothing, you don't have nothing to lose"). Keep in mind that bankruptcy is not without financial cost. You need to go through a bankruptcy trustee, which carries a fee of around $1,500–$1,800. And, needless to say, this is not forgiven in your bankruptcy filing.

An alternative to bankruptcy may be a consumer proposal allowing you to offer a proposal to pay off a portion of your debts. Although carrying many of the same negative effects as a bankruptcy, along with restrictions as they relate to your student loans and time out of school, it may have a shorter term negative effect on your credit rating. At the same time it may require you to come up with some cash to put in should your proposal be accepted. A credit counsellor can assist you in weighing the implications of each option as they pertain to your situation.

Student Bankruptcy: The Times They Are A-changing.

With bankruptcy's increasing appeal to over-burdened students ("Let's see, I walk across the stage, get my diploma, listen to the alumni guy plead for donations and then file for bankruptcy") the federal government decided to change the rules regarding bankruptcy and student debt. They have tightened the rules so that if you declare bankruptcy within seven years of graduating then you are still responsible for the student loans portion of your debt (you may however, apply for a hardship provision after five years). The rationale for this is that the new funding, along with interest and debt-relief measures of the Repayment Assistance Program, will be enough to prevent these huge debts from forcing students into bankruptcy.

Mom's advice when you trucked off to school applies equally to debt: "Keep in touch." Keep in touch with all parties: lenders, credit counsellors, government loans officers, etc. And watch for any new relief measures or changes to existing relief programs. And, oh yes, don't forget to still keep in touch with Mom!

Credit repair

For those of you whose credit rating is, let's say, badly broken, there are quick "fixers" ready to help you with your money . . . taking it that is. For fees of as much as $700 or more, they claim to be able to remove those bad marks on your rating. However, the major credit bureaus claim that they pay no attention to these "credit fixers." Bottom line: they are a scam to be avoided at all costs. Any errors that have occurred can be resolved without cost by checking your credit rating directly at a major credit bureau such as Equifax, 1-800-465-7166, or Trans Union of Canada, 1-866-525-0262 or 1-877-713-3393 (Quebec).

CHAPTER 17

When It's Over

A sense of pride and accomplishment often accompanies that expensive piece of paper you receive for toiling away the last few years. But with it also comes a sudden, chilling question: where do I go from here? In fact, graduation day is a lot like New Year's Day after the big party you hosted: you can recall some up-and-down moments, lots of celebrations, and a few near-disasters, but it was worth it. However, now that the party's over, you must face the worst part of all: cleaning up. With a little rearranging though, a little clearing out, and some strategic sweeps of the fiscal broom, you can put your financial house in order for the years ahead.

Regardless of your course major, past experience, and personal interests, graduation will leave you in one of four situations: unemployed, underemployed, back at school for another round, or employed and heading out to work. Whatever your situation, there are many things you can do to manage your money wisely.

Unemployment or Underemployment

While this may seem like a pessimistic way to look at the future, there is a possibility that you may be temporarily unemployed or underemployed after graduation. That's not to say that employers won't be beating a path to your door, but just in case they've misplaced your address, you should be prepared. Your general strategy will probably be similar to what it's been the last few years: debt avoidance. This is your chance to test that intro psych theory . . . delayed gratification.

Even If You Don't Have Debts

A smart spending strategy is to hold your expenses down after graduation. Avoid any debt (or any more than you already have). You may have to postpone the trappings of wealth a bit longer, but when you do get a job, you'll be able to spend your new earnings on the things you've been postponing buying for what must seem like a millennium. Some debt may be entirely unavoidable, but the following suggestions may help you achieve your goal of low or no debt:

- Buy only necessities. If you can live and work (or apply for work) without it, put off buying it. Obviously food, equipment, and clothing for your job fall under this category.

- See if you can continue to live in shared accommodation past graduation. A roommate may be the last thing you want right now, but the few hundred you save each month may provide the cash you need to pay loans and other expenses.

- Move back home if its an option. This may be the lowest choice on your list, or it may mean a grateful return to the pampering you once received. Either way, moving home may be the temporary option that will allow you to repair your budget and prepare for the years ahead.

- Avoid credit cards unless absolutely necessary. Stick with good old-fashioned cash.

- Sell the things you don't need if you can get cash for them. It may help you bridge the gap between school and employment.

- If you're heading off for an extended period of time on that world trek you've been planning, you may want to unload anything you have that's depreciating in value, such as a computer or a car.

- If you're heading back to school, your strategies will probably be similar to those you've been using, particularly if its another undergraduate or diploma degree. If it's grad school that calls, you may have a whole new funding trough to feed from through awards and grants for graduate students, depending on your area of study. So head to the graduate studies office and see what's on the menu.

The Wonderful World of Work

Planning for Retirement: Loans versus RRSPs

If you're now a working person, you may be bringing in some very long-awaited income. This means you'll have the option of contributing to a tax sheltered Registered Retirement Savings Plan (RRSP). So you are faced with a dilemma: do you pay down as much as you can on your loans and skip the RRSP, or do you invest in an RRSP and pay the minimum on your loans? Well, the best thing may be both. You can take out an RRSP and, with the money you'll save on taxes, pay off an additional amount of your student loan. For example, a $3,000 RRSP contribution would likely get you a tax refund of around $660 (assuming a 22% tax bracket) which you could use to pay off part of your loan.

Another option is an RRSP loan. While taking on more debt is normally not advisable, an RRSP loan can be a worthwhile step, but only if you are going to pay if off within a year. The reason is that you can lower your taxable income by taking out an RRSP (and thus benefit from tax savings). However, if you stretch out the repayment period past a year, the increased interest costs of borrowing tend to offset the tax savings. The interest rate on these loans tends to be lower than on most, and you'll thus be able to take advantage of the RRSP tax savings.

Okay, retirement seems like light years away—so an RRSP may seem crazy. But keep in mind that it is also a tax-sheltered income that you may be able to access much earlier for a house down payment, a return to school (oh no, not again!), income during unemployment or travelling sabbatical, or capital to start your own business. Although you may be taxed on what you withdraw, you may end up paying little or no tax on it. For example, if you were to withdraw money when you started a business, you would likely have little or no income during the first couple of years (most businesses aren't profitable at the start). At the same time you would probably have multiple business deductions and write-offs, helping to reduce taxable income during start-up. In the case of returning to school you would have education deductions to help further reduce a probably low taxable income at that time. The government now allows you to borrow from your RRSP for continuing education through the Lifelong Learning Plan (in addition to a first home down payment) without being taxed on the withdrawal. In any of these cases you still need to weigh the benefit of using the cash outside the RRSP versus having it continue to earn tax free within it.

Timing is Everything

How important is it that you start slipping a little money into your RRSP early? The following example will give you an idea.

Say we have two recent grads—Amber has graduated and is virtually debt-free (having read *The Debt-Free Graduate* several times, of course). She starts working and is able to throw $3,000 a year into an RRSP starting at age 22. She does this for five years and then decides to stop contributing.

Brian graduates with a pile of debts that have accumulated over his three years at school (he just never got around to picking up his copy of *The Debt-Free Graduate*). Although he too is beginning a full-time job, he finds that after he's made his payments on his loans he has no money left to put towards an RRSP. He therefore delays it until he is 31 and then begins his contributions by putting in $3,000 a year for the next 34 years until he's 65.

So who will come out with the bigger bundle at

retirement? (We'll assume for this example, a 10% annual rate of return.) Even though she contributed for only five years, compared with Brian's 34 years, Amber will end up with slightly more savings by the time she retires at age 65. A huge benefit of graduating debt-free and contributing early!

But let's carry it a bit further. What happens if Amber continues to contribute at the same rate until she's 65? What difference will that make? The chart below illustrates. How will debt affect your savings?

What a difference an early start can make ... a $1,221,492 difference!

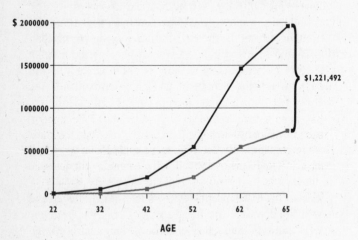

	22	32	42	52	62	65
Amber	3000	52593	189006	542829	1460556	1954923
Brian	0	3000	52593	189006	542829	733431

Little Pain, Lots of Gain: Starting Your Savings Plan

Regardless of how much you make, it always seems there is never enough cash left to start saving. Those new shoes, larger screen TV, latest iPhone, etc., always seem more appealing than putting the money into something you can't see, hear, eat or enjoy now. Instant gratification almost always seems to win over delayed rewards. But saving now could mean future returns many times greater.

Set out your future financial goals. Consider how much you will need to put aside to get there (e.g. $100/month or $300/month) along with the annual return you will need to get you there (5% per year or 12% per year). Also take into account how comfortable you are with risk. A good financial advisor, planner, or broker should help you work this out and give you an idea of how realistic your goals are (35% annual return with no risk doesn't exist . . . except perhaps on sleazy late night infomercials).

Here are a few strategies to get you started:

- Set up an automatic savings plan so that a certain amount each month goes into some form of savings. When it comes out automatically you don't see it—so chances are you won't miss it. Regardless of whether you put it into a guaranteed-interest type of savings or stock mutual fund, savings of $100–$150/month will add up over time.

- When faced with the choice of saving in or outside of your RRSP, the tax shelter advantage of an RRSP normally makes it the better choice when you are saving long-term. The automatic savings plan also helps you avoid the year-end scramble to find some money to get your RRSP tax break.

- Take advantage of tax shelters. Outside of your RRSP your first investment vehicle should be within an Tax Free Savings Account (TFSA). Start now as even a small initial investment builds over time - and besides you just never know when the government will change it's mind (mmm... didn't there used to be $100,000 personal capital gains exemption that vanished?). While it is ideal to leave your money to grow within a TFSA, these plans offer the flexibility to make withdrawals without incurring a tax hit.

- If you are starting a savings plan, decide what your investment goals are at different intervals and when you want to be there: modestly secure in 10 years, well off in 20 years, a egotistical real estate guy / reality show mogul with bad hair in 30 years, a wealthy philanthropist in 40 years.

- Shop around and interview a financial planner who you trust and who can develop an investment strategy that is consistent with your goals and risk comfort level. The guy that is scouting out the next big diamond mining stock might not fit with your goal of steady predictable growth. Ask for references from friends as to who they recommend. Also make sure that they are willing to give you time even though your initial investment may be small. Be choosy since you are, in effect, hiring that person to manage your hard-earned cash.

- Keep track of any carry-forward tax credits from when you were a student. You'll appreciate the deductions now that you have some real income the government can grab a chunk of. Also make sure you are aware of new found tax credits such as the interest paid on your Government Student Loans. And be sure to use them

As a recent grad your cash to invest may not be much, but the point is to start a plan and start it early. Not only will it build over time, but it will also foster a habit bound to reward you later.

Selling Off Your Student Trappings

It's amazing to see the things you've collected: numerous piles of photocopied notes, buttons and stickers promoting every event and social cause imaginable; copies of every underground newspaper printed in the last few years; a collection of pens and pencils that don't work and never will; a wall full of questionably obtained signs, flags, parking gates and posters covering up the peeling paint; a library of essay drafts, research notes, and journal articles you'll probably never read again; stacks of three-year-old library books the library has long since given up on. You may want to build a big bonfire and say a proper farewell to many of these treasures, but there are probably also a few things that could bring in a bit of desperately needed cash. Here are some tips for cashing in on the clutter:

- Sell those textbooks you still have around. Sure, there are classic works you may want to keep, or sentimental favourites from your best-loved classes, but get rid of that algebra text (left over from when you thought you liked math), and those soon-to-be-outdated sociology books.

- Get rid of any equipment or lab supplies you no longer need. Some other student could probably use them.

- You may as well sell anything that you think you wont want once you have put the student lifestyle aside. The lava lamp and grunge-rock CDs may have been great at the time . . . but why not take the money and run?

Footloose and Furniture Free

Sell or give away anything else you don't want to move or store. That overstuffed couch that's seen more petting than the Winnipeg zoo might be first on the list. Not only will you be able to shore up your weary bank account, but you may also be able to help some student who's in the same situation you were a few years ago.

Avoiding the New Grad Traps

You may have won the battle, but you haven't won the war. Sure, you sidestepped the lure of those retailers, merchants, advertisers, and corporations that badly wanted a piece of your cash while you were a student, but they haven't gone away. While you've been ignoring their hooks, lures, and traps, they've been re-arming and getting ready for an even bigger assault on your bankbook. Yes, you're a graduate now and they want your money even more.

You'll find your name is now on marketing lists, magazine lists, insurance lists, e-mail lists... any place that could sell you something. They'll even be phoning you and trying to peddle their wares. There's nowhere to hide—or is there? Here are a few things you can do:

- Swear Off Junk Mail—Unless you really like having a full mail box, ask the marketing companies to discontinue this trash. To get off their contact lists you can register for The Do Not Contact service for free at: **http://www.the-cma.org/consumers/do-not-contact** or call 1-866-580- 3625 for further information.

- Shop in Secret—Avoid giving personal information at stores and/or pay by cash. With the technology adopted by so many businesses, your purchases are traced by such methods as customer loyalty cards and specialty retail cards to determine your buying habits. Companies that sell merchandise you're apt to buy will then target you. Your personal information is stored and often shared with other retailers and services.

- Decline Ballots—Avoid filling out ballots for a lot of contests, promotions, etc. Sure, you may pass up the one-in-a-million chance of winning that Teflon frying pan, but you'll avoid being bombarded by sales pitches later.

- Boycott the Phone Book—You can save yourself a lot of sales pitches by having an unlisted phone number. It'll cost a little more, but it may be worth it. You can also register your phone number on the Do Not Call list at **www.lnnte-dncl.gc.ca/insnum-regnum-eng**.

- Say No to the Nosy—Some forms have the nerve to ask your income range. Unless its required, N/A or NIL is your best answer here. The more they think you have, the more they'll try to sell you.

- Turn off the ads. Add a free downloadable software program to keep the advertising out of your on-line experience. AdBlock Plus blocks the ads that hound us to spend more.

More Grad Trap-Avoidance Strategies

- If you're starting a job, don't assume you're suddenly rich. Some people end up spending half their yearly salaries before the ink is even dry on their contracts. Before you buy, add up how much it will cost to get the things you really need, and then figure out whether you can afford some of the other things you want. Prioritize the list and set a time frame for making purchases.

- Hold off on major purchases for eight to 12 months unless you really need them. You may end up despising your sales job at House of Hairpieces and want to quit, but it will be a difficult thing to do if you're already committed to car payments, furniture payments, mortgage, etc. This will also give you time to get a better sense of how secure your job may be, as well as build up a bit of cash in case of an emergency. Defaulting on car payments or having to sell suddenly due to an employment interruption could end up costing you thousands.

- Avoid the life insurance pitch. Sales reps love to talk about planning for the future, security, and so on, but life insurance is probably one of the worst investments for a single person with no dependants. If you're not looking after anyone, why buy it? The only good reason to buy it now while you are healthy may be to ensure you can get it later. In this case, go with renewable term insurance that sets out a maximum rate for future renewals. It's not only cheaper, but it gives you the option of renewing at a pre-determined rate even if you get sick. Take what you would have spent on a whole life policy and put it into a good mutual fund where the money will likely grow faster. Remember that some employers may already provide insurance for you. If you're covered at work, kindly thank these insurance peddlers and promptly refer them to your enemies . . . er, I mean other people.

- Rather than purchasing a car, look into the growing popularity of car sharing through auto co-ops. Often run as non profit programs, they allow you access to a car at a much cheaper rate than owning. Most auto share organizations require you to be at least 23 years of age, although some will let you join at age 21. Check out **www.autoshare.com/ca/city_list.html** to see if there is an auto share organization in your city.

Continuing Your Financial Smarts

Even though you've left your undergrad lifestyle behind you ("You mean I really lived in that dump?"), that doesn't mean you have to leave your financial smarts there too. Obviously, as you start hauling in the bucks, you'll want to splurge and treat yourself to some of the comforts and luxuries you've put off during the last few years. You deserve it. And clearly, if you're working, you may not have the luxury of going to cheap afternoon movies. But why suddenly discard your smart consumer habits, or intelligent purchasing strategies? These things can continue to keep your finances fit, giving you more money for other indulgences. Keep the following strategies in mind:

- Modify the strategy to your situation. You may not pack a lunch all the time to cut your costs, but you might want to buy some good, medium-priced packaged lunches for work as a cheaper alternative to eating out every day.

- Even though you may be rolling in money, remember that many cost-cutting measures may also mean doing a favour for the environment. Using homemade kitchen formulas (instead of chemical detergents) for cleaning, riding public transport (instead of driving yourself), or turning your thermostat down when you're away will all benefit this planet we share.

- Use wise banking and credit practices. Just because your finances are doing well doesn't mean you should feel you have to give banks and credit card companies extra money in service fees or interest charges. Let me assure you that most of these places are doing OKAY.

- One more plug for savings: even though planning for retirement seems like an abstract concept when you're just starting a new job, start your RRSP as soon as you can. Our generation is unfortunate in that government money for retirement might not be there for us. The government probably knows that, which perhaps explains why they are raising the age for receiving some government retirement benefits to 67 for those born in 1963 or later and offering tax shelters such as RRSPs and TFSAs. Basically, so we'll save ourselves. Take advantage of it. Its one of the few remaining tax shelters the miserly government gives us, and it will make an enormous difference in the money you end up with later on.

- Continue to shop at places that give you the best value. Cheap is in! After all, its the discount retailers who are making the big profits these days. Again, you may want to modify your choices. You may still use discount flights but decide to join a nicer health club, as opposed to sweating away at a school gym or in the basement.

- You can continue to develop your consumer smarts and investment savvy. Free on-line magazines such as *The MoneyRunner* **www.moneyrunner.ca**, give you tips and strategies to make and save money beyond your campus years.

- Your lost identity . . . student identity that is. Now that you're a grad many of the student deals are gone for such things as student banking, discount tickets, etc. But shopping around and negotiating can still give you some savings. For example if the bank, credit union, or trust company hikes your fees, negotiate for a reduced rate. If they won't cut you a deal, survey and negotiate with the others. The better off you are and/or the more potential future business they can see from you, the more leverage you have to use. Remember you're not just "a recent grad"—you're a success story in the making—and therefore are increasing your buying power.

- Even though you've graduated, many businesses such as magazines and newspapers will continue to give you student rates without your even asking. After all, are we not all students of life?

Each of us is different in our tastes, needs, wants, interests, and pleasures. Splurging to one person may mean a double fudge sundae, to someone else a trip to the beach, and to yet another a big-screen TV. The good news is that you can still spend wisely, and save, without giving up your pleasures and passions. Treat yourself—you deserve it! After all, you've worked hard to become a debt-free graduate!

Addendum

Addendum 1 – The exemption is for up to the amount of the scholarship income (scholarship, fellowship or bursary) that was intended to support your enrolment in the program.

Addendum 2 – Budget 2011 introduced measures to the Canada Student Loan Program to benefit part-time students through the following:

i) Eliminating the in-study interest rate for part-time students, bringing it down from prime plus 2.5 percent to zero.

ii) Doubling the weekly in-study income exemption from $50 per week to $100 per week for students who work while in school.

Addendum 3 – In addition to the federally funded Canadian Education Savings Grants (CESG), there are also Provincial Education Savings Programs in the following Provinces:

Alberta: The Alberta Centennial Education Savings Plan (ACES Plan). (eae.alberta.ca/funding/aces.aspx/). Toll free 1-866-515-2237 or ACES@gov.ab.ca.

Saskatchewan: The Saskatchewan Advantage Grant for Education Savings (SAGES) plan. (www.saskatchewan.ca/live/education-learning-and-child-care/saving-for-post-secondary-education). Administered by the Government of Canada. Phone toll-free at 1-888-276-3624 or cesp-pcee@hrsdc-rhdcc.gc.ca

Quebec: The Quebec Education Savings Incentive (QESI) program (www.revenuquebec.ca/en/sepf/publications/in/in-129.aspx) or Services Québec at 1-877-644-4545

British Columbia: The BC Training and Education Savings Grant (BCTES Grant) program. (www2.gov.bc.ca/gov/topic.page?id=25F4770A761640E99BDB035DD395BFD0) Phone: 250-356-7270 or BCTESP@gov.bc.ca

Index

Index

MURRAY BAKER
... on the platform

One of Canada's leading speakers ...
Murray Baker frequently appears on the platform
speaking to students and parent groups on the topic of
student finance and debt. He focuses on the bottom
line—financial management, planning and investing
strategies, and managing your money. His advice is
blended with humour that captures the fun and follies
of the campus experience. From money saving tactics
and student jobs, to tax breaks, scholarship strategies
and travelling on the cheap—he covers it all!

For information on Murray Baker's presentations
contact Money$marts at (604) 738-2115 or
mbaker@debtfreegrad.com

Visit us at:

www.debtfreegrad.com

Stories, News and Updates on:
Making, Saving, Spending and
Investing Your Money;

Getting More Money, Getting
More For Your Money

And best of all: It's FREE!

Also sign up for your free subscription
to *The Money Runner*; Your #1 on-line
Student Money Magazine!

Loaded with info on:

- Money Saving Tips
- New Scholarships, Bursaries & Awards
- Money Managing Tips and Strategies
- Travelling on the Cheap
- Consumer Tips and Independent Product Reviews
- Summer and Part-time Job Updates
- Investing Info (making your money Grow and
  Grow and Grow!)
- Where to Get Things Free
- Textbook trading and thrifty recipe search sections

Anything to do with students
and saving and making Money!